Anonymous

Annual Illustrated Catalogue and Price-List of Cast, Steel, and Chilled Plows, Planters, Cultivators and Harrows

Season 1899-1900

Anonymous

Annual Illustrated Catalogue and Price-List of Cast, Steel, and Chilled Plows, Planters, Cultivators and Harrows
Season 1899-1900

ISBN/EAN: 9783337328467

Printed in Europe, USA, Canada, Australia, Japan

Cover: Foto ©ninafisch / pixelio.de

More available books at **www.hansebooks.com**

SEVENTY-FOURTH
ANNUAL ILLUSTRATED CATALOGUE
AND PRICE-LIST

—OF—

B. F. AVERY & SONS'
INCORPORATED.

CAST, STEEL, AND CHILLED

PLOWS,

PLANTERS, CULTIVATORS, AND HARROWS.

SEASON 1899-1900   SEASON 1899-1900

FACTORY AND OFFICES:

FIFTEENTH, MAIN, CROP, AND ROWAN STREETS,

LOUISVILLE, KY.

OUR BRANCH HOUSES.

Please address our house nearest you. Our branches are equipped with goods and prices to supply you equally well as our factory.

NASHVILLE, TENN., - 306-316 Broad St.
For Middle Tennessee Trade.
KANSAS CITY, MO., - 1203 Union Ave.
Our Western Branch.
DALLAS, TEX., Cor. Wood and Market Sts.
The largest Plow and Vehicle Warehouse in the country. Our branch for TEXAS, OKLAHOMA, INDIAN, and NEW MEXICO TERRITORIES.

NEW YORK CITY, - - 66-70 Beaver St.
Our Eastern States and Export Office.
NEW ORLEANS, LA., - - 430 Canal St.
Carry a large stock of our general line of goods, and particularly a very complete stock of SUGAR, RICE, COTTON, CORN, and TRUCKERS' TOOLS.
MEMPHIS, TENN., - - - - - Union St.

JOBBING AGENTS

For genuine Avery goods are located in nearly every principal city in the United States and throughout the world.

WE DESIRE AN ACTIVE MERCHANT AGENT WHERE WE ARE NOT ALREADY REPRESENTED.

JOHN P. MORTON & COMPANY, LOUISVILLE, KY.

LOUISVILLE, KY.

B. F. AVERY & SONS' PLOW FACTORY, CORNER FIFTEENTH, MAIN, CROP, AND ROWAN STREETS, LOUISVILLE, KENTUCKY, U. S. A.

RULES OF BUSINESS.

All previous Catalogues and Price Lists are Superseded by this issue.

FIRST—Warranty—We warrant goods only against breakage caused by manifest defects in material or workmanship. Reclamations must be made promptly, and defective parts must be retained to show to our travelers, or credit can not be given for them.

SECOND—Quotations—All prices and quotations are subject to change without notice. All prices quoted are for goods at factory.

THIRD—Insurance—We do not insure river or ocean shipments unless specially instructed in each order. Insurance, when authorized, will be charged in invoice at current rates.

FOURTH—Shipper's Responsibility—A clear shipping receipt for goods relieves us of all responsibility and places it with the carriers. In no instance is the payment subject to the arrival of goods at destination. Claims for lost and damaged goods should be made against the carriers.

FIFTH—Terms—No goods furnished on commission. All bills payable with exchange on Louisville or New York. Express remittances must be prepaid. Notes required in settlement for all time sales. All past due notes and accounts subject to interest from maturity at legal rates. Sight drafts will be drawn for all unpaid open accounts as they fall due.

SIXTH—Right Hand plows and repairs are always shipped unless Left Hand are specified in each and every order.

SEVENTH—Wood Beam plows and repairs are always shipped unless Steel Beam are specified in each and every order.

We have frequent complaints from persons who have been defrauded into the purchase of imitations of our plows and other tools and parts thereof; therefore be careful to look on every plow or part you purchase for "Avery," "B. F. Avery," or "B. F. Avery & Sons," which is plainly branded on all goods of our manufacture. Also look for above trade-mark on all castings, steel points and parts, and buy points and parts only from merchants who handle the Genuine Avery Plows and Implements. Imitation points and repairs, besides not fitting well, are invariably of INFERIOR MATERIAL and workmanship. Demand the GENUINE AVERY. A picture of B. F. Avery, founder of this factory, is on the beam or handle of every Genuine Avery Plow.

Order specifically, according to our marks cast or stamped in the metal parts, or stenciled on the wood parts, and you will then be sure to get true and exact-fitting duplicates and repairs.

NOTICE.

We make a specialty of Plows and Implements for export, as also for Sugar Cultivation. Write for these special catalogues.

B. F. AVERY & SONS. LOUISVILLE, KY.

AVERY'S STEEL PLOWS.

"NEW CLIPPER"—GENERAL PURPOSE PLOW.
(PATENTED.)

Patent adjustable chilled heel.
Beam and handles painted red, black tipped.
Extra hardened soft center steel moldboard, point, and slide.
Wrought steel standard and cap, attached to beam by two bolts.
Moldboard double shinned on face, which triples the lasting qualities.
Handles strongly braced by two wood rounds, one iron rod, and one iron set brace.
Frog and land bar is welded in one piece, the frog being extra wide, making a solid bearing for the moldboard and point.
The point brace, bolted to the point, mold, and landside, prevents the point from springing, no matter how hard and sudden the jar.

An extra high grade, strong, heavy plow, suited for general purpose work, particularly in clay, stiff, and stubble lands, and in heavy bottom lands.

Its turning qualities are perfect. It will turn the sod entirely under in timothy, clover, and bluegrass, while in stubble or old ground will turn sufficient to cover all trash and weeds, and leave the land in excellent shape for pulverizing with a harrow. The long easy mold offers very little resistance to be overcome; it is light draft, a useful style, and its construction particularly adapted for deep and heavy work.

Chilled points made for all sizes.

Fin cutters can be furnished for all sizes steel points. Cost extra.

B. F. AVERY & SONS.  LOUISVILLE, KY.

AVERY'S STEEL PLOWS.

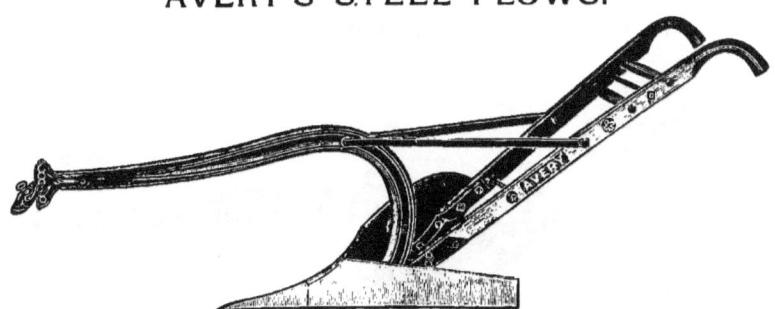

"NEW CLIPPER"—GENERAL PURPOSE PLOW. LANDSIDE VIEW.
(PATENTED.)

Double beaded steel beam, high curve.
For general description see preceding page.
Beam painted green, handles red, black tipped.

PRICE LIST—WOOD BEAM.
Right and Left Hand.   Without Extra Point.

Number and Name.	Code Word.	Cut.	Weight.	Price.	Fin Cutter with Bolts.	Straight Knife Coulter.	Gauge Wheel.	Jointer.
No. 10, New Clipper, W. B.	Jabber.	10 in.	84 lbs.	$13 50	$0 70	$1 50	$1 50	$2 50
No. 12, New Clipper, W. B.	Jacket.	12 in.	96 lbs.	15 75	70	1 75	1 50	2 50
No. 14, New Clipper, W. B.	Jaconet.	14 in.	110 lbs.	18 25	70	1 75	1 50	2 50
No. 16, New Clipper, W. B.	Jagger.	16 in.	131 lbs.	20 50	70	1 75	1 50	2 50

PRICE LIST—STEEL BEAM.
Right and Left Hand.   Without Extra Point.

Number and Name.	Code Word.	Cut.	Weight.	Price.	Fin Cutter with Bolts.	Straight Knife Coulter.	Gauge Wheel.	Jointer.
No. 10, New Clipper, S. B.	Jambee.	10 in.	91 lbs.	$14 75	$0 70	$1 50	$1 20	$2 50
No. 12, New Clipper, S. B.	Janus.	12 in.	99 lbs.	17 25	70	1 75	1 20	2 50
No. 14, New Clipper, S. B.	Jardes.	14 in.	122 lbs.	20 00	70	1 75	1 20	2 50
No. 16, New Clipper, S. B.	Jaspoid.	16 in.	135 lbs.	22 50	70	1 75	1 20	2 50

REPAIR PRICE LIST—WOOD BEAM.

No.	Steel Point.	Chilled Point.	Mold-board.	Steel Slide.	Frog and Land Bar.	Stand-ard.	Heel.	Clevis.	Handle Braces, each.	Finished Beam.	Finished Handles, per pair.
10	$2 00	$0 60	$4 50	$1 25	$1 50	$2 00	$0 25	$0 40	$0 40	$1 50	$1 00
12	2 50	65	5 00	1 50	1 50	2 00	25	40	40	1 75	1 25
14	3 00	75	5 50	1 75	1 75	2 25	25	50	40	2 00	1 50
16	3 50	80	6 00	2 00	1 75	2 25	25	50	40	2 25	1 75

REPAIR PRICE LIST—STEEL BEAM.
When ordering repairs state "for Steel Beam Plow."

No.	Steel Point.	Chilled Point.	Mold-board.	Steel Slide.	Frog and Land Bar.	Heel.	Clevis.	Handle Braces, each.	Finished Beam.	Finished Handles, per pair.
10	$2 00	$0 60	$4 50	$1 25	$1 50	$0 25	$0 50	$0 40	$4 50	$1 00
12	2 50	65	5 00	1 50	1 50	25	50	40	4 75	1 25
14	3 00	75	5 50	1 75	1 75	25	60	40	5 00	1 50
16	3 50	80	6 00	2 00	1 75	25	60	40	5 50	1 75

In ordering repairs always state whether for "Clipper" or "New Clipper." Clipper Plows and repairs are different from New Clipper Plows and repairs.

B. F. AVERY & SONS.   LOUISVILLE, KY.

AVERY'S STEEL PLOWS.

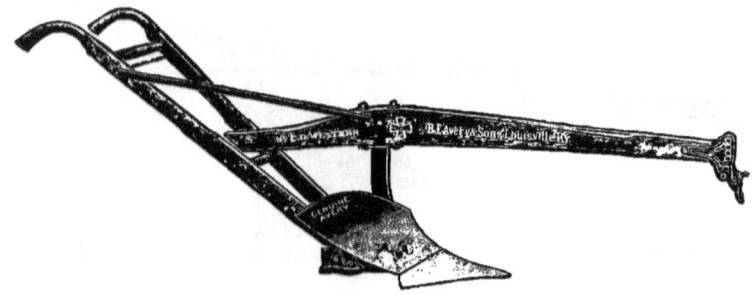

"WESTERN" GENERAL PURPOSE PLOW.
(PATENTED.)

Patent malleable frog.
Patent adjustable chilled heel.
Beam and handles painted red, black tipped.
Extra hardened soft center steel moldboard, point, and slide.
Wrought steel standard and cap, attached to beam by two bolts.

An excellent light draft general purpose plow that will do splendid work in all clay, loam, and ordinary soils, and in wheat, corn, tobacco, and cotton stubble can not be excelled.
Has ample moldboard and turning power, and works nicely in old ground, turning bluegrass, timothy, or clover admirably.
Chilled points made for all sizes.
Fin cutters can be furnished for all sizes steel points. Cost extra.

PRICE LIST—WOOD BEAM.

*Right and Left Hand; all others Right Hand only.   With Extra Steel Point.

Number and Name.	Code Word.	Cut.	Weight.	Price.	Fin Cutter with Bolts.	Straight Knife Coulter.	Gauge Wheel.
No. Pony, Western, W. B.	Jazel.	7 in.	44 lbs.	$7 00	$0 60	$1 00	$1 50
No. A.O., Western, W. B.	Jegget.	8 in.	52 lbs.	8 50	60	1 00	1 50
No. B.O., Western, W. B.	Jerbo.	9 in.	55 lbs.	10 00	70	1 00	1 50
No. C.O., Western, W. B.*	Jester.	10 in.	80 lbs.	12 00	70	1 50	1 50
No. D.O., Western, W. B.*	Jetty.	11 in.	82 lbs.	13 00	70	1 50	1 50
No. E.O., Western, W. B.*	Jiggish.	12 in.	97 lbs.	14 00	70	1 75	1 50

REPAIR PRICE LIST.

Number.	Soft Center Steel Point.	Chilled Point.	Soft Center Steel Moldboard.	Soft Center Steel Slide.	Frog.	Heel.	Clevis.	Handle Braces.	Standard Welded to Landbar with Steel Slide and Bolts.	Finished Beam.	Finished Handles, per pair.
Pony	$1 10	$0 25	$2 00	$0 75	$0 50	$0 20	$0 15	$0 35	$2 25	$0 90	$0 75
A.O	1 10	30	2 50	75	50	20	15	35	2 50	1 00	75
B.O	1 35	35	3 00	90	50	20	20	35	2 75	1 10	80
C.O	1 50	40	3 50	1 00	85	25	40	40	3 50	1 20	1 00
D.O	1 75	50	4 00	1 10	85	25	40	40	3 75	1 35	1 00
E.O	2 00	65	5 00	1 25	1 00	25	50	40	4 00	1 85	1 25
F.O	2 25	85	5 00	1 25	1 00	25	50	40	4 50	2 25	1 50

NOTE.—In ordering extra beams for Nos. C.O., D.O., E.O., and F. O., state whether for top or side clevis.

B. F. AVERY & SONS.   LOUISVILLE, KY.

AVERY'S STEEL PLOWS.

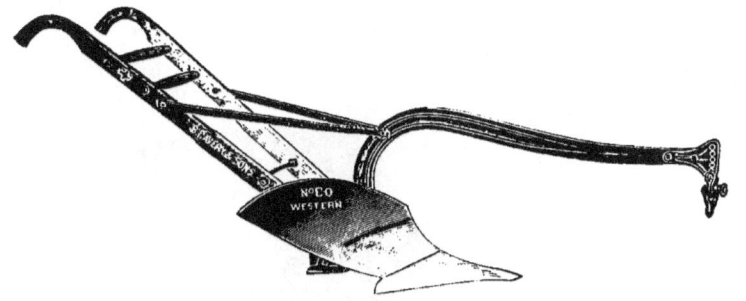

"WESTERN"—GENERAL PURPOSE PLOW.
(PATENTED.)

Wrought steel frog.
Patent adjustable chilled heel.
Double beaded steel beam, high curve.
Beam and handles painted red, black tipped.
Extra hardened soft center steel moldboard, point, and slide.
Straight handles, interchangeable on all plows of same size and pattern.

This series of plows is very strong, and is constantly growing in popularity on account of being adapted for a great variety of work, lightness of draft, and excellent pulverizers, leaving the ground with smooth, even surface.
Chilled points made for all sizes.
Fin cutters can be furnished for all sizes steel points. Cost extra.

PRICE LIST—STEEL BEAM.

*Right and Left Hand; all others Right Hand only.   With Extra Steel Point.

Number and Name.	Code Word.	Cut.	Weight.	Price.	Fin Cutter with Bolts.	Straight Knife Coulter.	Gauge Wheel.
No. Pony, Western, S. B.	Jockey.	7 in.	60 lbs.	$9 50	$0 60	$1 00	$1 10
No. A.O., Western, S. B.	Jogger.	8 in.	71 lbs.	11 00	60	1 00	1 10
No. B.O., Western, S. B.	Joiner.	9 in.	72 lbs.	13 00	70	1 00	1 20
No. C.O., Western, S. B.*	Joker.	10 in.	90 lbs.	15 00	70	1 50	1 20
No. D.O., Western, S. B.*	Jorum.	11 in.	96 lbs.	16 00	70	1 50	1 20
No. E.O., Western, S. B.*	Jowter.	12 in.	108 lbs.	17 50	70	1 75	1 20

REPAIR PRICE LIST.

When ordering repairs state "for Steel Beam Plow."

Number.	Soft Center Steel Point.	Chilled Point.	Soft Center Steel Moldboard.	Soft Center Steel Slide.	Frog and LandBar.	Heel.	Clevis.	Handle Braces.	Finished Beam.	Finished Handles, per pair.
Pony	$1 10	$0 25	$2 00	$0 75	$0 60	$0 20	$0 35	$0 35	$3 00	$0 75
A.O.	1 10	30	2 50	75	60	20	35	35	3 00	75
B.O.	1 35	35	3 00	90	75	20	35	35	3 50	80
C.O.	1 50	40	3 50	1 00	85	25	40	40	4 00	1 00
D.O.	1 75	50	4 00	1 10	85	25	40	40	4 00	1 00
E.O.	2 00	65	5 00	1 25	1 00	25	40	40	5 00	1 25
F.O.	2 25	85	5 00	1 25	1 00	25	40	40	5 00	1 50

B. F. AVERY & SONS.   LOUISVILLE, KY.

AVERY'S STEEL PLOWS.

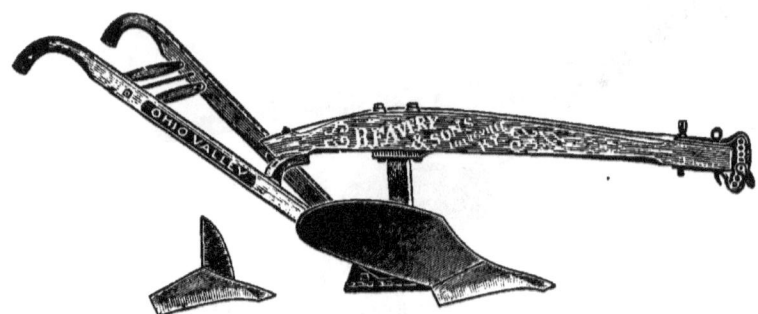

"OHIO VALLEY"—GENERAL PURPOSE PLOW. OUR "BLUE LINE."

Extra heavy cast frog.
Steel moldboard, point, and slide.
Beam and handles painted blue, red tipped.
Point fastened to frog by big bolts, easily removed for repairs.
Wrought steel standard and cap, attached to beam by two bolts.
Index beam rest between handles, permitting adjustment for land.
Straight handles, interchangeable on all plows of same size and pattern.
Handles strongly braced by two wood rounds, one iron rod, and index beam rest.

This line of plows is especially adapted for the soils of the Ohio Valley and similar districts. A general purpose plow of light draft and perfect shape, and very desirable for clay and loam soils, clover, bluegrass, and timothy sod, and for wheat and corn lands, etc. The construction is simple and strong.
Chilled points made for all sizes.

PRICE LIST—WOOD BEAM.

Right and Left Hand.   **With Plain or Fin Cutter Extra Steel Point.**

Number and Name.	Code Word.	Cut.	Weight.	Price.	Straight Knife Coulter.	Gauge Wheel.
No. 8, Ohio Valley, W. B.	Judger.	8 in.	60 lbs.	$8 25	$1 50	$1 50
No. 9, Ohio Valley, W. B.	Julep.	9 in.	78 lbs.	9 00	1 50	1 50
No. 10, Ohio Valley, W. B.	Juno.	10 in.	100 lbs.	11 00	1 50	1 50
No. 11, Ohio Valley, W. B.	Jurist.	11 in.	105 lbs.	12 00	1 75	1 50
No. 12, Ohio Valley, W. B.	Jutty.	12 in.	107 lbs.	13 50	1 75	1 50

REPAIR PRICE LIST.

No.	Plain Steel Point.	Fin Cut'r Steel Point.	Chilled Point.	Mold-board.	Steel Slide.	Frog with Land Bar.	Stand-ard.	Clevis.	Beam Rest.	Finished Beam.	Finished Handles, per pair.
8	$1 25	$1 50	$0 50	$3 25	$1 00	$1 60	$1 00	$0 25	$0 30	$1 10	$0 80
9	1 50	1 75	55	3 75	1 00	1 60	1 00	25	30	1 10	80
10	1 75	2 00	60	4 00	1 25	2 00	1 25	30	35	1 20	1 00
11	2 00	2 25	65	4 50	1 25	2 00	1 35	30	40	1 25	1 00
12	2 00	2 25	70	5 00	1 25	2 00	1 50	30	50	1 75	1 25

B. F. AVERY & SONS.   LOUISVILLE, KY.

AVERY'S STEEL PLOWS.

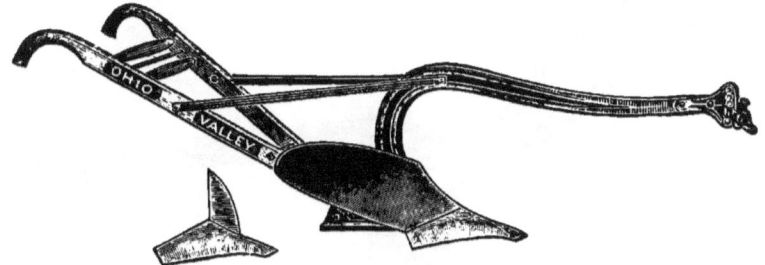

"OHIO VALLEY"—GENERAL PURPOSE PLOW. "OUR BLUE LINE."

Extra heavy cast frog.
Steel moldboard, point, and slide.
Double beaded steel beam, high curve.
Beam and handles painted blue, red tipped.
Point fastened to frog by big bolts, easily removed for repairs.
Straight handles, interchangeable on all plows of same size and pattern.
Handles strongly braced by two wood rounds, one iron rod, and an iron set brace.

In shape, finish, and general construction, except the beam, this plow is the same as the wood beam series described on preceding page, and will be found to possess all the excellent qualities which go to make up a first-class plow.

Chilled points made for all sizes.

PRICE LIST—STEEL BEAM.

Right and Left Hand.   With Plain or Fin Cutter Extra Point.

Number and Name.	Code Word.	Cut.	Weight.	Price.	Straight Knife Coulter.	Gauge Wheel.
No. 8, Ohio Valley, S. B	Kaolin.	8 in.	85 lbs.	$9 75	$1 50	$1 20
No. 9, Ohio Valley, S. B	Keeler.	9 in.	89 lbs.	10 75	1 50	1 20
No. 10, Ohio Valley, S. B	Keeve.	10 in.	104 lbs.	12 75	1 50	1 20
No. 11, Ohio Valley, S. B	Kerf.	11 in.	112 lbs.	13 75	1 75	1 20
No. 12, Ohio Valley, S. B	Kevel.	12 in.	116 lbs.	15 75	1 75	1 20

REPAIR PRICE LIST.

When ordering repairs state "for Steel Beam Plow."

No.	Plain Steel Point.	Fin Cut'r Steel Point.	Chilled Point.	Mold-board.	Steel Slide.	Frog, with Land Bar.	Clevis.	Handle Braces, each.	Finished Beam.	Finished Handles, per pair.
8	$1 25	$1 50	$0 50	$3 25	$1 00	$1 60	$0 40	$0 35	$3 50	$0 80
9	1 50	1 75	55	3 75	1 00	1 60	40	35	3 50	80
10	1 75	2 00	60	4 00	1 25	2 00	40	40	4 00	1 00
11	2 00	2 25	65	4 50	1 25	2 00	40	40	4 00	1 00
12	2 00	2 25	70	5 00	1 25	2 00	40	40	5 00	1 25

B. F. AVERY & SONS.  LOUISVILLE, KY.

AVERY'S STEEL PLOWS.

GENUINE AVERY "PONY"—ONE-HORSE PLOW. AVERY'S WORLD-RENOWNED SERIES.
(PATENTED.)

Patent malleable iron frog.
Patent adjustable chilled heel.
Hardened steel mold, point, and slide.
Beam and handles varnished, black tipped.
Wrought steel standard and cap, attached to beam by two bolts.

The banner one-horse plow, being the most perfect general purpose steel plow of its size ever designed.

Beware of imitations. None genuine without our name and trade-mark on beam and parts.
Chilled point can be furnished when desired.
Fin cutters can be furnished for steel points. Cost extra.

PRICE LIST—WOOD BEAM.

Right Hand Only. **With Extra Steel Point.**

Number and Name.	Code Word.	Cut.	Weight.	Price.	Fin Cutter with Bolts.	Straight Knife Coulter.	Gauge Wheel.
No. Pony, W. B.....	Kicker.	7 in.	43 lbs.	$5 00	$0 60	$1 00	$1 50

REPAIR PRICE LIST.

No.	Steel Point.	Chilled Point.	Mold-board.	Steel Slide.	Frog.	Heel.	Standard weld'd to Land Bar with St'l Slide and Bolts.	Clevis.	Finished Beam.	Finished Handles, per pair.
Pony.	$0 60	$0 25	$1 75	$0 50	$0 50	$0 20	$2 00	$0 15	$0 90	$0 75

NOTE.—In ordering extra handles for Pony plows, be sure to state whether wide or narrow distance handles are wanted. The distance between handles at the bottom has been widened, and the right hand handle is now bolted to steel handle lug. Old style handles were bolted to lugs on malleable frog.

B. F. AVERY & SONS.   LOUISVILLE, KY.

AVERY'S STEEL PLOWS.

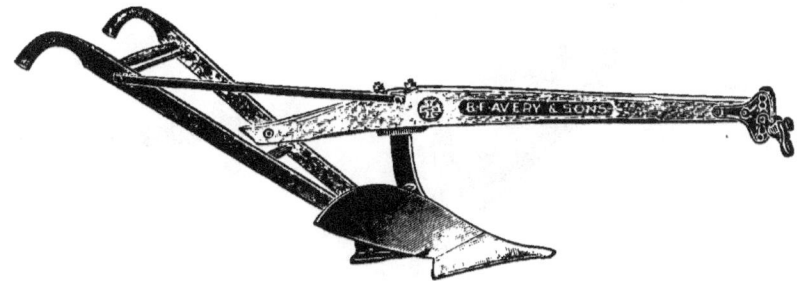

No. C. O. "GENUINE AVERY"—GENERAL PURPOSE PLOW.
(PATENTED.)

Patent malleable iron frog.
Patent adjustable chilled heel.
Hardened steel mold, point, and slide.
Beam and handles varnished, black tipped.
Wrought steel standard and cap, attached to beam by two bolts.

    This series of plows is of very light draft, and will do fine work in sandy, loam, and clay soils. They have great turning capacity, and will turn the weeds, trash, and stubble under perfectly, pulverizing the ground almost the same as if harrowed.
    Chilled points made for all sizes.
    Fin cutters can be furnished for all sizes steel points. Cost extra.

PRICE LIST—WOOD BEAM.

Right Hand Only.   With Extra Steel Point.

Number.	Code Word.	Cut.	Weight.	Price.	Fin Cutter with Bolts.	Straight Knife Coulter.	Gauge Wheel.
No. A.O., W.B	Killas.	8 in.	48 lbs.	$6 25	$0 60	$1 00	$1 50
No. B.O., W.B	Kindler.	9 in.	53 lbs.	7 50	70	1 00	1 50
No. C.O., W.B	Kiosk.	10 in.	82 lbs.	10 40	70	1 50	1 50
No. D.O., W.B	Kiver.	11 in.	84 lbs.	11 40	70	1 50	1 50
No. E.O., W.B	Knawel.	12 in.	101 lbs.	13 00	70	1 75	1 50

REPAIR PRICE LIST.

Number.	Steel Point.	Chilled Point.	Mold-board.	Steel Slide.	Frog.	Standard Welded to Land Bar with Steel Slide and Bolts.	Heel.	Clevis.	Handle Braces.	Finished Beam.	Finished Handles, per pair.
A.O.	$0 70	$0 30	$2 00	$0 60	$0 50	$2 25	$0 20	$0 15	$0 35	$1 00	$0 75
B.O.	90	35	2 75	60	50	2 50	20	20	35	1 10	80
C.O.	1 00	40	3 25	75	85	3 25	25	25	40	1 20	1 00
D.O.	1 10	50	4 00	75	85	3 50	25	40	40	1 35	1 00
E.O.	1 50	65	4 50	85	1 00	3 75	25	50	40	1 85	1 25
F.O.	2 00	85	5 00	85	1 00	4 25	25	50	40	2 25	1 50

    NOTE.—In ordering repair handles for A.O., B.O., C.O., D.O., E.O., and F.O. plows, be sure to state whether old or new style are wanted. The handles now used are wide apart at base and are bolted to steel handle lug. Old style handles were bolted to lugs on malleable frog. Also in ordering extra beams for Nos. C.O., D.O., E.O., and F.O., state whether same are to be used with top or side clevis.

B. F. AVERY & SONS.   LOUISVILLE, KY.

AVERY'S STEEL PLOWS.

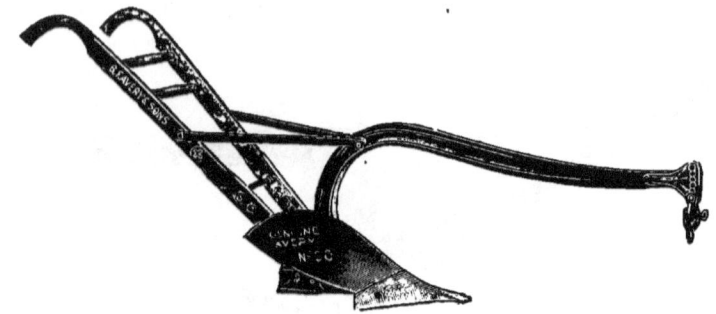

No. C.O. "GENUINE AVERY"—GENERAL PURPOSE PLOW.
(PATENTED.)

Wrought steel frog.
Patent adjustable chilled heel.
Hardened steel mold, point, and slide.
Double beaded steel beam, high curve.
Beam painted green, handles red, black tipped.
Straight handles, interchangeable on all plows of same size and pattern.

This series of Steel Beam Plows is adapted for the same class of work as the Wood Beam Series described on preceding page.
Chilled points made for all sizes.
Fin cutters can be furnished for all sizes steel points. Cost extra.

PRICE LIST—STEEL BEAM.

Right Hand Only.   With Extra Steel Point.

Number.	Code Word.	Cut.	Weight.	Price.	Fin Cutter with Bolts.	Straight Knife Coulter.	Gauge Wheel.
No. Pony, S. B.	Knight.	7 in.	57 lbs.	$7 00	$0 60	$1 00	$1 10
No. A.O., S. B.	Knobby.	8 in.	68 lbs.	8 50	60	1 00	1 10
No. B.O., S. B.	Knout.	9 in.	70 lbs.	10 00	70	1 00	1 20
No. C.O., S. B.	Kokob.	10 in.	88 lbs.	11 75	70	1 50	1 20
No. D.O., S. B.	Labefy.	11 in.	97 lbs.	12 75	70	1 50	1 20
No. E.O., S. B.	Laccine.	12 in.	105 lbs.	14 50	70	1 75	1 20

REPAIR PRICE LIST.
When ordering repairs state "for Steel Beam Plow."

No.	Steel Point.	Chilled Point.	Mold-board.	Steel Slide.	Frog and Land Bar.	Heel.	Clevis.	Handle Braces, each.	Finished Beam.	Finished Handles, per pair.
Pony	$0 60	$0 25	$1 75	$0 50	$0 60	$0 20	$0 30	$0 35	$3 00	$0 75
A.O.	70	30	2 00	60	60	20	30	35	3 00	75
B.O.	90	35	2 75	60	75	20	30	35	3 50	80
C.O.	1 00	40	3 25	75	85	25	40	40	4 00	1 00
D.O.	1 10	50	4 00	75	85	25	40	40	4 00	1 00
E.O.	1 50	65	4 50	85	1 00	25	40	40	5 00	1 25
F.O.	2 00	85	5 00	85	1 00		40	40	5 00	1 50

The moldboards of new series C.O. and D.O. steel beam plows (beginning November 1, 1890) are marked C.O.X. or D.O.X. Specify clearly in ordering these moldboards whether C.O. or C.O.X. is wanted, etc.

B. F. AVERY & SONS. LOUISVILLE, KY.

AVERY'S STEEL PLOWS.

"TINY TIM"—ONE HORSE.
(COPYRIGHTED AND PATENTED.)

Malleable iron frog.
Patent adjustable chilled heel.
Wrought steel standard and cap, attached to beam by two bolts.
Steel moldboard, point, and slide.
Beam and handles varnished, black tipped.

A popular plow for light breaking and for cultivating cotton, corn, tobacco, and gardens. Chilled points can be furnished.

"CADET"—ONE HORSE.
(PATENTED.)

Chilled landside.
Cast standard and frog.
Steel moldboard and point.
Patent adjustable chilled heel.
Beam and handles painted red, black tipped.

A good plow for bedding cotton or rounding corn, and for general light breaking and cultivating.

PRICE LIST.

Right Hand Only. / With Extra Steel Point.

Number and Name.	Code Word.	Cut.	Weight.	Price.	Fin Cutter with Bolts.
Tiny Tim	Lackey.	6 in.	35 lbs.	$5 00	$0 60
No. 6, Cadet	Lactic.	6 in.	35 lbs.	4 00	
No. 7, Cadet	Ladkin.	7 in.	37 lbs.	4 25	

REPAIR PRICE LIST.

Number and Name.	Steel Point.	Chilled Point.	Mold-board.	Steel Slide.	Frog.	Heel.	Stand-ard.	Standard weld'd to Land Bar with St'l Slide and Bolts.	Clevis.	Finished Beam.	Finished Handles, per pair.
Tiny Tim	$0 50	$0 25	$1 70	$0 55	$0 50	$0 20		$2 00	$0 15	$0 75	$0 65
No. 6, Cadet	50		1 25			20	$1 00		15	80	70
No. 7, Cadet	60		1 35			20	1 00		15	80	70

B. F. AVERY & SONS.      LOUISVILLE, KY.

AVERY'S STEEL PLOWS.

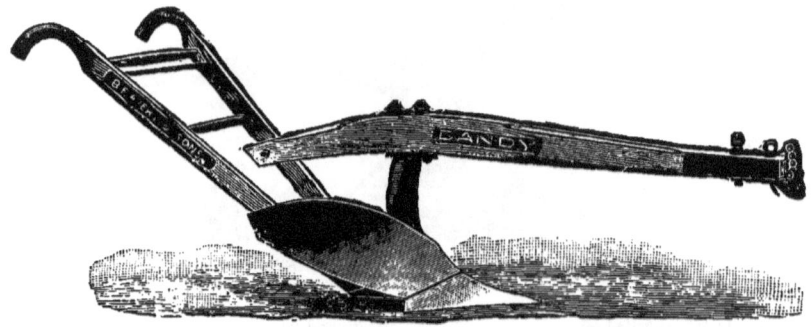

"DANDY," "STAR," AND "BIG BOLT" SERIES.

Steel moldboard.
Solid steel landside.
Special extra hard crucible steel point.
Beam and handles painted red, black tipped.
Malleable iron standard, attached to beam by two bolts, and is of such shape that it readily clears itself of trash.
The points of Nos. 6½, 7, and 8X are fastened by one bolt, and Nos. 9 and 10 by two bolts, and are all on the face, which makes it very easy to remove and replace points.

A strong, simple, common-sense plow, with few parts. (Only four pieces compose the entire base of this plow.)

We specially recommend this plow to corn, cotton, and sugar planters and truckers. They have the lightest possible draft, and will scour in almost any soil. Good breaking and cultivating plows especially for the "bottoms," but good for the hills and general purposes also.

PRICE LIST—WOOD BEAM.

Right Hand Only.   **With Extra Steel Point.**

Number and Name.	Code Word.	Cut.	Weight.	Price.	Straight Knife Coulter.
No. 6½, Dandy	Lagoon.	6½ in.	49 lbs.	$5 75	$1 00
No. 7, Dandy	Lamel.	7 in.	50 lbs.	6 50	1 00
No. 8X, Dandy	Lamin.	8 in.	55 lbs.	7 00	1 00
No. 9, Dandy	Lamprey.	9 in.	82 lbs.	10 50	1 00
No. 10, Dandy	Landau.	10 in.	86 lbs.	11 50	1 50

REPAIR PRICE LIST.

Number and Name.	Steel Point.	Steel Moldboard.	Steel Landside.	Standard.	Clevis.	Finished Beam.	Finished Handles, per pair.
6½, Dandy	$0 70	$1 50	$0 75	$1 30	$0 20	$0 80	$0 70
7, Dandy	80	1 75	80	1 40	20	80	70
8X, Dandy	90	2 00	90	1 50	20	1 00	75
9, Dandy	1 00	2 75	1 00	1 70	25	1 10	90
10, Dandy	1 25	3 00	1 10	2 00	25	1 25	90

The points of the No. 8 Dandy are not interchangeable with the No. 8X Dandy. In ordering, be careful to state if points are wanted for No. 8 or No. 8X Dandy.

B. F. AVERY & SONS.  LOUISVILLE, KY.

AVERY'S STEEL PLOWS.

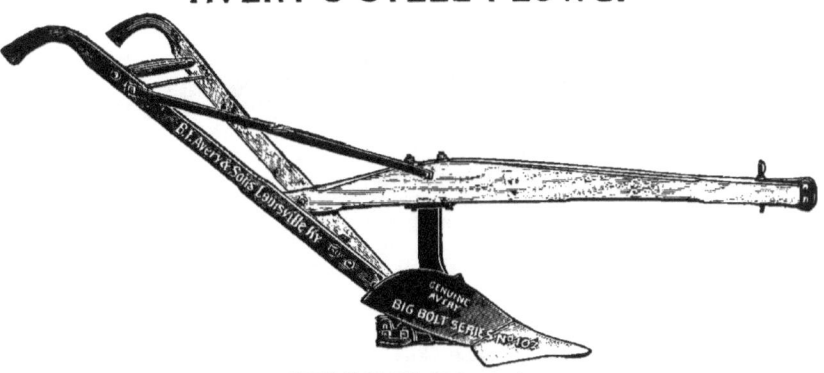

"BIG BOLT"—Patented.

Solid steel landside.
Patent adjustable chilled heel.
Beam and handles painted red, black tipped.
Wrought steel standard and cap, attached to beam by two bolts. Wrought steel frog.

    This plow in general outline of moldboard and in turning capacity is similar to our world-famous Pony Series. The point is attached with one large half-inch bolt, thus enabling the operator to very readily take off the old point; also all the other bolts used in the bottom of the plow are one-half inch.

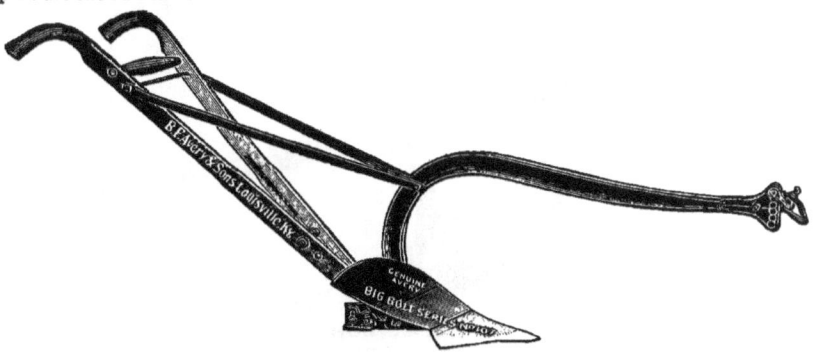

"BIG BOLT"—Patented.

This plow answers the description given above in every particular excepting the steel beam.

PRICE LIST.

Right Hand Only.   With Extra Steel Point.

Number and Name.	Code Word, Wood Beam.	Code Word, Steel Beam.	Cut.	Weight, Wood Beam.	Weight, Steel Beam.	Wood Beam Plow.	Steel Beam Plow.
No. 107, Big Bolt	Landslip.	Larch.	7 in.	58 lbs.	77 lbs.	$5 75	$7 50
No. 108, Big Bolt	Lanner.	Larker.	8 in.	62 lbs.	84 lbs.	6 75	9 00
No. 109, Big Bolt	Lapel.	Lasher.	9 in.	65 lbs.	85 lbs.	7 50	10 00

REPAIR PRICE LIST.

No.	Steel Point.	Mold-board.	Solid Steel Landside.	Frog.	Standard Only.	Heel.	Clevis, Wood Beam.	Clevis, Steel Beam.	Finished Wood Beam.	Finished Steel Beam.	Finished Handles, per pair.
107	$0 70	$1 75	$0 75	$0 60	$1 25	$0 20	$0 15	$0 30	$0 90	$3 00	$0 75
108	80	2 00	85	60	1 50	20	15	30	1 00	3 00	75
109	90	2 75	95	60	1 75	20	15	30	1 10	3 50	80

B. F. AVERY & SONS. LOUISVILLE, KY.

AVERY'S STEEL PLOWS.

"RAINBOW"—AN EXTRA HIGH GRADE PLOW.

Wrought steel frog.
Extra hardened soft center steel moldboard.
Beam and handles painted red, green tipped.
Solid steel landside, with extra hardened steel heel welded on.
Wrought steel standard and cap, attached to beam by two bolts.
Point brace, bolted to point and landside, prevents the point from springing, no matter how hard or sudden the jar.
All bolts used in the bottom are one-half inch diameter and are easily removed, facilitating the fitting on of duplicate parts.

    Avery's Rainbow plows have been made especially for use in the black, sticky lands of Mississippi, Texas, and other waxy, stiff soils. They will do perfect work in the bottoms of the Delta and elsewhere, and in buckshot anywhere, and will scour or shed satisfactorily in the most stubborn soils. These plows are so constructed as to have all necessary strength, and the draft is very light for the amount of work.

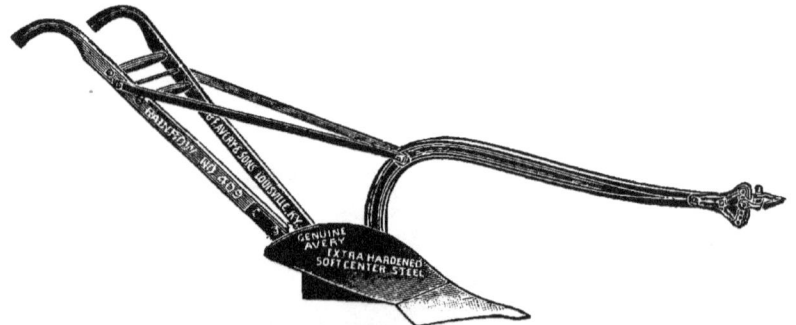

"RAINBOW"—AN EXTRA HIGH GRADE PLOW.

This plow answers the description given above in every particular excepting the steel beam.

Right Hand Only.   **PRICE LIST.**   With Extra Steel Point.

Number and Name.	Code Word, Wood Beam.	Code Word, Steel Beam.	Cut.	Weight, Wood Beam.	Weight, Steel Beam.	Wood Beam Plow.	Steel Beam Plow.
No. 407, Rainbow	Latch.	Launch.	7 in.	66 lbs.	81 lbs.	$9 00	$11 50
No. 408, Rainbow	Lathe.	Lautu.	8 in.	74 lbs.	87 lbs.	10 00	12 50
No. 409, Rainbow	Latrant.	Lavolta.	9 in.	89 lbs.	99 lbs.	11 50	14 50
No. 410, Rainbow	Laud.	Laxity.	10 in.	93 lbs.	100 lbs.	12 50	16 00

REPAIR PRICE LIST.

Number.	Steel Point.	Moldboard.	Solid Steel Landside.	Frog.	Standard Only.	Clevis, W. B.	Clevis, S. B.	Finished Wood Beam.	Finished Steel Beam.	Finished Handles, per pair.
No. 407	$1 10	$2 50	$1 20	$1 50	$2 00	$0 20	$0 40	$1 25	$3 00	$1 00
No. 408	1 10	3 00	1 30	1 50	2 00	40	40	1 50	3 50	1 25
No. 409	1 35	3 50	1 50	1 75	2 25	40	40	1 75	3 75	1 25
No. 410	1 50	4 00	1 75	1 75	2 25	40	40	2 00	4 00	1 25

B. F. AVERY & SONS.  LOUISVILLE, KY.

AVERY'S STEEL PLOWS.

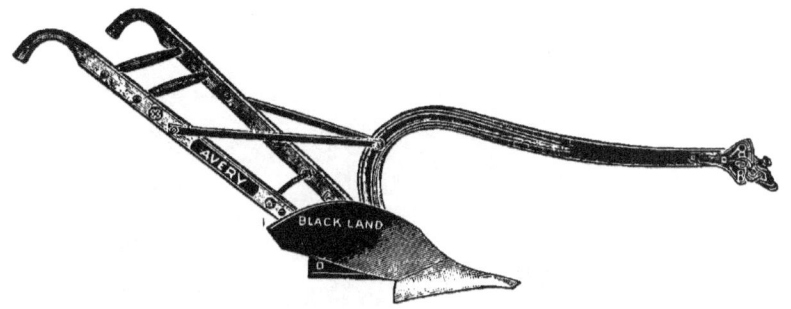

"IMPROVED" BLACKLAND PLOW.

Wrought steel frog.
Double beaded steel beam, high curve.
Beam and handles painted red, black tipped.
Special extra hard crucible steel point and slide.
Extra hardened soft center steel convex moldboard.
Straight handles, interchangeable on all plows of same size and pattern.
Wrought steel point brace, preventing the point from springing, no matter how hard or sudden the jar.

This series of Plows is designed for and work excellently in the sticky, waxy, hard-to-scour red clay, buckshot, and black or sticky, stiff soils of Texas, in bottom lands, etc. Come nearer scouring or shedding than any Blackland Plow made; widely used where other plows will not shed or take the ground.

No clogging or loading up, nor balling up in the bottom.

PRICE LIST—STEEL BEAM.

Right Hand Only.   With Extra Steel Point.

Number and Name.	Code Word.	Cut.	Weight.	Price.	Straight Knife Coulter.	Gauge Wheel.
No. 7, Improved Blackland.	Leach.	7 in.	71 lbs.	$11 50	$1 25	$1 10
No. 8, Improved Blackland.	Leaf.	8 in.	72 lbs.	12 50	1 25	1 20
No. 9, Improved Blackland.	Leaper.	9 in.	85 lbs.	14 50	1 50	1 20
No. 10, Improved Blackland.	Leather.	10 in.	89 lbs.	16 00	1 50	1 20
No. 11, Improved Blackland.	Leaver.	11 in.	99 lbs.	17 00	1 75	1 20
No. 12, Improved Blackland.	Ledger.	12 in.	102 lbs.	19 00	1 75	1 20

REPAIR PRICE LIST.

No.	Steel Point.	Steel Slide.	Mold-board.	Frog and Land Bar.	Handle Braces, each.	Point Brace.	Clevis.	Finished Beam.	Finished Handles, per pair.
7	$1 10	$0 80	$2 50	$1 25	$0 35		$0 40	$3 00	$1 00
8	1 10	85	3 00	1 25	35	$0 20	40	3 50	1 25
9	1 35	1 00	3 50	1 50	35	25	40	3 75	1 25
10	1 50	1 15	4 00	1 50	40	25	40	4 00	1 25
11	1 75	1 25	4 15	1 50	40	30	40	4 25	1 25
12	2 50	1 25	4 25	1 50	40	30	40	4 50	1 25

B. F. AVERY & SONS.      LOUISVILLE, KY.

AVERY'S STEEL PLOWS.

"X" SERIES BLACKLAND PLOWS.
(PATENTED.)

Malleable iron frog.
Patent adjustable chilled heel.
Hardened steel convex moldboard.
Beam and handles painted red, black tipped.
Special extra hard crucible steel point and slide.
Wrought steel standard and cap, attached to beam by two bolts.
Handles strongly braced by two wood rounds, one iron rod, and one iron set brace.

These plows are made the lightest possible draft and strong; will reasonably turn and shed the black, waxy, and hog-wallow lands, or any class of sticky lands. Thousands in use on plantations giving satisfaction. One of our old reliable series.

We make a Special Sugarland series of these Blackland plows, heavier throughout; to be ordered "Special Sugarland."

Chilled points made for all sizes.

PRICE LIST—WOOD BEAM.

Right Hand Only.   **With Extra Steel Point.**

Number and Name.		Code Word.	Cut.	Weight.	Price.	Straight Knife Coulter.	Gauge Wheel.
No. 61	X, Blackland, W. B.	Legato.	7 in.	55 lbs.	$7 50	$1 00	$1 50
No. 62	X, Blackland, W. B.	Legist.	8 in.	74 lbs.	9 00	1 25	1 50
No. 62½	X, Blackland, W. B.	Lemma.	9 in.	78 lbs.	10 50	1 50	1 50
No. 63	X, Blackland, W. B.	Lenient.	10 in.	82 lbs.	12 00	1 50	1 50
No. 64	X, Blackland, W. B.	Leonine.	11 in.	101 lbs.	18 50	1 75	1 50
No. 65	X, Blackland, W. B.	Lessee.	12 in.	124 lbs.	16 00	1 75	1 50
No. 65	X, Blackland, W. B.	Lettuce.	14 in.	127 lbs.	18 00	1 75	1 50

REPAIR PRICE LIST.

No.	Steel Point.	Chilled Point.	Mold-board.	Steel Slide.	Frog.	Standard Welded to Land Bar with Steel Slide and Bolts	Heel.	Clevis.	Finished Beam.	Finished Handles, per pair.
61 X	$0 80	$0 25	$2 00	$0 65	$1 00	$2 00	$0 20	$0 20	$1 00	$0 90
62 X	90	35	2 50	65	1 05	2 50	25	40	1 30	90
62½ X	1 15	40	2 75	75	1 05	2 75	25	40	1 80	1 00
63 X	1 25	50	3 00	75	1 10	3 50	25	40	1 80	1 00
64 X	1 50	70	3 50	1 00	1 20	4 00	25	50	2 00	1 25
65 X	2 00	80	4 00	1 00	2 20	4 00	25	50	3 00	1 50
65 X	2 25	90	4 00	1 00	2 20	4 00	25	50	3 00	1 50

In ordering repairs be careful to state whether for Nos. 62, 63, 64, or 65 plows, or for 62X, 63X, 64X, and 65X.

B. F. AVERY & SONS.  LOUISVILLE, KY.

AVERY'S STEEL PLOWS.

"X" SERIES BLACKLAND PLOWS.
(PATENTED.)

Wrought steel frog.
Patent adjustable chilled heel.
Hardened steel convex moldboard.
Double beaded steel beam, high curve.
Beam painted green, handles red, black tipped.
Special extra hard crucible steel point and slide.
Straight handles, interchangeable on all plows of same size and pattern.

The X series of Steel Beam Blackland plows possesses all the excellent qualities of the wood beam series, with the additional advantage of the steel beam, and will be found to meet the requirements of the most difficult soil in a highly satisfactory manner.

Chilled points made for all sizes.

PRICE LIST—STEEL BEAM.

Right Hand Only.   **With Extra Steel Point.**

Number and Name.	Code Word.	Cut.	Weight.	Price.	Straight Knife Coulter.	Gauge Wheel.
No. 61 X, Blackland, S. B.	Levee.	7 in.	67 lbs.	$9 50	$1 00	$1 10
No. 62 X, Blackland, S. B.	Levite.	8 in.	77 lbs.	11 00	1 25	1 20
No. 62½ X, Blackland, S. B.	Lexical.	9 in.	87 lbs.	12 50	1 50	1 20
No. 63 X, Blackland, S. B.	Libation.	10 in.	90 lbs.	13 50	1 50	1 20
No. 64 X, Blackland, S. B.	Liberate.	11 in.	103 lbs.	15 00	1 75	1 20
No. 65 X, Blackland, S. B.	Licit.	12 in.	122 lbs.	18 00	1 75	1 20
No. 65 X, Blackland, S. B.	Liege.	14 in.	126 lbs.	20 00	1 75	1 20

REPAIR PRICE LIST.
When ordering repairs state "for Steel Beam Plow."

No.	Steel Point.	Chilled Point.	Mold-board.	Steel Slide.	Land Bar.	Heel.	Frog.	Clevis.	Handle Braces, each.	Finished Beam.	Finished Handles, per pair.
61 X	$0 80	$0 25	$2 00	$0 65	$0 75	$0 20	$0 50	$0 30	$0 35	$3 00	$0 90
62 X	90	35	2 50	65	80	25	60	40	35	3 50	90
62½X	1 15	40	2 75	75	1 00	25	60	40	35	3 50	1 00
63 X	1 25	50	3 00	75	1 00	25	75	40	40	4 00	1 00
64 X	1 50	70	3 50	1 00	1 35	25	75	40	40	5 00	1 25
65 X	2 00	80	4 00	1 00	2 20	25	90	40	40	6 00	1 50
65 X	2 25	90	4 00	1 00	2 20	25	1 00	40	40	6 00	1 50

In ordering repairs be careful to state whether for Nos. 62, 63, 64, or 65 plows, or for 62X, 63X, 64X, and 65X.

B. F. AVERY & SONS.   LOUISVILLE, KY.

AVERY'S STEEL PLOWS.

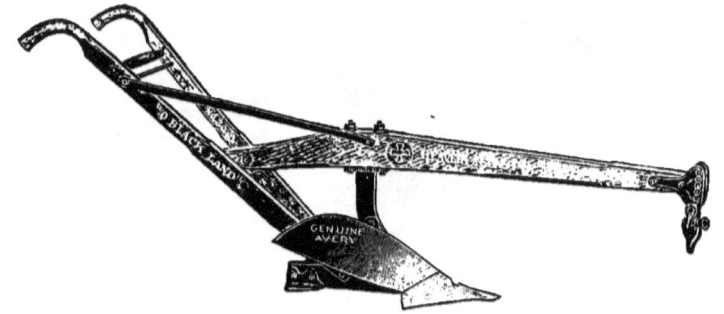

"O" OR "OUGHT" SERIES BLACKLAND PLOWS.
(PATENTED.)

Patent malleable iron frog.
Patent adjustable chilled heel.
Hardened steel convex moldboard.
Beam and handles varnished, black tipped.
Special extra hard crucible steel point and slide.
Wrought steel standard and cap, attached to beam by two bolts.

This old series of Blackland plows is very popular. A good general purpose plow for black land. Light, trim, and comparatively easy draft. Imitated by many, equaled by none.

PRICE LIST—WOOD BEAM.

Right Hand Only. **With Extra Steel Point.**

Number and Name.	Code Word.	Cut.	Weight.	Price.	Straight Knife Coulter.	Gauge Wheel.
No. 20-O, Blackland, W.B.	Lifter.	6½ in.	50 lbs.	$7 50	$1 00	$1 50
No. 30-O, Blackland, W.B.	Lighter.	7½ in.	70 lbs.	9 00	1 25	1 50
No. 40-O, Blackland, W.B.	Lignify.	8½ in.	72 lbs.	11 00	1 50	1 50

REPAIR PRICE LIST.

No.	Steel Point.	Mold-board.	Steel Slide.	Frog.	Standard Welded to Land Bar with Steel Slide and Bolts.	Heel.	Clevis.	Handle Braces, each.	Finished Beam.	Finished Handles, per pair.
20-O	$0 80	$2 00	$0 65	$0 65	$2 00	$0 20	$0 20	$0 35	$1 00	$0 90
30-O	90	2 50	70	80	2 50	20	40	35	1 30	90
40-O	1 00	2 75	75	80	2 75	25	40	35	1 80	1 00

B. F. AVERY & SONS.   LOUISVILLE, KY.

AVERY'S STEEL PLOWS.

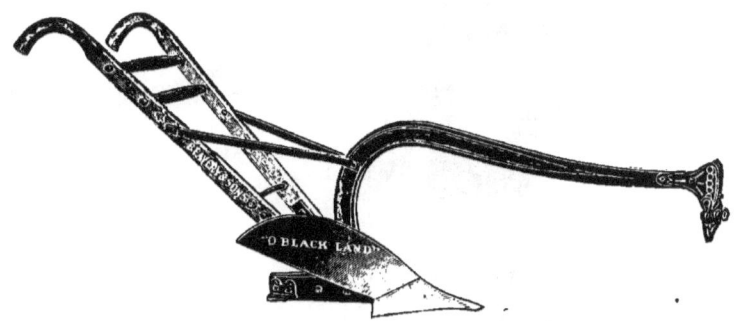

"O" OR "OUGHT" SERIES BLACKLAND PLOWS.
(PATENTED.)

Wrought steel frog.
Patent adjustable chilled heel.
Hardened steel convex moldboard.
Double beaded steel beam, high curve.
Beam painted green, handles red, black tipped.
Special extra hard crucible steel point and slide.
Straight handles, interchangeable on all plows of same size and pattern.

After years of severe test, they stand as an old reliable series, and as good, easy workers in sticky land.

PRICE LIST—STEEL BEAM.

Right Hand Only. **With Extra Steel Point.**

Number and Name.	Code Word.	Cut.	Weight.	Price.	Straight Knife Coulter.	Gauge Wheel.
No. 20-0, Blackland, S. B	Lingo.	6½ in.	66 lbs.	$9 00	$1 00	$1 10
No. 30-0, Blackland, S. B	Linnet.	7½ in.	76 lbs.	10 50	1 25	1 20
No. 40-0, Blackland, S. B	Lisbon.	8½ in.	87 lbs.	12 50	1 50	1 20

REPAIR PRICE LIST.

When ordering repairs state "for Steel Beam Plow."

No.	Steel Point.	Mold-board.	Steel Slide.	Land Bar.	Frog.	Heel.	Clevis.	Handle Braces, each.	Finished Beams.	Finished Handles, per pair.
20-0	$0 80	$2 00	$0 65	$0 75	$0 50	$0 20	$0 30	$0 35	$3 00	$0 90
30-0	90	2 50	70	80	60	20	40	35	3 50	90
40-0	1 00	2 75	75	90	60	25	40	35	3 50	1 00

B. F. AVERY & SONS.   LOUISVILLE, KY.

AVERY'S STEEL PLOWS.

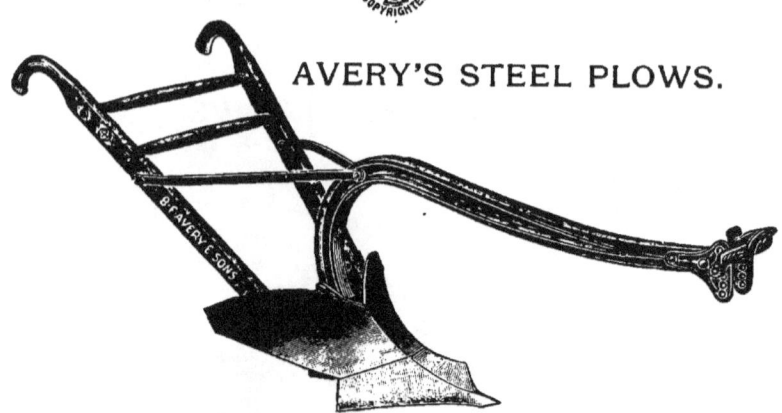

"STEEL BEAM MIDDLE BURSTER."

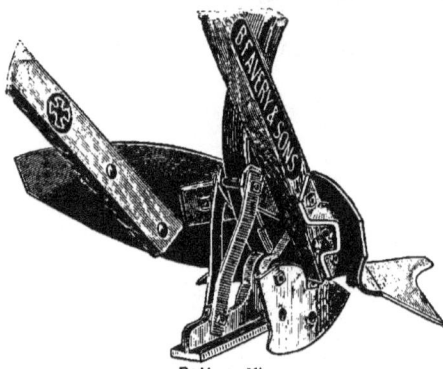

Bottom View.

Very strongly built and braced.
Double beaded steel beam, high curve.
Extra hardened soft center steel moldboard.
Beam and handles painted red, black tipped.
Perfect steel rudder to guide and steady plow.
Special extra hard crucible steel point, with an extra thick and deep penetrating nose.
The easy-running and perfect-working qualities of these bursters have put them far in the lead of every other series designed for middle bursting, etc. Take the ground, hug it and run exceedingly steady, no matter how stiff the soil nor how frequent the obstructions.
They are especially adapted for the bursting of corn or cotton ridges and plowing out quarter drains. Many of our friends using them write us they find these plows to keep steady to the work, running the entire length of long ridges, bursting them out perfectly, without requiring the plow handles to be touched after starting. For Riding Middle Bursters, see pages 45 and 47.

PRICE LIST.
With Extra Steel Point.

Number and Name.	Code Word.	Cut.	Extreme Width of Moldboards.	Weight.	Price.
No. 9, Middle Burster, S. B	Liver.	9 in.	16 in.	78 lbs.	$16 00
No. 10, Middle Burster, S. B	Loach.	10 in.	16½ in.	88 lbs.	16 50
No. 12, Middle Burster, S. B	Loaves.	12 in.	18½ in.	91 lbs.	17 50
No. 14, Middle Burster, S. B	Loch.	14 in.	22½ in.	99 lbs.	22 50
No. 16, Middle Burster, S. B	Lockey.	16 in.	23 in.	102 lbs.	27 50
No. 18, Middle Burster, S. B	Lodger.	18 in.	25 in.	118 lbs.	32 50
No. 20, Middle Burster, S. B	Logic.	20 in.	26½ in.	120 lbs.	37 50

REPAIR PRICE LIST.

No.	Steel Point.	Moldboard, Right or Left.	Steel Rudder.	Frog.	Heel.	Clevis.	Handle Braces, each.	Finished Beam.	Finished Handles, per pair.
9	$2 50	$2 00	$1 50	$1 50	$0 40	$0 40	$0 40	$3 50	$0 90
10	3 00	2 00	1 50	1 50	40	40	40	3 50	90
12	3 50	2 25	1 60	1 60	40	40	40	3 50	90
14	4 00	2 50	1 75	1 75	50	40	40	4 00	1 00
16	4 50	3 25	2 00	2 00	50	40	40	4 50	1 00
18	5 00	4 00	2 25	2 00	60	40	40	4 75	1 25
20	5 50	4 50	2 25	2 25	60	40	40	5 00	1 50

B. F. AVERY & SONS.   LOUISVILLE, KY.

AVERY'S STEEL PLOWS.

"ADVANCE"—DOUBLE MOLDBOARD PLOW.

Malleable iron frog.
Solid steel moldboards.
Removable cast iron runner.
Special extra hard crucible steel point.
Beam and handles painted red, black tipped.

Is specially adapted for bursting corn, garden, and cotton ridges, for hilling potatoes and making trenches for irrigation, also used for opening up a furrow for planting as well as for plowing out quarter drains, etc. In bursting ridges they save half the labor and leave the bed often in better shape than many a turning plow. In opening the cane row, etc., for planting, its work is perfect. It is also used in opening or splitting the middle of the row during the cultivating season, turning the furrow evenly to each side of the bed and giving perfect drainage.

We make a straight knife coulter which is quite extensively used. (See No. 52x, page 107.)
We also make three, four, six, and eight mule sizes of "Advance" Double Moldboard Plows. Ask specially for these.

PRICE LIST—WOOD BEAM.

With Plain or Fin Cutter Extra Point as ordered.

Number and Name.	Size.	Code Word.	Cut.	Extreme Width of Moldboards.	Weight.	Price.	Straight Knife Coulter.
No. ½, Advance	1 Horse.	Loiter.	10 in.	15 in.	60 lbs.	$9 00	$1 00
No. 1, Advance	2 Horse.	Longeval.	12 in.	16½ in.	65 lbs.	11 00	1 00

REPAIR PRICE LIST.

No.	Plain Steel Point.	Fin Cutter Steel Point.	Moldboard, Right or Left Hand.	Standard.	Frog.	Clevis.	Finished Beam.	Finished Handles, per pair.
½	$1 50	$2 25	$2 00	$1 50	$1 00	$0 15	$0 90	$0 75
1	1 75	2 50	2 25	1 50	1 00	15	1 00	75

B. F. AVERY & SONS.   LOUISVILLE, KY.

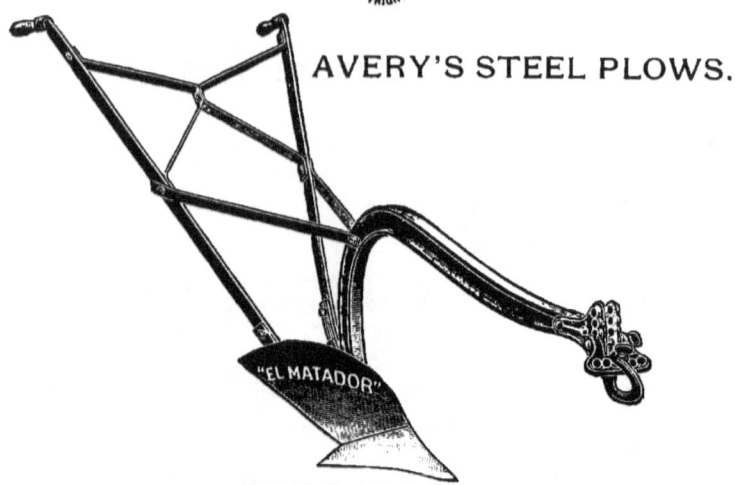

AVERY'S STEEL PLOWS.

"EL MATADOR"—Patented.

Wrought steel frog.
Patent adjustable chilled heel.
Beam and handles painted red, black tipped.
Wrought steel handles, strongly braced, with wood-lined handholds.
Double beaded steel beam, high curve.
Hardened steel moldboard, point, and slide.
Fin cutters can be furnished if desired.   Cost extra.

Right Hand Only.   **PRICE LIST.**   **With Extra Steel Point.**

Name.	Code Word.	Cut.	Weight.	Price.	Fin Cutter with Bolts.	Straight Knife Coulter.	Gauge Wheel.
El Matador	Lonish.	7 inch.	62 lbs.	$7 50	$0 60	$1 00	$1 10

REPAIR PRICE LIST.

Steel Point.	Chilled Point.	Mold-board.	Steel Slide.	Frog and Land Bar.	Heel.	Clevis.	Handle Braces, each.	Finished Beam.	Iron Handles, per pair.
$0 60	$0 25	$1 75	$0 50	$0 60	$0 20	$0 30	$0 35	$3 00	$1 00

"ORANGE" PLOW—Patented.

Malleable iron frog.
Patent adjustable chilled heel.
Wrought steel standard and cap attached to beam by two bolts.
Steel moldboard, point, and slide.
Beam and handles painted red, black tipped.

A light but strong general purpose plow that works well wherever there is a light or sandy soil; especially built and adjusted for shallow plowing, to meet the wants of orange growers and horticulturists generally; for general orchard and vineyard work, and for thoroughly turning over and wrapping under orchard grass, trash, etc.

Right Hand Only.   **PRICE LIST.**   **With Extra Steel Point.**

Number and Name.	Code Word.	Cut.	Weight.	Price.
No. 11, Orange	Loom.	11 inch.	57 lbs.	$7 50

REPAIR PRICE LIST.

Steel Point.	Mold-board.	Land-side.	Frog.	Heel.	Standard.	Clevis.	Handle Braces, each.	Finished Beam.	Fin. Handles, per pair.
$1 50	$3 00	$0 70	$0 85	$0 20	$1 50	$0 20	$0 40	$1 00	$0 80

B. F. AVERY & SONS.  LOUISVILLE, KY.

AVERY'S STEEL PLOWS.

RAILROAD OR GRADING PLOW.

Beam and handles painted red, black tipped.
Solid steel moldboard, point, and landside, extra thick.
Beam extra heavy, of choice, tough, seasoned white oak.
Heavy wrought steel handles, strongly braced by two heavy set rods.
A very strong and heavy cutter is attached to each plow, giving it additional strength.
Extra heavy wrought steel standard welded to cap, and attached to beam by two super-strong bolts.
Underneath the beam runs a heavy iron strap, attached to the standard and running to the end of beam, forming draft rod for clevis.

A monster for plowing up macadam streets, city and county roads, and the like. The strongest plow on the market. Made especially for hard, rough work. Used by railroad and other heavy contractors throughout the country.

PRICE LIST—WOOD BEAM.

Gauge Slide or Gauge Wheel supplied, as preferred, without extra charge.

Right Hand Only.   With Extra Steel Point.

Number and Name.	Code Word.	Cut.	Weight.	Price.
No. 1, Railroad	Lopper.	10 in.	235 lbs.	$30 00

REPAIR PRICE LIST.

Steel Point.	Draft Rod.	Landside.	Moldboard.	Coulter.	Gauge Wheel.	Standard with Frog.	Finished Beam.	Iron Handles, per pair.
$2 50	$5 00	$1 75	$4 00	$1 75	$1 00	$5 00	$6 00	$6 00

B. F. AVERY & SONS. LOUISVILLE, KY.

AVERY'S STEEL PLOWS.

"HARD PAN" BEET DIGGER AND SUBSOIL PLOW.

Dial clevis.
Strongly braced.
Heavy draft rod.
Beam and handles painted red, black tipped.
Wrought steel frog and land bar, welded together.
Heavy steel standard, plated out in front to act as a cutter.
Extra hardened soft center steel moldboard, point, and slide, extra heavy.
Wood beam made in two sections and bolted together, giving additional strength.

SUBSOILER.—Designed to follow in the furrow of an ordinary turning plow and loosen up the hard subsoil without bringing up and turning over the subsoil, but allowing it to fall back in its own furrow, thoroughly pulverized, and leaving the soil in excellent condition for free access of moisture and air to the roots of the growing crops, and to retain the moisture. After thorough trials and experiments in Nebraska and other sections, we are in position to offer our "Hard Pan" with the assurance that they will do this in the most complete and satisfactory manner, loosening and breaking up the soil to the depth of sixteen to nineteen inches. They will scour in any soil and do deep plowing without clogging.

BEET DIGGER.—To obtain best results, the ground for beets must be subsoiled, and after the crop is matured the beets must be dug. This plow serves both purposes, and has proven to be a better tool for getting the beets out of the ground than the beet puller or any other device that has been tried. The great advantage which this plow has is that it goes below the beets and raises them up without cutting or breaking them off, leaving the beets still standing loosely in their natural position in the ground unexposed, but handy to be taken out and laid in rows ready for topping.

INSTRUCTIONS.—To dig beets, allow the standard to run close as possible to the beets without damaging them, and the share to run under them.

Chilled points made for both sizes.

PRICE LIST—WOOD BEAM.

Right and Left Hand.   With Extra Steel Point.

Number and Name.	Size.	Code Word.	Weight.	Price.
No. 6, Hard Pan	2 Horse.	Lotus.	98 lbs.	$12 50
No. 8, Hard Pan	3 or 4 Horse.	Lovage.	103 lbs.	15 00

REPAIR PRICE LIST.

No.	Steel Point.	Chilled Point.	Mold-board.	Steel Slide.	Land Bar.	Standard	Draft Rod with Pendulum.	Dial Clevis Castings.	Finished Beam.	Finished Handles, per pair.
6	$1 50	$0 75	$1 50	$1 25	$1 15	$2 75	$2 00	$1 00	$1 50	$0 85
8	1 75	75	2 00	1 50	1 25	3 00	2 00	1 00	1 75	1 00

B. F. AVERY & SONS.  LOUISVILLE, KY.

AVERY'S STEEL PLOWS.

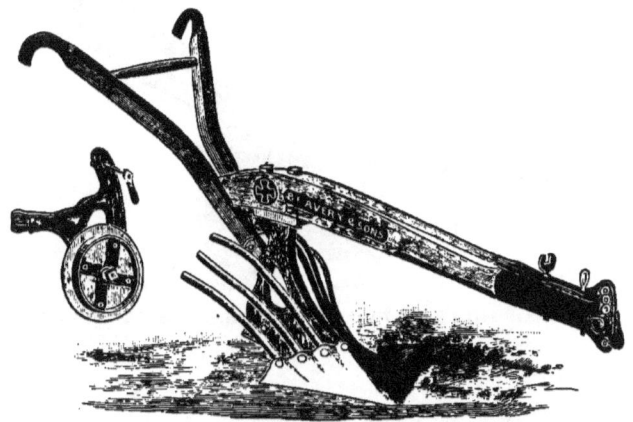

"POTATO DIGGER"—WITH VINE CUTTER.

Beam and handles painted red, black tipped.
Cast standard, attached to beam by two bolts.
Adjustable steel heel or rudder, forcing plow to take any depth or hardness of ground.
Steel point has a ribbed surface, which causes the ground to gather in and follow the grooves, separating from the potatoes.
Fingers are of superior stiff spring steel, the upper side of which being rounding, the potatoes are lifted to the surface without being cut or bruised.

The Vine Cutter shown is a solid wheel with knife in the center of same, preventing cutting too deep, steadies the plow and does not cut the potatoes, but cuts the vines and weeds, preventing them choking the plow.

Chilled points can be furnished when desired.

PRICE LIST.

Extra Point not included in price of Digger.

Name.	Code Word.	Cut.	Weight.	Without Vine Cutter or Extra Point.
Potato Digger	Lovely.	17 in.	80 lbs.	$10 00
Vine Cutter	Lowery.		20 lbs.	2 50

REPAIR PRICE LIST.

Steel Point.	Chilled Point.	Standard with Rudder.	Fingers, each.	Clevis.	Finished Beam.	Finished Handles, per pair.
$3 00	$1 25	$2 50	$0 35	$0 30	$1 50	$0 90

Cast points for old style Avery Potato Digger supplied, when ordered, at $1.50 each.

B. F. AVERY & SONS. LOUISVILLE, KY.

AVERY'S STEEL PLOWS.

"IDEAL" HILLSIDE PLOW. REVERSIBLE SIDE HILLER.

Cast frog and shoe.
Wide steel standard.
Beam and handles painted red, black tipped.
Special extra hard crucible cast steel moldboard.
Chilled point on plow with cast cast-steel extra point.
Eccentric hand lever device for "landing" beam of plow to take the "land" as desired.
The spring trip for changing plow from right to left is simple and strong, and can be easily operated by a slight pressure of the foot.

These are modern and popular hillside plows of very excellent construction. Are also widely used by gardeners and truckers on level lands as "reversible plows," and by farmers and horticulturists generally in terracing.

PRICE LIST—WOOD BEAM.
With Extra Cast Cast-Steel Point.

Number and Name.	Code Word.	Cut.	Weight.	Price.
No. 26, Ideal Hillside (one or light two-horse)	Loyal.	8 in.	87 lbs.	$10 00
No. 28, Ideal Hillside (two-horse)	Lucre.	10 in.	125 lbs.	12 00

REPAIR PRICE LIST.

No.	Chilled Point.	Cast Cast-Steel Point.	Mold-board.	Shoe.	Frog.	Clevis.	Handle Braces, each.	Finished Beam.	Finished Handles, per pair.
No. 26	$0 75	$2 00	$2 50	$0 60	$0 60	$0 25	$0 20	$1 25	$0 80
No. 28	1 00	2 50	3 00	80	75	25	20	1 50	1 00

REPAIRS FOR HILLSIDE PLOWS NOT NOW MADE.

Number and Name.	Chilled Point.	Cast Cast-Steel Point.	Steel Point.	Mold-board.	Finished Beam.	Finished Handles, per pair.
No. 22, Steel Hillside	$0 75	$2 00		$2 50	$1 25	$0 80
No. 24, Steel Hillside	1 00	2 50		3 00	1 50	1 00
No. 1, Steel Hillside			$1 50			
No. 2, Steel Hillside			2 00			
No. 1, Cast Hillside	75					
No. 2, Cast Hillside	1 10					

The points of Nos. 26 and 28 will interchange with old series of Nos. 22 and 24, respectively.
The cast cast-steel point furnished as extra point for the above plows can be sharpened under the hammer, but great care should be taken that a slow heat is used and that they are only heated to a cherry red. If these instructions are carefully observed, no difficulty will be experienced.

B. F. AVERY & SONS. LOUISVILLE, KY.

AVERY'S CHILLED PLOWS.

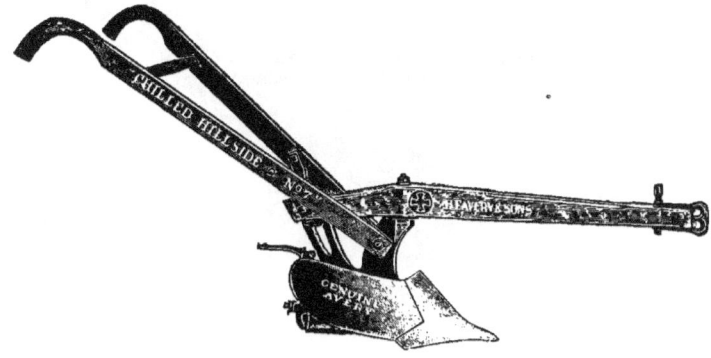

No. 7 CHILLED "HILLSIDE" PLOW. REVERSIBLE SIDE HILLER.

Strong cast standard.

Chilled moldboard and point.

Beam and handles painted red, black tipped.

A medium light one-horse plow of deservedly great popularity.

Chilled shoe running full length of landside; renewable when worn.

Has a very strong simple spring and wrought steel hook for reversing, and can be so set that plow will take land on the steepest hills.

    Are widely used also by gardeners and truckers on level lands as gardeners' reversible plows, and by farmers and horticulturists generally in terracing.

PRICE LIST—WOOD BEAM.

With Extra Chilled Point.

Number and Name.	Code Word.	Cut.	Weight.	Price.
No. 7, Hillside	Lugger.	7 in.	64 lbs.	$6 50

REPAIR PRICE LIST.

Point.	Moldboard.	Standard.	Shoe.	Clevis.	Handle Braces, each.	Finished Beam.	Finished Handles, per pair.
$0 40	$1 50	$2 00	$0 60	$0 15	$0 20	$1 10	$1 00

B. F. AVERY & SONS.      LOUISVILLE, KY.

AVERY'S CHILLED PLOWS.

"AMERICAN."

Beam and handles painted red, black tipped.
Index beam rest between handles, permitting adjustment for land.
Straight handles, strongly braced by two wood rounds, one index beam rest, and one iron set brace.
All parts guaranteed to interchange with other makes of the same numbers.

No pains are spared to make this the best and strongest Chilled Plow on the market. They are made from the best brands of car wheel iron and chilled by the latest and best methods, and are guaranteed to do equally as good work, under the same conditions, as any other plow of the same number now on the market.

Jointers and gauge wheels can be supplied. Cost extra.

PRICE LIST—WOOD BEAM.

*Right and Left Hand; all others Right Hand only.   With Extra Chilled Point.

Number and Name.	Code Word.	Capacity.	Weight.	Price.	Jointer, Complete.	Gauge Wheel, Complete.
No. AX, American, W. B.	Lumbric.	4½ x 8 in.	47 lbs.	$4 50	$2 00	$1 10
No. BX, American, W. B.	Lunar.	5 x 10 in.	68 lbs.	6 00	2 00	1 10
No. 10X, American, W. B.	Lupine.	5¼ x 11 in.	72 lbs.	7 00	2 00	1 20
No. 13X, American, W. B.	Luscious.	6 x 11 in.	80 lbs.	8 00	2 00	1 20
No. 19X, American, W. B.*	Luster.	6½ x 12 in.	102 lbs.	8 50	2 00	1 20
No. 20X, American, W. B.*	Lyam.	7 x 13 in.	117 lbs.	9 00	2 00	1 20
No. 40X, American, W. B.*	Lyric.	9 x 16 in.	134 lbs.	9 50	2 00	1 20
No. ZX, American, W.B., Middle Burster	Macaw.	16 in. spread	75 lbs.	8 00		

Nos. AX, BX, and ZX are furnished with plain points, all other sizes with cutter points.

REPAIR PRICE LIST.

Number and Name.	Plain Point.	Cutter Point.	Land-side.	Mold-board.	Stand-ard.	Clevis.	Beam Rest.	Finished Beam.	Finished Handles, per pair.
No. AX, American	$0 25		$0 40	$1 25	$1 25	$0 25	$0 25	$1 00	$1 25
No. BX, American	25		60	1 75	1 50	25	30	1 00	1 25
No. 10X, American		$0 35	60	2 00	2 00	25	30	1 00	1 25
No. 13X, American		35	65	2 25	2 25	35	30	1 25	1 50
No. 19X, American		40	75	2 50	2 25	35	50	1 25	1 75
No. 20X, American		40	75	2 75	2 25	35	50	1 25	1 75
No. 40X, American		40	75	3 00	2 50	35	50	1 25	1 75
No. ZX, American	40			2 50	2 25	35	25	1 00	1 25

All repairs for Steel Beam American Plows interchange with Wood Beam, excepting the Landsides.

B. F. AVERY & SONS.      LOUISVILLE, KY.

AVERY'S CHILLED PLOWS.

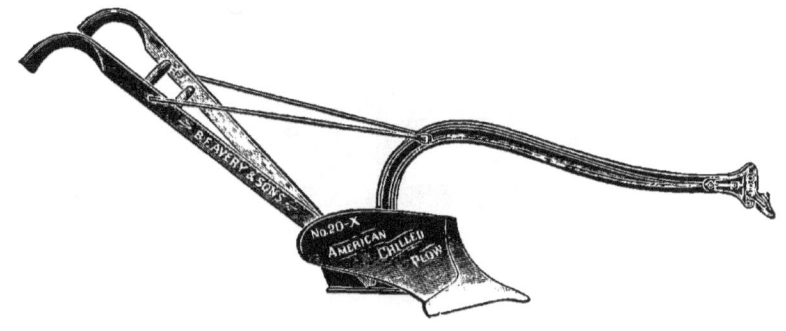

"AMERICAN."

Double beaded steel beam, high curve.
Beam and handles painted red, black tipped.

No pains are spared to make this the best and strongest Chilled Plow on the market. They are made from the best brands of car wheel iron and chilled by the latest and best methods, and are guaranteed to do equally as good work as any other plow of the same number now on the market, under the same conditions.

Jointers and gauge wheels can be supplied. Cost extra.

PRICE LIST—STEEL BEAM.

*Right and Left Hand; all others Right Hand only.   With Extra Chilled Point.

Number and Name.	Code Word.	Capacity.	Weight.	Price.	Jointer Complete.	Gauge Wheel Complete.
No. BX, American, S. B.	Macigno.	5 x 10 in.	89 lbs.	$7 00	$2 00	$1 10
No. 10X, American, S. B.	Madefy.	5½ x 11 in.	93 lbs.	8 00	2 00	1 20
No. 13X, American, S. B.	Maggot.	6 x 11 in.	103 lbs.	9 00	2 00	1 20
No. 19X, American, S. B*	Magma.	6½ x 12 in.	120 lbs.	9 50	2 00	1 20
No. 20X, American, S. B*	Magnifio.	7 x 13 in.	126 lbs.	10 00	2 00	1 20
No. 40X, American, S. B*	Maguey.	9 x 16 in.	154 lbs.	10 50	2 00	1 20

No. BX is furnished with plain points, all other sizes with cutter points.

REPAIR PRICE LIST.

When ordering repairs state "for Steel Beam Plow."

Number and Name.	Plain Point.	Cutter Point.	Landside.	Mold-board.	Clevis.	Handle Braces.	Finished Beam.	Finished Handles, per pair.
No. BX, American	$0 25	....	$0 60	$1 75	$0 40	$0 35	$3 50	$1 25
No. 10X, American	....	$0 35	60	2 00	40	35	3 50	1 25
No. 13X, American	....	35	65	2 25	40	40	3 50	1 50
No. 19X, American	....	40	75	2 50	40	40	4 00	1 75
No. 20X, American	....	40	75	2 75	40	40	4 00	1 75
No. 40X, American	....	40	75	3 00	40	40	4 50	1 75

All repairs for Steel Beam American Plows interchange with Wood Beam, excepting the Landsides.

B. F. AVERY & SONS.   LOUISVILLE, KY.

AVERY'S CHILLED PLOWS.

"GRANITE"—SHOWING WITH JOINTER AND GAUGE WHEEL.
(PATENTED.)

Beam and handles painted black.
Have good moldboard capacity and wrap under weeds and trash thoroughly.
We make a variety of points with degrees of penetration for any and every kind and condition of soil.
Patent adjustable chilled heel, greatly reducing the wear on the landside and restoring the pitch or suck of the plow.

    Jointers and gauge wheels can be supplied. Cost extra.
    Our Vineyard Plow in this series is perfectly adapted for the work indicated.

PRICE LIST.

Plain, without Jointer or Gauge Wheel.

Right Hand Only.   With Extra Chilled Point.

Number and Name.	Code Word.	Cut.	Turning Capacity.	Weight.	Price.
No. 14, Granite	Mainor.	6½ in.	7 in.	53 lbs.	$4 50
No. 14½, Granite	Maize.	7 in.	8 in.	59 lbs.	5 00
No. 15, Granite	Maki.	8 in.	9 in.	68 lbs.	6 00
No. 15, Granite Vineyard Plow	Malate.	8 in.	9 in.	72 lbs.	7 00

PRICE LIST, GAUGE WHEEL, JOINTER, AND KNIFE COULTER.

Number and Name.	Code Word.	For Size Plow.	Weight.	Price.
No. A, 6-in. wheel	Progress.	Nos. 14, 14½, 15.	11 lbs.	$1 10
No. 12, Jointer	Profusion.	Nos. 14, 14½, 15.	8 lbs.	1 75
No. 50, Knife Coulter	Pretty.	Nos. 14, 14½, 15.	6 lbs.	75

REPAIR PRICE LIST.

Number.	Chilled Point.	Slip Nose Point.	Cast Cast Steel Point.	Shins.	Mold-board.	Stand-ard.	Land-side with Heel.	Heel.	Beam Rest.	Clevis.	Fin-ished Beam.	Finished Handles, per pair.
No. 14	$0 25				$1 25	$1 25	$0 40	$0 20	$0 20	$0 20	$0 50	$0 75
No. 14½	25				1 25	1 35	40	20	20	25	1 00	85
No. 15	35				1 50	1 50	55	20	20	25	1 00	90
No. 15, Vineyard	35				1 50	2 00	55	20	20	25	1 00	90
No. 16	40	$0 60	$1 50	$0 20	2 00	2 00	75	20	30	30	1 25	1 10
No. 16½	40	60	1 60	20	2 00	2 25	75	20	35	30	1 25	1 25
No. 17	45	70	1 75	20	2 50	2 50	75	20	40	30	1 50	1 35
No. 18	45	75	2 00	20	2 50	2 50	75	20	50	35	1 50	1 35

B. F. AVERY & SONS.      LOUISVILLE, KY.

AVERY'S CHILLED PLOWS.

No. 8 CHILLED—ONE-HORSE.
(PATENTED.)

Patent adjustable chilled heel.
Beam and handles painted red.

    The chilled iron is of superior quality and highly polished.
Has the same shaped moldboard as our old No. 8 Cast Plow so long and favorably known.
Cast cast-steel points can be furnished. Cost extra.

No. 12 CHILLED—TWO-HORSE.
(PATENTED.)

Beam and handles painted red.

    Above cut shows our patent landside construction with patent adjustable chilled heel.
An excellent plow for corn, cotton, and general breaking, cultivating, and bedding.

PRICE LIST.

Right Hand Only.   With Extra Chilled Point.

Number and Name.	Code Word.	Cut.	Weight.	Price.
No. 8, Chilled Plow	Malet.	7 in.	47 lbs.	$3 60
No. 12, Chilled Plow	Malison.	9 in.	67 lbs.	5 75

REPAIR PRICE LIST.

Number and Name.	Chilled Point.	Cast Cast-Steel Point.	Moldboard	Standard.	Heel.	Clevis.	Finished Beam.	Finished Handles, per pair.
8, Chilled	$0 25	$0 85	$1 10	$1 50	$0 20	$0 15	$0 75	$0 70
12, Chilled	45	....	1 50	2 00	20	20	1 20	95

B. F. AVERY & SONS.  LOUISVILLE, KY.

AVERY'S CAST PLOWS.

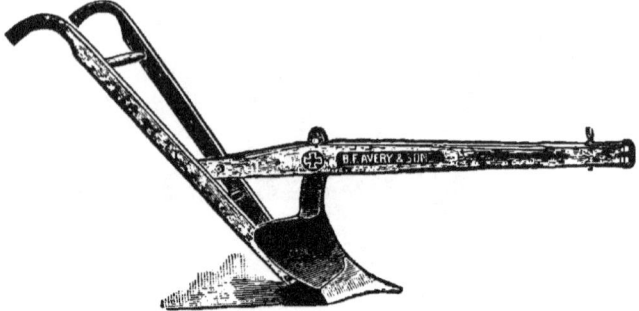

No. 8, OLD SERIES. The Original B. F. Avery Model.

Beam and handles varnished.
Cast cast-steel points can be supplied when wanted, which will cost extra.
The most popular cotton bedder in the world, bluff of moldboard, strong and durable.
  The No. 12 of this series is a two-horse plow, having a very high and bold moldboard.

No. ½. NEW SERIES.

Beam and handles varnished.
  The No. ½ has more gradual turning power than our No. 8, and is preferred in some sections.
Cast cast-steel points can be supplied when wanted, which will cost extra.

PRICE LIST.

*Right and Left Hand; all others Right Hand only.

Number and Name.	Code Word.	Cut.	Weight.	With Extra Cast Point. Price.
No. 8, Old Series	Malodor.	7 in.	39 lbs.	$3 35
No. 12, Old Series	Mammal.	9 in.	57 lbs.	5 00
No. ½, New Series	Manatus.	7 in.	38 lbs.	3 35
No. 1, New Series	Mangaby.	8 in.	42 lbs.	3 75
No. 2, New Series	Manicon.	8½ in.	47 lbs.	4 25
No. 3, New Series*	Manikin.	9 in.	58 lbs.	5 00

REPAIR PRICE LIST.

Number and Name.	Cast Point.	Cast Cast-Steel Point.	Mold-board.	Landside.	Clevis.	Finished Beam.	Finished Handles, per pair.
No. 8, Old Series	$0 20	$0 85	$1 40	$0 30	$0 15	$0 70	$0 65
No. 12, Old Series	40		2 50	45	20	1 00	90
No. ½, New Series	20		1 40	30	15	70	65
No. 1, New Series	20	85	1 50	40	15	75	70
No. 2, New Series	30	85	2 00	50	20	90	75
No. 3, New Series	35		2 75	60	20	90	80

B. F. AVERY & SONS.   LOUISVILLE, KY.

AVERY'S CAST PLOWS.

"VETERAN"—ONE-HORSE.
(PATENTED.)

Chilled moldboard. Patent adjustable chilled heel.
Beam and handles painted blue. Cast standard, point, and landside.

A series of cast plows with bluff moldboard, and similar to the No. 8 Cast Plow. A good cotton bedder and general purpose light one-horse plow.

"RED PONY"—ONE-HORSE.

Chilled point.
Cast moldboard and landside.
Beam and handles painted red.
Wrought steel standard, frog, and cap, attached to beam by two bolts.
  Constructed on the model of our world-renowned "Pony" Steel Plow.
  Steel points can be furnished when desired. Cost extra.

PRICE LIST.
Right Hand Only.
Veteran with Extra Cast Point.   Red Pony with Extra Chilled Point.

Number and Name.	Code Word.	Cut.	Weight.	Price.
No. 6½ Veteran	Manna.	6½ in.	44 lbs.	$3 50
No. 7 Veteran.	Mansion.	7 in.	45 lbs.	4 00
Red Pony	Mantle.	7 in.	41 lbs.	4 00

REPAIR PRICE LIST.

Number and Name.	Cast Point.	Chilled Steel Point.	Cast Point.	Cast Moldboard.	Chilled Moldboard.	Standard.	Standard with Frog.	Cast Landside.	Heel.	Clevis.	Finished Beam.	Finished Handles, per pair.
No. 6½ Veteran	$0 20				$1 00	$1 00			$0 20	$0 15	$0 75	$0 65
No. 7 Veteran	25				1 15	1 15			20	15	75	75
Red Pony		$0 25	$0 60	$1 00			$1 40	$0 30		15	90	75

B. F. AVERY & SONS. LOUISVILLE, KY.

AVERY'S NEW GROUND PLOWS.

"OLD STYLE." WITH JUMPING COULTER.

Standard is well braced.
Blade fastened to standard by two bolts.
Beam, handles, and standard varnished.
Coulter is held firmly in place by a notched plate and band.
Thick steel blade, reinforced by a steel bar welded to back of blade.

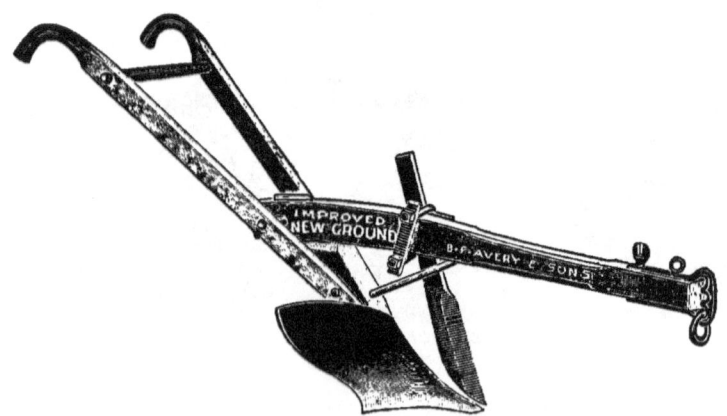

"IMPROVED." WITH EITHER JUMPING OR STRAIGHT COULTER.

Wrought clevis and ring.
Extra thick double shinned steel blade.
Beam, handles, and standard varnished.
Has a short steel landside to steady plow.
Blade is fastened to standard by two bolts.
Coulter is held firmly in place by a notched plate and band.
In ordering, state whether jumping or straight knife coulter is wanted.
Wrought strap under beam, the strap being securely bolted to the standard and taking much of the strain from the beam.

PRICE LIST.
Right Hand Only.

Number and Name.	Code Word.	Cut.	Weight.	Price.
No. 1, Old Style New Ground.	Manumit.	5 in.	55 lbs.	$5 00
No. 1, Improved New Ground.	Maracan.	6 in.	52 lbs.	5 00
No. 2, Improved New Ground.	Marcasite.	8 in.	57 lbs.	6 00

For Repair Price List, see next page.

AVERY'S NEW GROUND PLOWS.

"SAMSON"—WITH REVERSIBLE COULTER.

Wrought clevis and ring.
Blade is fastened to standard by two bolts.
Beam and standard extra heavy and well braced.
Beam, handles, and standard painted red, black tipped.
The mold is of the most approved shape, with a steel bar welded to the landside edge of same.
Reversible or double-edged coulter, which can be used either as a jumping or straight coulter, is adjustable, and firmly held in place by a notched plate and band.

Will be found to meet the wants for a first class new ground plow, the general construction being of the very best and strongest.

PRICE LIST.

Right and Left Hand.

Number and Name.	Code Word.	Cut	Weight.	Price.
No. 8, Samson New Ground	Margarin.	6 in.	59 lbs.	$7 00
No. 9, Samson New Ground	Mariner.	7 in.	64 lbs.	8 00

REPAIR PRICE LIST.

Old Style New Ground Plow.	No. 1.	Old Style New Ground Plow.	No. 1.
Blade ¼ inch, with two bolts	$1 75	Finished Beam, 3¾x2½x56 inches	$1 00
No. 61 Jumping Coulter, complete	2 00	Finished Standard, 3½x2½ inches	1 00
Standard Brace	50	Finished Handles, per pair	80
Clevis	25		

REPAIR PRICE LIST.

Improved New Ground Plow.	No. 1.	Improved New Ground Plow.	No. 2.
Blade 5-16 inch, with two bolts	$2 00	Blade 5-16 inch, with two bolts	$2 25
No. 64 Jumping Coulter	2 00	No. 64 Jumping Coulter	2 00
No. 58 Straight Coulter	1 25	No. 58 Straight Coulter	1 25
Brace and Beam Strap	75	Brace and Beam Strap	1 00
Wrought Clevis	30	Wrought Clevis	30
Finished Beam, 4½x2½x52½ inches	1 00	Finished Beam, 4½x2½x52½ inches	1 25
Finished Standard, 3¾x2½ inches	75	Finished Standard, 4⅜x2¾ inches	1 00
Finished Handles, per pair	80	Finished Handles, per pair	85

REPAIR PRICE LIST.

Samson New Ground Plow.	No. 8.	Samson New Ground Plow.	No. 9.
Blade ¼ inch, with two bolts	$2 00	Blade ¼ inch, with two bolts	$2 50
No. 70 Reversible Coulter	2 00	No. 70 Reversible Coulter	2 00
Standard Brace	50	Standard Brace	50
Clevis	25	Clevis	25
Finished Beam, 4½x2 11-16x57 inches	1 50	Finished Beam, 5x2 13-16x60 inches	1 75
Finished Standard, 4½x2 11-16 inches	1 25	Finished Standard, 4½x2 11-16 inches	1 50
Finished Handles, per pair	1 00	Finished Handles, per pair	1 00

B. F. AVERY & SONS. LOUISVILLE, KY.

AVERY'S NEW GROUND PLOWS.

"GRUBBER"—WITH JUMPING COULTER. RIGHT HAND ONLY.

Iron handles.
Extra heavy steel beam.
Beam and handles painted green, black tipped.
The coulter is held firmly in place by brace and band.
Mold has a steel bar welded to landside edge and extended so as to allow mold to be braced to it, giving additional strength to mold.

Has a very successful record in the field, and is a most excellent breaker and turner in new ground.

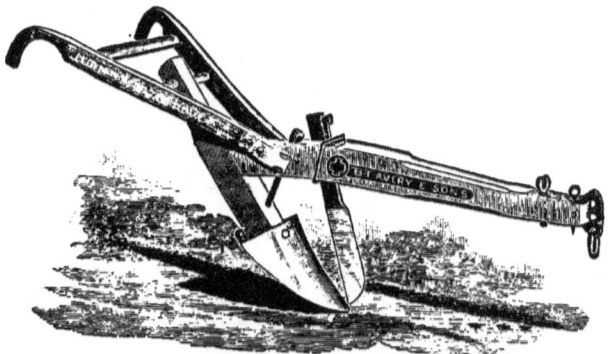

"JUMPING SHOVEL"—WITH JUMPING COULTER.

Wrought clevis and ring.
Wrought strap under beam.
Heavy beam and standard, thoroughly braced.
Beam, handles, and standard painted red, black tipped.
Extra thick blade attached to standard by one heavy bolt.
Coulter is held firmly in place by passing through beam strap, beam, and wrought plate on top of beam and securely wedged.

PRICE LIST.

Number and Name.	Code Word.	Cut.	Weight.	Price Complete.	Price Stock without Blade and Coulter.
No. 8, Grubber	Marl.	9 in.	85 lbs.	$10 00	
No. 15, Jumping Shovel	Marrer.		48 lbs.	5 00	$3 00
No. 16, Jumping Shovel	Mars.		57 lbs.	6 00	3 50

REPAIR PRICE LIST—FOR JUMPING SHOVEL PLOWS.

No. 15.	Blade No. 133, 9 x 12 x 5-16, with 1 Bolt	$1 00	No. 16.	Blade No. 133, 12 x 15 x 5-16, with 1 Bolt	$1 25
No. 15.	No. 63 Coulter and Band	1 25	No. 16.	No. 63 Coulter and Band	1 25
No. 15.	Finished Beam, 4⅝ x 2½ x 53 inches	1 25	No. 16.	Finished Beam, 4⅝ x 2 13-16 x 56 inches	1 50
No. 15.	Finished Standard, 4 x 2½ inches	1 00	No. 16.	Finished Standard, 4⅝ x 2 13-16 inches	1 25
No. 15.	Standard Brace	50	No. 16.	Standard Brace	50
No. 15.	Clevis	30	No. 16.	Clevis	30
No. 15.	Handles, per pair	80	No. 16.	Handles, per pair	90

B. F. AVERY & SONS. LOUISVILLE, KY.

"Louisville" Double-edge Stalk Cutter.

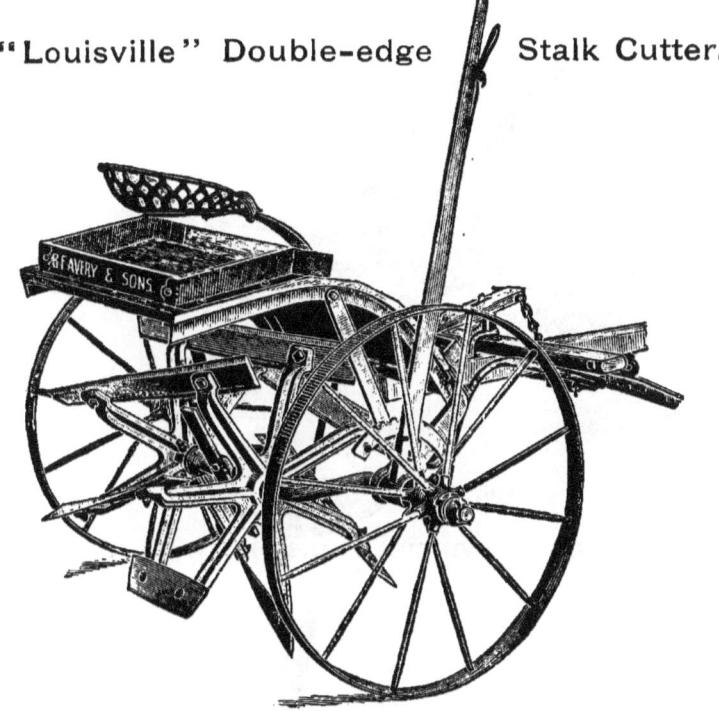

WITH EITHER SPIRAL OR STRAIGHT KNIVES.

Cuts the stalk into twelve-inch pieces.
Axles are of the finest cold rolled steel.
Wheels and cylinder spider both have removable boxes.
Has seven (7) double-edged and reversible spiral knives.
High steel wheels 34 inches in diameter, with 2-inch tires.
The most successful and satisfactory stalk cutter in the field.
Is practically all steel and wrought iron; has no castings that break.
The drag hooks are raised or lowered by pressure upon the foot treadle.
With the spring seat and the easy motion of the spiral knives there is no jolting.
Cylinder revolves on the axle, and the axle itself does not revolve, hence there is no danger of vines or trash winding about the axle; it is non-cloggable.
A simple attachment on the axle brushes away any trash that might have a tendency to clog or gather between the knives.
The steel cover is carried completely over the knives, protecting the driver both from the danger of falling on the knives and from flying dirt and stalks.
Any degree of penetration can be given the knives by means of the lever, by which the entire weight of machine and driver can be forced on the knives, which, in case of damp or heavy stalks, can be increased by putting such weight in weight-box as may be found necessary.

Straight Knife Stalk Cutter.—Those preferring a straight knife stalk cutter, we can furnish same mounted on the same carriage used for our spiral knife cutter.

Directions for setting up on page 152.   For prices on Repairs, see pages 152 and 153.

PRICE LIST.

No.	Style.		Code Word.	Weight.	Price.
1	Spiral Knives	With Wood Doubletree, Steel Singletrees, and Steel Neckyoke	Marvel.	478 lbs.	$17 00
2	Spiral Knives	Without Wood Doubletree, Steel Singletrees, and Steel Neckyoke	Masker.	455 lbs.	15 00
3	Straight Knives	With Wood Doubletree, Steel Singletrees, and Steel Neckyoke	Mastery.	478 lbs.	47 00
4	Straight Knives	Without Wood Doubletree, Steel Singletrees, and Steel Neckyoke	Matachin.	455 lbs.	45 00

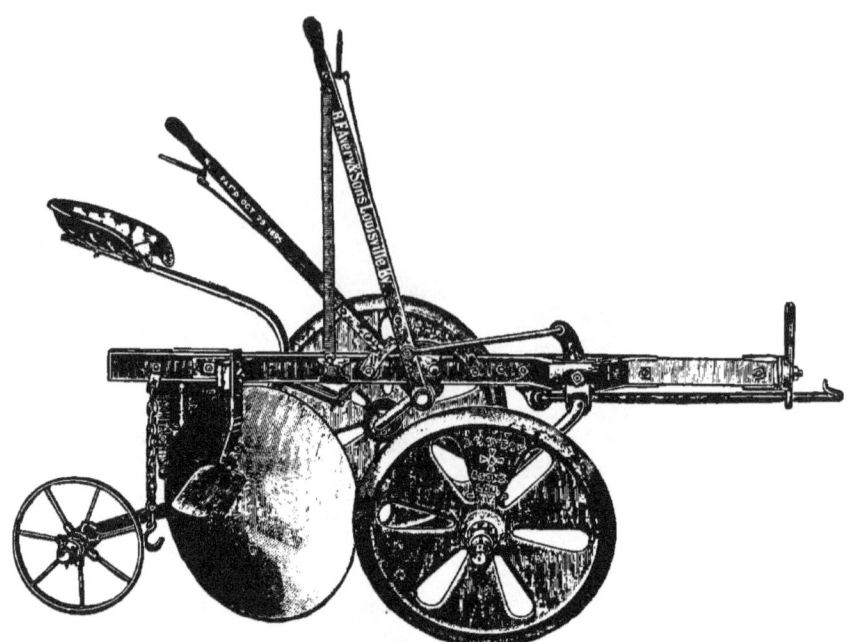

AVERY'S "INVINCIBLE" DISC PLOW No. 15.
(Patented.)

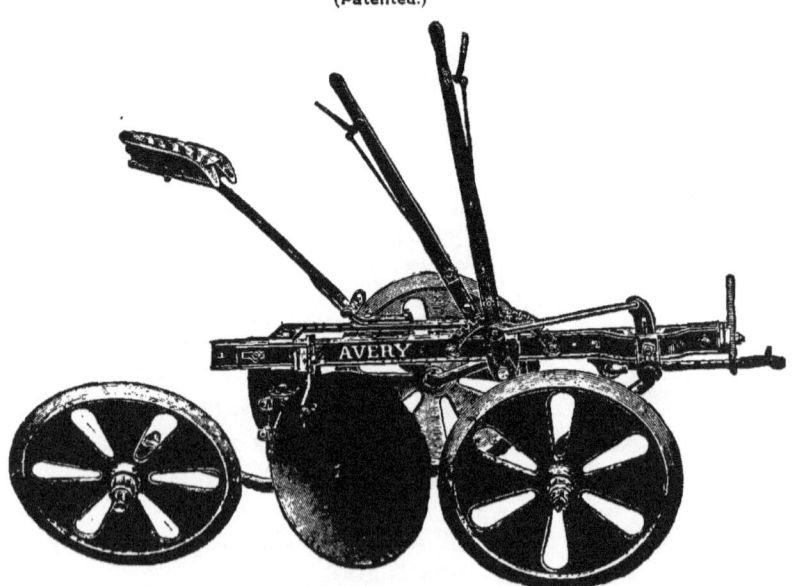

AVERY'S "INVINCIBLE" DISC PLOW No. 10.
(Patented.)

B. F. AVERY & SONS.  LOUISVILLE, KY.

AVERY'S "INVINCIBLE" DISC PLOWS.
(Patented.)

In the two years that the Invincible Disc Plow has been made it has been very largely sold in all parts of the world, and severely tried in all kinds of soil and under varying conditions. Reports received from both dealers and farmers are that they have given very general satisfaction. With the improvements made this season we are prepared to offer our Invincible Disc Plow to the dealer with every assurance of it being the best Disc Plow on the market, and that it will do good and satisfactory work.

There having been a demand in some sections for a Disc Plow that will turn a square corner either to the right or left, we have constructed our No. 15, which will do so with the disc in or out of the ground, thereby enabling the user to back-furrow perfectly, something which has never been accomplished before with a Disc Plow. The rear wheel is a perfect caster, and requires no attention whatever from the operator while turning.

On both Disc Plows the seat has been slightly lowered and its position changed, making it more convenient for the operator to get on or off, and to ride with perfect comfort and ease.

A new scraper has also been attached, which is very much simpler than the former one, besides being more durable and stronger; it can be easily adjusted to handle all kinds and conditions of soil.

The following general description will apply to both Nos. 10 and 15 Disc Plows.

THE FRAME is our celebrated Invincible Sulky frame, made of channel steel trussed together, forming a bracket on each side ; abundantly strong and rigid without excessive weight.

THE WHEELS are car-wheel iron, with oil holes and removable boxes; the rims of the wheels are V-shaped ; will not ball up even in sticky ground.

THE DISC STANDARD has a removable chilled box, closed on the end, forming a reservoir to retain the oil, in which the disc hub, which is made of chilled iron, revolves. The oil is conveyed to this reservoir through a pipe (which is capped) extending close to the top of standard so as to facilitate oiling. The bearings are perfectly protected from dust, insuring long life in good condition. Being removable, they can, when worn from long use, be quickly and easily replaced.

THE DISC. The wear on a disc is so slight that it is very durable. Being self-sharpening, it saves delay and expense incidental to repairing old style plows. Disc has perfect smooth surface, being fastened to flange by countersunk bolts.

THE HITCH is easily adjusted to give any desired "land" or penetration. Our dial clevis can be moved upward or downward, right or left, by simply loosening one nut, giving any required adjustment.

THE DRAFT is as light, if not lighter, than any other Disc Plow of the same capacity. A Disc Plow is practically harrowing as well as plowing the land, thus accomplishing more work than a Moldboard Sulky.

THE LEVERS. The plow is operated and controlled perfectly and easily by the levers within easy reach, and by which the plow may be leveled to suit any surface or depth. When the depth is once adjusted to soil it is never necessary to touch the adjusting lever.

CONDITION OF SOIL. The Invincible Disc Plow will scour and turn perfectly in any soil ; the stickiest black, waxy lands of Texas, and in foul, weedy land where the trash is abundant and hard to cover. We do not claim it to be a perfect sod plow, but will guarantee it to handle sod land as well as any disc can be made to do.

THE FURROW. The Invincible Disc Plow leaves a broad and clean furrow, unusual for a Disc Plow, enabling the lead horse to walk in the furrow without difficulty.

THE CUT. To adjust width of cut move front furrow wheel in or out on axle. When the front furrow wheel is set to cut any given width of furrow, adjust the clevis until the front furrow wheel tracks in the marks left by rear furrow wheel of furrow previously plowed ; thus the operator can tell at a glance when he is cutting more or less than intended, and whether the plow is doing proper work.

INVINCIBLE MOLDBOARD SULKY. To those already having our Invincible Disc Plow we can furnish the necessary parts so same can readily be converted into a Moldboard Sulky.

We also make a two-furrow Disc Gang Plow on the same general lines as the above.

Directions for setting up and operating on page 141.

PRICE LIST.

Single Furrow furnished with Steel Tripletrees, Double Furrow with No. 1 Four-Horse Eveners, Monkey Wrench, Malleable Wrench, and Oil Can.

Number and Name.	Code Word.	Weight.	Price.
No. 15, Invincible Disc Plow, with 26 in. Disc	Mate.	692 lbs.	$65 00
No. 10, Invincible Disc Plow, with 26 in. Disc	Materiate.	777 lbs.	65 00
Two-Furrow Invincible Disc Gang Plow, with two 26 in. Discs	Mathesis.	1006 lbs.	85 00
No. 15, Back-Furrowing Attachment complete to attach on No. 10	Maudlin.	97 lbs.	8 50
Attachments complete to convert Disc Plow into a Moldboard Sulky	Mawkish.	300 lbs.	31 00
Extra Disc, 26 in	Maying.	20 lbs.	6 00

B. F. AVERY & SONS.      LOUISVILLE, KY.

AVERY'S "INVINCIBLE" SULKY PLOWS.
(Patented.)

No. 5 INVINCIBLE SULKY.

With lever attachment to the rear wheel so that the same can be lifted entirely out of the ground, thus enabling the plow to turn a perfectly square corner, either to the right or left, with the plow in the ground when back-furrowing.

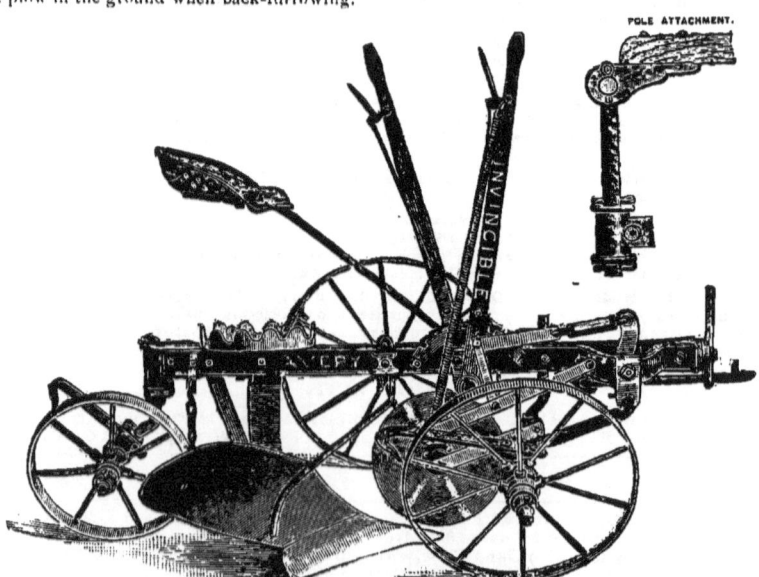

No. 1 INVINCIBLE SULKY.

The Nos. 1 and 5 Invincible Sulkies are constructed alike in every particular, omitting the lever on rear furrow wheel of No. 5, which alone distinguishes it from the No. 1.

B. F. AVERY & SONS.   LOUISVILLE, KY.

AVERY'S INVINCIBLE SULKY PLOWS.
(Patented.)

CONSTRUCTION. The Invincible is constructed practically entirely of steel and wrought iron. It is very simple in construction, and we guarantee it to be perfect in point of strength and durability, and to withstand any strain that may be put upon it. The frame is of two pieces of channel steel trussed together, forming a bracket on each side of the furrow and land wheel axle, making the strongest possible construction without excessive weight. The wheels are of steel, with removable boxes. The wheel axles are made of polished cold-rolled steel.

IN QUALITY OF WORK, lightness of draft, ease of adjustment and handling, it is far superior to any offered to the trade. Any boy who can drive a team can do perfect work with the "Invincible."

THE DRAFT. The plow is rigid in the frame, and being carried on the three wheels prevents any landside or bottom friction, which necessarily makes it of very light draft.

THE CUT. The Invincible Sulky will open a furrow from one to seven inches. The width of cut is varied by moving the front furrow wheel in or out on axle.

THE HITCH is easily adjusted to give any desired "land" or penetration. Our dial clevis can be moved upward or downward, right or left, by simply loosening one nut, giving any required adjustment. The horses are hitched direct to the end of the beam. Two, three, or four horses may be hitched abreast. It works as well without as with a pole. Pole, with necessary attachments, can be furnished, when wanted, at a small additional cost. The pole swivels in every direction, consequently there is no neck draft on the horses' necks.

THE LEVERS are within easy reach of the operator, by which it can be perfectly controlled without having to leave the seat. The right lever raises and lowers the plow and rolling coulter and regulates the depth of plowing; having a spring lifting attachment, it is very easily raised. The left hand lever adjusts the wheel on the land so as to level the plow when plowing at different depths. By bringing both furrow and land levers to last notch in ratchets, plow can be raised from the ground to transport sulky to and from the field. The No. 5 Invincible Sulky has also a third or rear-wheel lever attachment to the rear wheel so that the same can be lifted entirely out of the ground, thus enabling the plow to turn a perfectly square corner with the plow in the ground when back-furrowing.

CONDITION OF SOIL. We make a variety of bottoms, suitable for any soil, which are guaranteed to do satisfactory work in the soil intended for. See description of these bottoms below.

The front and rear furrow wheels are angled so as to run in the corner or angle of furrow. By setting in this manner the plow is held firmly to its work, especially when the ground is hard. When ground is extremely hard sulky can be changed to cut one or two inches less, if desired to lighten the work, by moving collars inward on front furrow wheel.

There is abundance of clearance between the plow and front furrow wheel, which prevents clogging in the foulest of land.

When using weed hook no weeds or trash are high enough to choke plow or prevent being covered entirely.

STYLE OF BOTTOM TO ORDER: Made right and left hand, with various styles of bottoms to do satisfactory work in any soil, as follows, viz:

NEW CLIPPER BOTTOM: With soft center steel moldboard and point extra hardened and highly polished, for loose, sandy, clay, or loam soils and stubble work.

TEXAS BOTTOM: With soft center steel moldboard and point extra hardened and polished, for all tough, sticky, obstinate soils difficult to turn or shed, including buckshot, tough river bottoms, and for sod plowing.

SILVER BOTTOM: With chilled iron moldboard and point, for loose, sandy, or clay soils that are suited to chilled plow work.

Extra chilled points can be furnished for any of the above bottoms.

ATTACHMENTS: The owner of an "INVINCIBLE" Sulky can, at a small additional cost, procure the Disc Plow Attachment, or Middleburster Attachment, or both, which enables him to own the three complete machines at much less expense than if bought separately.

For setting up and operating directions, see page 144.

For prices on repairs, see pages 142 and 143.

B. F. AVERY & SONS. LOUISVILLE, KY.

AVERY'S "INVINCIBLE" SULKY PLOWS.
(Patented.)

PRICE LIST.

With 15 inch Rolling Coulter, Weed Hook, Wheel Scraper, Steel Tripletrees, Wrench, Oil Can, and Extra Steel Point. Pole costs extra.

Size and Name.	No. 5.			No. 1.		
	Code Word.	Weight.	Price.	Code Word.	Weight.	Price.
With 10 inch New Clipper Bottom	Meacock.	477 lbs.	$58 00	Melrose.	444 lbs.	$58 00
With 12 inch New Clipper Bottom	Meander.	483 lbs.	58 00	Memento.	450 lbs.	58 00
With 14 inch New Clipper Bottom	Mease.	504 lbs.	58 00	Memphian.	471 lbs.	58 00
With 16 inch New Clipper Bottom	Meathe.	510 lbs.	58 00	Mender.	477 lbs.	58 00
With 12 inch Texas Bottom	Meconic.	484 lbs.	58 00	Mensal.	451 lbs.	58 00
With 14 inch Texas Bottom	Mediant.	497 lbs.	58 00	Mercer.	454 lbs.	58 00
With 16 inch Texas Bottom	Medicate.	500 lbs.	58 00	Mercury.	459 lbs.	58 00
With 12 inch Silver Bottom	Medullin.	505 lbs.	55 00	Meritot.	472 lbs.	55 00
Pole and attachments	Melanite.	44 lbs.	6 00	Melanite.	44 lbs.	6 00
Jointer and attachments	Melligo.	13 lbs.	2 50	Melligo.	13 lbs.	2 50

DISC ATTACHMENT (INCLUDING WHEELS) COMPLETE, TO ATTACH TO INVINCIBLE SULKY FRAME.

Number and Name.	Code Word.	Weight.	Price.
No. 10 Disc Attachment to Invincible Sulky	Mersion.	512 lbs.	$37 00
No. 15 Disc Attachment to Invincible Sulky	Meslin.	464 lbs.	37 00

MIDDLE BURSTER ATTACHMENT COMPLETE, TO ATTACH TO INVINCIBLE SULKY FRAME—WITHOUT EXTRA POINT.

Size and Name.	Code Word.	Weight.	Price.
14 inch Middle Burster Attachment	Mesole.	54 lbs.	$23 00
16 inch Middle Burster Attachment	Mestizo.	58 lbs.	27 00

EXTRA PLOW BOTTOMS—WITHOUT EXTRA POINTS.

Size and Name.	Code Word.	Weight.	Price.
10 inch New Clipper Bottom for Invincible Sulky	Metalist.	57 lbs.	$19 00
12 inch New Clipper Bottom for Invincible Sulky	Metatome.	62 lbs.	20 00
14 inch New Clipper Bottom for Invincible Sulky	Meter.	77 lbs.	21 50
16 inch New Clipper Bottom for Invincible Sulky	Metope.	80 lbs.	23 50
12 inch Texas Bottom for Invincible Sulky	Mezereon.	61 lbs.	20 00
14 inch Texas Bottom for Invincible Sulky	Mico.	62 lbs.	21 50
16 inch Texas Bottom for Invincible Sulky	Midge.	72 lbs.	23 50
12 inch Silver Bottom for Invincible Sulky	Midway.	81 lbs.	17 00

PRICE LIST OF EXTRAS.
In ordering state whether for right or left hand plow.

Articles.	10 inch.	12 inch.	14 inch.	16 inch.
15 inch Caster Rolling Coulter, with attachments	$5 00	$5 00	$5 00	$5 00
No. 1 Steel Tripletrees	4 40	4 40	4 40	4 40
Steel Point, with bolts for New Clipper or Texas	2 00	2 50	3 00	3 50
Steel Point, with bolts for Middle Burster			4 00	4 50
Chilled Point, with bolts for New Clipper or Texas	60	65	75	80
Chilled Point, with bolts for Silver		70		
Steel Moldboard, with bolts for New Clipper or Texas	4 50	5 00	5 50	6 00
Steel Moldboard, with bolts for Middle Burster, R or L, each			2 50	3 25
Chilled Point, with bolts for Silver		3 00		
Steel Landside, with bolts for New Clipper or Texas	1 25	1 50	1 75	2 00
Chilled Landside, with bolts for Silver		1 10		

For prices on repairs, see pages 142 and 143.

B. F. AVERY & SONS.  LOUISVILLE, KY.

Avery's "Invincible" Sulky—With Middle Burster Bottom.
Patented.

Above represents our Invincible Sulky Frame with Middle Burster attached, which in bursting out middles is a great labor-saving implement, as it does the work of several walking-plows, with less labor on the team and plowman, and with better results.

Being held firmly and steadily to its work by three wheels, it enables the operator to make a straight, even bed, which is more easily cultivated and kept clean.

With it the planter can make a complete cotton bed at one "through," instead of plowing from four to eight furrows as formerly.

It makes a perfect lister, making a complete bed for corn, cotton, etc., at one "through." This feature alone will more than pay for the sulky in one year.

Ditching—One "through" with the Middle Burster makes a splendid water furrow, which will generally serve the same purpose as ditching.

Fall Plowing—With one furrow the old bed can be reversed, entirely burying all pea vines, stalks, and other trash.

It has been demonstrated by successful cotton growers that the best results, at the least cost of preparing land for cotton, is to cut the stalks, as soon after picking as practicable, with a Stalk Cutter, then with the Sulky Middle Burster, running it through the old bed; the furrow is thrown out both ways and the stalks completely buried (which act as a fertilizer), and a complete cotton bed is made at one "through"; this, freshened up just before planting with a Disc Cultivator or Harrow, is then ready for planting.

The Invincible Sulky can be converted into a Sulky Middle Burster by simply unbolting turning plow bottom and substituting Middle Burster Bottom. No other change is necessary.

For directions for setting up and operating, see page 144.
For prices on repairs, see pages 142 and 143.
For prices on extras, see page 41.

PRICE LIST.
With Steel Tripletrees, Wrench, Oil Can, and Extra Steel Point.

Name and Size.	Attached to No. 5 Invincible Sulky.			Attached to No. 1 Invincible Sulky.		
	Code Word.	Weight.	Price.	Code Word.	Weight.	Price.
Invincible Sulky with 14-inch Middle Burster Bottom	Mildew.	480 lbs.	$61 00	Millrea.	430 lbs.	$61 00
Invincible Sulky with 16-inch Middle Burster Bottom	Militia.	485 lbs.	61 00	Milter.	435 lbs.	61 00
Pole and attachments	Melanite.	44 lbs.	6 00	Melanite.	44 lbs.	6 00

PRICE LIST—EXTRA MIDDLE BURSTER BOTTOMS.
Without Extra Point.

Name and Size.	Code Word.	Weight.	Price.
14-inch Middle Burster Bottom for Invincible Sulky	Mesole.	54 lbs.	$23 00
16-inch Middle Burster Bottom for Invincible Sulky	Mestizo.	58 lbs.	27 00

B. F. AVERY & SONS.  LOUISVILLE, KY.

AVERY'S "SIMPLE" SULKY PLOW.
(Patented.)

Simple, light, and strong.
Turns a perfectly square corner with the plow in the ground.
The only sulky which can be used either as a straight or cant wheel.
Both the pole and plow bottom are adjustable to right or left as desired.
Furrow wheel can be set at four different angles to suit various conditions of work and soil.
The leveling attachment will regulate the carriage to ride over uneven ground, while the plow will run level, making bottom of furrow even and level, regardless of uneven surface.
It is the simplest and by far the best two-wheel sulky in the field; it is easy of adjustment and handling, has no gearing, cogs, or cranks; in fact, there is nothing to get out of order.
The carriage is so constructed that the plow can be removed and a steel beam middle burster or stalk cutter attachment attached, as can also any plow that is of sufficient height.
Landing attachment can be furnished, which will cost extra.
    For setting up and operating directions, see page 150.
    For prices on repairs, see pages 146 and 147.
    For price list of extras, see page 48.

PRICE LIST.
With Steel Tripletrees and Neckyoke, Rolling Coulter, Weed Hook, Wrench, Oil Can, and Extra Steel Point.

Name.		10 inch.	12 inch.	14 inch.	16 inch.
Simple Sulky with New Clipper Bottom	Price	$45 00	$45 00	$47 50	$47 50
	Code Word	Mincing.	Mineral.	Ministry.	Miocene.
	Weight	522 lbs.	527 lbs.	544 lbs.	548 lbs.
Simple Sulky with Texas Bottom	Price		$45 00	$47 50	$47 50
	Code Word		Miniate.	Mintage.	Mirror.
	Weight		530 lbs.	534 lbs.	537 lbs.

PRICE LIST—EXTRA PLOW BOTTOMS.
Plow Bottom with Rolling Coulter, Weed Hook, and Clevis, fitted ready to attach. Without Extra Point.

Name		10 inch.	12 inch.	14 inch.	16 inch.
New Clipper Bottom for Simple Sulky	Price	$20 00	$20 00	$22 50	$22 50
	Code Word	Miscast.	Miscible.	Miser.	Misletoe.
	Weight	148 lbs.	153 lbs.	170 lbs.	174 lbs.
Texas Bottom for Simple Sulky	Price		$20 00	$22 50	$22 50
	Code Word		Miscreant.	Mishna.	Missile.
	Weight		156 lbs.	160 lbs.	163 lbs.

B. F. AVERY & SONS. LOUISVILLE, KY.

AVERY'S "SIMPLE" SULKY.

WITH MIDDLE BURSTER BOTTOM.

Above represents our Simple Sulky with Middle Burster attached, which in bursting out middles is a great labor-saving implement, as it does the work of several walking plows, with less labor on the team and plowman, and with better results.

Fall Plowing—With one furrow the old bed can be reversed, entirely burying all pea vines, stalks, and other trash.

Ditching—One "through" with the Middle Burster makes a splendid water furrow, which will generally serve the same purpose as ditching.

It makes a perfect lister, making a complete bed for corn, cotton, etc., at one "through;" this feature alone will pay for the sulky many times each year.

Planters using them freely state that the benefit derived from turning under the cotton and cornstalks has been worth to them at least two dollars for each and every acre.

It has been demonstrated beyond question that this style of ridge plowing is better than any other way of doing same.

For directions to attach Middle Burster attachment to Simple Sulky, see page 150.
For prices on repairs, see page 148.   For price list of extras, see page 48.

PRICE LIST.

With Four-Horse Eveners, Neckyoke, Wrench, Oil Can, and Extra Steel Point.

Name and Size.	Code Word.	Weight.	Price.
Simple Sulky with 14-inch Middle Burster Bottom	Mistily.	563 lbs.	$50 00
Simple Sulky with 16-inch Middle Burster Bottom	Mitten.	569 lbs.	50 00
Simple Sulky with 18-inch Middle Burster Bottom	Mizzy.	573 lbs.	52 50
Simple Sulky with 20-inch Middle Burster Bottom	Mockage.	578 lbs.	55 00
Simple Sulky with 22-inch Middle Burster Bottom	Modicum.	584 lbs.	57 50

PRICE LIST—EXTRA MIDDLE BURSTER BOTTOMS.

Extra Bottom is Sent Fitted Ready to Attach. Without Extra Steel Point.

Size and Name.	Code Word.	Weight.	Price.
14-inch Middle Burster Bottom for Simple Sulky	Modus.	154 lbs.	$25 00
16-inch Middle Burster Bottom for Simple Sulky	Molar.	160 lbs.	25 00
18-inch Middle Burster Bottom for Simple Sulky	Molien.	164 lbs.	27 50
20-inch Middle Burster Bottom for Simple Sulky	Momier.	169 lbs.	30 00
22-inch Middle Burster Bottom for Simple Sulky	Monastic.	175 lbs.	32 50

B. F. AVERY & SONS.   LOUISVILLE, KY.

AVERY'S "SIMPLE" SULKY STALK CUTTER.

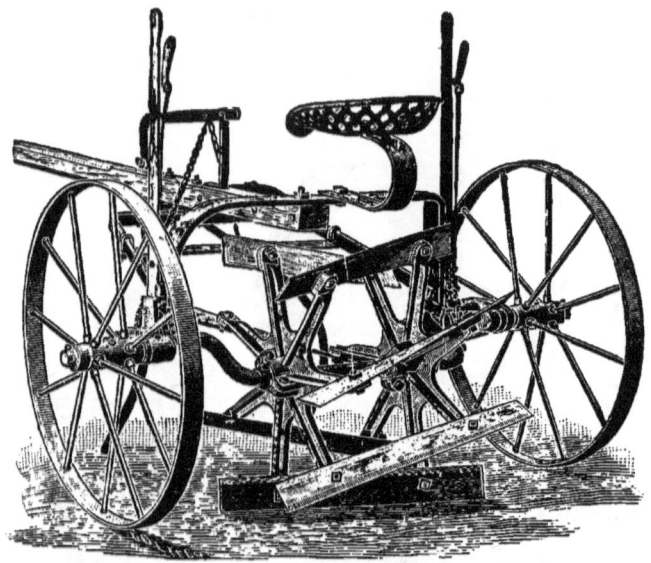

Above cut represents our Simple Sulky with Stalk Cutter attachment.
A keen, heavy, and sure cutter.
Cuts the stalk into twelve-inch pieces.
Has seven (7) double-edged and reversible spiral knives.
The drag hooks are raised or lowered by means of a lever in front of driver.
With the spring seat and the easy motion of the spiral knives there is no jolting.

Any degree of penetration can be given the knives by means of the lever, by which the entire weight of machine and driver can be forced on the knives, thus making it very desirable for heavy work.

For directions to attach Stalk Cutter attachment to Simple Sulky, see page 150.
For prices on repairs, see page 149.

PRICE LIST.

Stalk Cutters Complete Furnished with Steel Tripletrees and Neckyoke, Wrench, and Oil Can.
Simple Sulky Carriage Only Furnished with Steel Tripletrees, Wrench, and Oil Can.

Name.	Code Word.	Weight.	Price.
Simple Sulky with Stalk Cutter Attachment	Monger.	596 lbs.	$40 00
Stalk Cutter Attachment only	Monocrat.	222 lbs.	17 00
Simple Sulky, Carriage only	Monograph.	374 lbs.	25 00

PRICE LIST OF EXTRAS.

Order Name.	8-in.	10-in.	12-in.	14-in.	16-in.	18-in.	20-in.
Landing Attachment		$2 00	$2 00	$2 00	$2 00		
15-inch Caster Rolling Coulter, with attachments	$6 00	6 00	6 00	6 00	6 00		
Special 18-inch Pea Vine Cutter				7 00	7 00	$7 00	$7 00
No. 1 Steel Tripletrees		4 40	4 40	4 40	4 40		
Steel Point, with Bolts for New Clipper or Texas		2 00	2 50	3 00	3 50		
Steel Point, with Bolts for Black Prince	1 50	2 00	2 50	3 00	3 50		
Steel Point, with Bolts for Middle Burster				4 00	4 50	5 00	5 50
Chilled Point, with Bolts for New Clipper or Texas		60	65	75	80		
Chilled Point, with Bolts for Black Prince	70	75	85	90	1 00		
Steel Moldboard, with Bolts for New Clipper or Texas		4 50	5 00	5 50	6 00		
Steel Moldboard, with Bolts for Black Prince	4 00	4 50	5 00	5 50	6 00		
Steel Moldboard, with Bolts for Middle Burster—R. or L.				2 50	3 25	4 00	4 50
Steel Landside, with Bolts for New Clipper or Texas		1 25	1 50	1 75	2 00		
Steel Landside, with Bolts for Black Prince	1 00	1 00	1 00	1 25	1 25		

B. F. AVERY & SONS. LOUISVILLE, KY.

AVERY'S "INVINCIBLE" GANG PLOWS.

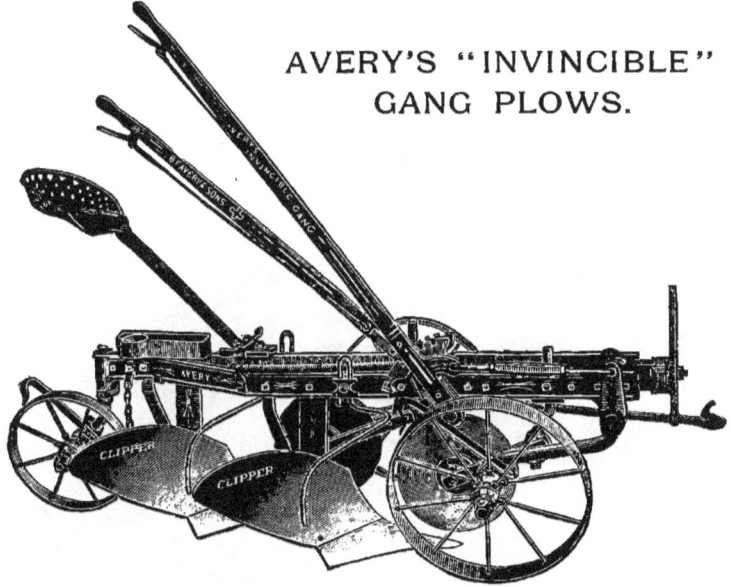

TWO FURROW.

The Invincible Gang Plow is constructed on the same principle as the Invincible Sulky, and is thoroughly excellent in every respect.

It will "open-up" the land six inches deep with the plows perfectly level.

The horses are hitched four abreast with one horse in furrow, three on land.

The plows are in front of the operator, where their work is constantly under his eye.

The frame is light, strong, well braced, and high up from the ground, giving ample clearance in trashy ground.

The weight of frame and the bottom friction of the plows are carried entirely on the wheels, thereby making a very light draft. Has no side friction.

Has the simplest and most perfect dial clevis made, and by which the line of draft can be shifted in any direction by loosening one nut.

Front and rear furrow wheels are canted, and hold the plow steady to its work, and turning a perfect square corner without taking plows out of the ground.

The rear furrow wheel swivels automatically when turning a corner with the plows in the ground and immediately resumes its proper position when plow is pulled forward.

The levers are within easy reach of the driver; has one lever to gauge the depth of furrow, and one to level the plow.

New Clipper Bottoms.—With soft center steel moldboard and point extra hardened and highly polished for loose, sandy, clay, or loam soils and stubble work. Right and left hand.

Texas Bottoms.—With soft center steel moldboard and point extra hardened and polished for all tough, sticky, obstinate soils difficult to turn or shed, including buckshot, tough river bottoms, and for sod plowing. Right and left hand.

Silver Bottoms.—With chilled iron moldboard and point for loose, sandy, or clay soils that are suited to chilled plow work. Right hand only.

Extra chilled points can be furnished for any of the above bottoms.

For setting up and operating directions, see page 151.

PRICE LIST.
Includes Riding Attachment, Rolling Coulters, Weed Hooks, Wheel Scrapers, Four-Horse Eveners, and Extra Points.

Name.		10 inch.	12 inch.	14 inch.
Invincible Gang, with New Clipper Bottoms	Price	$72 00	$75 00	$80 00
	Weight	676 lbs.	726 lbs.	758 lbs.
	Code Word	Monopoly.	Monster.	Monticle.
Invincible Gang, with Texas Bottoms	Price	$72 00	$75 00	$80 00
	Weight	676 lbs.	686 lbs.	736 lbs.
	Code Word	Moorage.	Mopus.	Morass.
Invincible Gang, with Silver Bottoms	Price		$68 00	
	Weight		716 lbs.	
	Code Word		Morgay.	
Steel Point, with Bolts for New Clipper or Texas		$2 00	$2 50	$3 00
Chilled Point, with Bolts for New Clipper or Texas		60	65	75
Chilled Point, with Bolts for Silver			70	

B. F. AVERY & SONS. LOUISVILLE, KY.

AVERY'S "NAPOLEON" GANG PLOWS.

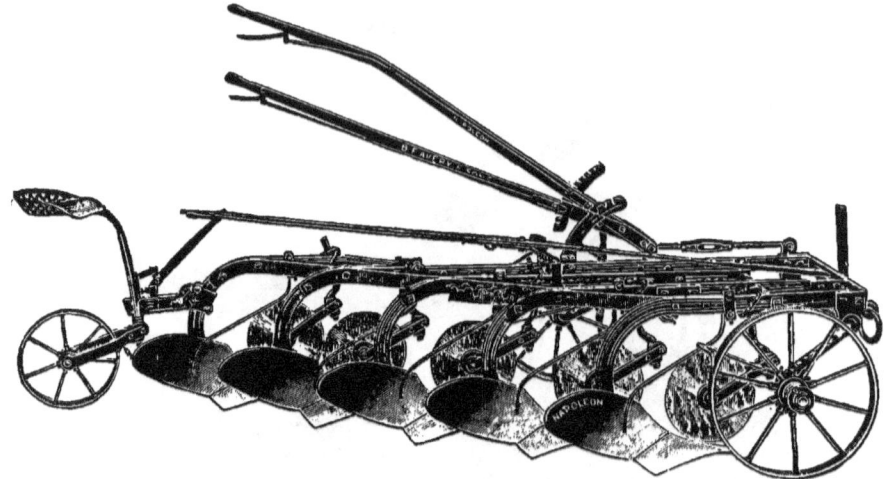

With or Without Seat Attachment, Rear Wheel, and Rolling Coulters.

Made in 2, 3, 4, and 5-Furrow Sizes. Furnished with 10, 12, and 14-inch Steel Bottoms.
Suited to every Soil.

For absolute strength, extreme simplicity, freedom from weak or undesirable points, and abundance of excellent working features throughout, Napoleon Gang Plows are unrivaled. They will do perfectly the work that can be expected of any gang plows, and are guaranteed to give satisfactory service in any soils and in every quarter of the earth, wherever gang plows can be expected to work at all, no matter how tough and difficult the work.

The only gang manufactured that has been able to stand the strain and to do satisfactory work in the world's toughest soils. Received first prize over all other gangs at the California State Fair, 1893, and at many other fairs. We ship them to all quarters of the earth. They are pulled by horse, mule, ox, elephant, and steam power.

FEATURES AND ADVANTAGES OF THESE PLOWS ARE:

Extra Strong and High Beams, being 23 inches in the clear, prevents clogging with trash.

High Wheels, A series 26 inches; B series 24 inches in diameter. Unusually strong.

Axles of cold-rolled steel. A series $1\frac{3}{8}$ inches; B series $1\frac{1}{4}$ inches in diameter. Strongest in use.

Braces, steel, $2\frac{1}{4} \times 1$ inch, fitted securely into grooved sides of the plow beams, thus holding the plows rigidly and securely together, making it impossible to rack or strain the gangs.

Bolts, nothing smaller than $\frac{5}{8}$ inch used in construction of these gang frames. Largest, safest bolts on any gang plows.

The Hitch is center draft, reaching from rear axle. A splendid new feature in the hitch is that it can be shifted in any direction, up or down, right or left, by simply loosening one nut.

The Quadrant has one single notch, which is the right and only spot for the main or lifting lever for plowing at any depth after the first furrow is opened.

The Lift is extra high and easy, and the lever so arranged that the operator can handle same easily without leaving his seat, or while walking at the side of the plow.

Turns a Square Corner with Perfect Ease; no other gang known to us does this. No strain on axles or wheels in turning corner.

Furnished with or without Seat Attachment and Rear Wheel (these two parts go on or off the plow together). The lever attachment furnished with the rear wheel gives the highest lift above ground and above ordinary obstructions of any plow known, being a superior advantage in transporting from field to field.

We make the Napoleon Gang in two sizes of frames: No. A being extra strong and heavy, and warranted to withstand the severest strain that it may be put to. The No. B is some lighter than No. A, yet stronger and heavier than any other gang in the market.

B. F. AVERY & SONS.   LOUISVILLE, KY.

AVERY'S "NAPOLEON" GANG PLOWS.

PRICE LIST.

Furnished with extra Steel or Chilled Points as preferred.

NOTICE.—Seat Attachment, Rear Wheel, Rolling Coulters, and Eveners cost extra.

Number, Size, and Name.	A SERIES.		
	Code Word.	Weight.	Price.
With New Clipper Bottoms for Sandy or Loose Soils.			
No. A, 2-Furrow 10-inch Napoleon Gang	Morose.	600 lbs.	$63 00
No. A, 2-Furrow 12-inch Napoleon Gang	Morsel.	635 lbs.	68 00
No. A, 2-Furrow 14-inch Napoleon Gang	Mortise.	655 lbs.	78 00
No. A, 3-Furrow 10-inch Napoleon Gang	Mosquito.	735 lbs.	90 00
No. A, 3-Furrow 12-inch Napoleon Gang	Motific.	765 lbs.	100 00
No. A, 4-Furrow 10-inch Napoleon Gang	Mounter.	960 lbs.	110 00
No. A, 4-Furrow 12-inch Napoleon Gang	Mouser.	1,000 lbs.	122 00
No. A, 5-Furrow 10-inch Napoleon Gang	Moyle.	1,185 lbs.	133 00
No. A, 5-Furrow 12-inch Napoleon Gang	Mucor.	1,250 lbs.	145 00
With Texas Bottoms for Tough or Sticky Soils.			
No. A, 2-Furrow 10-inch Napoleon Gang	Muffin.	600 lbs.	63 00
No. A, 2-Furrow 12-inch Napoleon Gang	Muleteer.	635 lbs.	68 00
No. A, 2-Furrow 14-inch Napoleon Gang	Multiplex.	655 lbs.	78 00
No. A, 3-Furrow 10-inch Napoleon Gang	Multitude.	735 lbs.	90 00
No. A, 3-Furrow 12-inch Napoleon Gang	Mumble.	765 lbs.	100 00
No. A, 4-Furrow 10-inch Napoleon Gang	Muncher.	960 lbs.	110 00
No. A, 4-Furrow 12-inch Napoleon Gang	Murex.	1,000 lbs.	122 00
No. A, 5-Furrow 10-inch Napoleon Gang	Murion.	1,185 lbs.	133 00
No. A, 5-Furrow 12-inch Napoleon Gang	Musculite.	1,225 lbs.	145 00

Number, Size, and Name.	B SERIES.		
	Code Word.	Weight.	Price.
With New Clipper Bottoms for Sandy or Loose Soils.			
No. B, 2-Furrow 10-inch Napoleon Gang	Musket.	515 lbs.	$60 00
No. B, 2-Furrow 12-inch Napoleon Gang	Mustard.	550 lbs.	62 00
No. B, 2-Furrow 14-inch Napoleon Gang	Multilous.	560 lbs.	70 00
No. B, 3-Furrow 10-inch Napoleon Gang	Mutton.	600 lbs.	82 00
No. B, 3-Furrow 12-inch Napoleon Gang	Myriad.	625 lbs.	90 00
No. B, 4-Furrow 10-inch Napoleon Gang	Mystics.	850 lbs.	100 00
No. B, 4-Furrow 12-inch Napoleon Gang	Naivete.	900 lbs.	110 00
No. B, 5-Furrow 10-inch Napoleon Gang	Namer.	1,000 lbs.	120 00
No. B, 5-Furrow 12-inch Napoleon Gang	Nappal.	1,050 lbs.	130 00
With Texas Bottoms for Tough or Sticky Soils.			
No. B, 2-Furrow 10-inch Napoleon Gang	Nariform.	525 lbs.	60 00
No. B, 2-Furrow 12-inch Napoleon Gang	Narwal.	550 lbs.	62 00
No. B, 2-Furrow 14-inch Napoleon Gang	Nathmore.	560 lbs.	70 00
No. B, 3-Furrow 10-inch Napoleon Gang	Naturist.	600 lbs.	82 00
No. B, 3-Furrow 12-inch Napoleon Gang	Nautilus.	625 lbs.	90 00
No. B, 4-Furrow 10-inch Napoleon Gang	Nazarean.	850 lbs.	100 00
No. B, 4-Furrow 12-inch Napoleon Gang	Neatherd.	900 lbs.	110 00
No. B, 5-Furrow 10-inch Napoleon Gang	Necklace.	1,000 lbs.	120 00
No. B, 5-Furrow 12-inch Napoleon Gang	Nectar.	1,050 lbs.	130 00
Riding Attachment (Seat and Rear Wheel)	Needle.	----------	10 00
15-inch Rolling Coulter with Attachments, each	Negatory.	----------	5 00
No. 1, Steel Tripletrees	Negotiant.	----------	4 40
Four-Horse Eveners with Steel Doubletrees	Neighbor.	----------	5 00
10-inch Steel Point	Neology.	----------	2 00
12-inch Steel Point — When ordering give name	Nepotist.	----------	2 50
14-inch Steel Point — and size of bottom	Nervure.	----------	3 00
10-inch Chilled Point — wanted for.	Nettle.	----------	60
12-inch Chilled Point	Neuter.	----------	65
14-inch Chilled Point	Newish.	----------	75

In ordering, state character of land to be plowed, as we make a variety of bottoms.

B. F. AVERY & SONS. LOUISVILLE, KY.

AVERY'S "COSMOPOLITAN" GANG PLOWS.

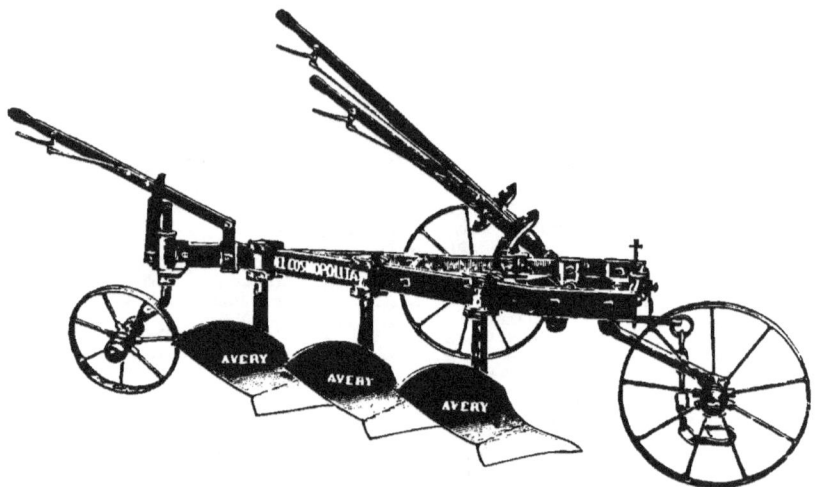

THREE FURROW. CUTS 24 INCHES.

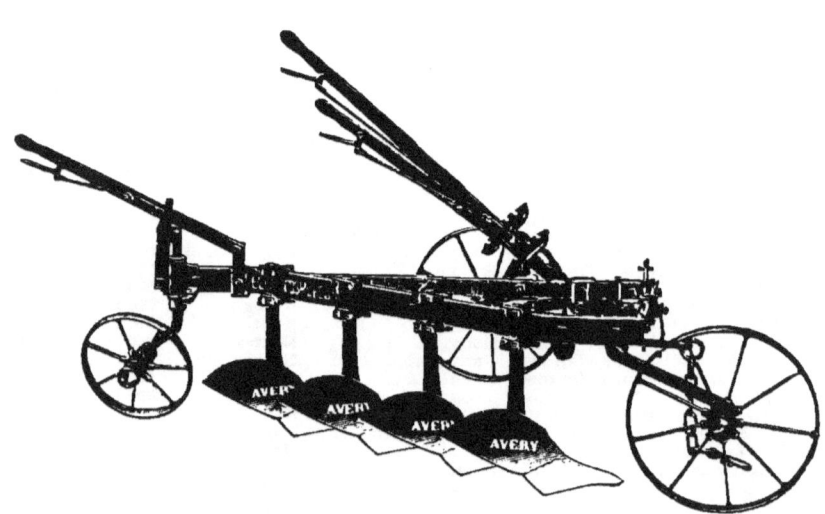

FOUR FURROW. CUTS 24 INCHES.

AVERY'S "COSMOPOLITAN" GANG PLOWS.

Patented.

These small gang plows are adapted for vineyard and orchard cultivation in California and elsewhere, as well as fall plowing in all light soils, and are especially adapted for all kinds of plowing in Mexico.

They are strongly built, practically entirely of steel and wrought iron, and in quality of work, lightness of draft, and ease of handling and adjusting they are far superior to any offered to the trade.

The special advantage of the "Cosmopolitan" Gang over all other light gangs is its levers; in all other makes it is necessary to change the position of the wheels by stepping and removing bolts to adjust the plow for its work, while the Cosmopolitan can be adjusted for any and all work required of it with its levers.

The right hand lever serves to adjust the depth and lifts the plow out of the ground.

The left hand lever adjusts the wheel on the land side to level the carriage or frame when plowing at different depths.

The levers are so arranged that the operator can handle them easily while walking at the side of the plow.

The Gang will turn a perfectly square corner to the left with plows in the ground without touching any levers, and will turn square to the right when plows are out of the ground by depressing rear lever or handle sufficiently to unlock rear wheel, thereby enabling the operator to successfully back-furrow (or plow from the center), an advantage no other light Gang possesses. For transportation the rear end of Gang can be elevated six inches, by depressing rear lever or handle.

The plows being rigid in the frame and being carried on three wheels prevents any landside or beam friction, which necessarily makes Gang of very light draft. Has no side friction.

The frame is high up from the ground, giving ample clearance in trashy ground.

They will "open-up" the land from two to six inches deep with the plows perfectly level.

The wheel nuts are covered to protect the axles from dust and dirt, thus insuring long service without wearing.

PRICE LIST.

Without Extra Points.

Size and Name.	Code Word.	Weight.	Price.
Three-Furrow Cosmopolitan Gang	Nibbler.	313 lbs.	$89 00
Four-Furrow Cosmopolitan Gang	Nickel.	390 lbs.	89 00
Extra 8-inch bottom, each	Niello.	21 lbs.	5 00
Extra 6-inch bottom, each	Nightcap.	14 lbs.	3 50
Extra Steel Point, 6-inch	Niotic	....	60
Extra Steel Point, 8-inch	Niobium.	....	80

B. F. AVERY & SONS. LOUISVILLE, KY.

Avery's "Perfection" "Center-Disc" Harrow.

WITH SOLID DISCS.

No side draft.
Perfect working cleaners.
Simple and strong in construction.
Is made of iron and steel throughout.
Hitch always remains central, which prevents side draft.
Leaves the surface perfectly level, cutting the center all away.
Having two levers, each gang can be worked independently of the other.
The pole is readily adjusted for three-horse hitch, and can be used either rigid or flexible, which assures no neck weight.

Can be furnished with sectional disc blades in place of the solid discs when specially ordered.

PRICE LIST.
With Two, Three, or Four-Horse Hitch as ordered, excepting No. 100, which has Two-Horse Hitch only.

Number and Name.	Code Word.	Width of Cut.	No. of Discs.	Size of Disc.	Weight.	Price.
No. 100, Perfection Disc Harrow.	Nitric.	4 feet	9	16 in.	417 lbs.	$46 00
No. 110, Perfection Disc Harrow.	Noachian.	5 feet	11	16 in.	440 lbs.	48 00
No. 120, Perfection Disc Harrow.	Noctiluca.	6 feet	13	16 in.	480 lbs.	50 00
No. 130, Perfection Disc Harrow.	Noddy.	7 feet	15	16 in.	505 lbs.	56 00
No. 210, Perfection Disc Harrow.	Nolition.	5 feet	11	20 in.	530 lbs.	54 00
No. 220, Perfection Disc Harrow.	Nominate.	6 feet	13	20 in.	565 lbs.	56 00
No. 230, Perfection Disc Harrow.	Nonagon.	7 feet	15	20 in.	600 lbs.	62 00

HALF SEEDERS.

Right Hand.	Code Word.	Price.	Left Hand.	Code Word.	Price.
No. 120	Nonjuror.	$11 00	No. 120	Noseless.	$11 00
No. 130	Nonsense.	12 00	No. 130	Notary.	12 00
No. 220	Nooning.	11 00	No. 220	Noter.	11 00
No. 230	Northing.	12 00	No. 230	Notional.	12 00

B. F. AVERY & SONS. LOUISVILLE, KY.

Avery's Improved "Tornado" Disc Harrow.

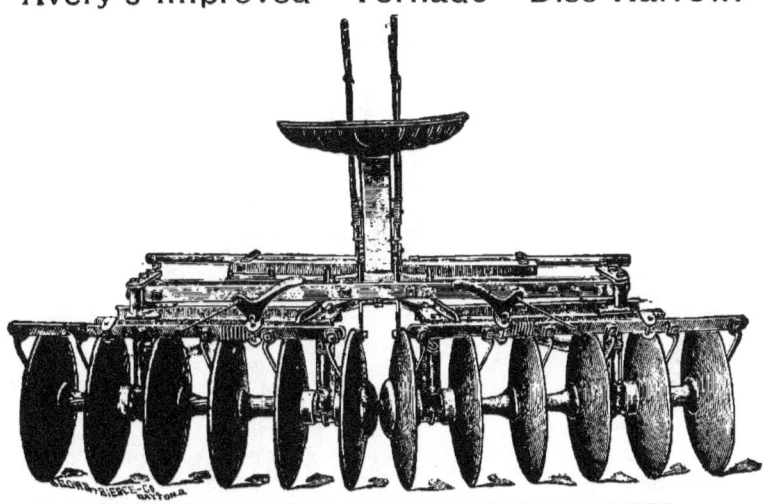

WITH SOLID DISC AND ANTI-FRICTION END WASHERS.

Has two levers.
No side draft whatever.
Perfect working cleaners.
Perfect two or three-horse center hitch. No neck weight.
Both gangs can be set at any angle while the team is in motion.
Tongue rigid or flexible; easily changed for either two or three horses.
Is flexible, with improved couplings, permitting each gang to vibrate and revolve independently.

Has anti-friction end washers that revolve independent of gangs, receiving the end pressure and preventing riding or locking of gangs and removing all strain from bearings and reducing the draft.
Is made of iron and steel throughout, and is strong and durable, simple of construction, and easy of operation.
Spring trip center tooth attachment can be furnished when desired.
Seeders can be furnished to be attached to all sizes excepting for the Nos. ½, 0, 5½, and 6.

PRICE LIST.

With Two, Three or Four-Horse Hitch as ordered, excepting on Nos. ½ and 5½, which Have Two-Horse Hitch only.

Number and Name.	Code Word.	Width of Cut.	No. of Discs.	Size of Disc.	Weight.	Price.
No. ½, Imp. Tornado Disc Harrow	Nourice.	4 feet.	8	16 inch.	351 lbs.	$42 00
No. 0, Imp. Tornado Disc Harrow	Novelist.	5 feet.	10	16 inch.	402 lbs.	44 00
No. 1, Imp. Tornado Disc Harrow	Nowel.	6 feet.	12	16 inch.	443 lbs.	46 00
No. 2, Imp. Tornado Disc Harrow	Numerator	7 feet.	14	16 inch.	500 lbs.	50 00
No. 3, Imp. Tornado Disc Harrow	Nunchion.	8 feet.	16	16 inch.	575 lbs.	54 00
No. 7X, Imp. Tornado Disc Harrow	Nurser.	6 feet.	12	18 inch.	455 lbs.	49 00
No. 5½, Imp. Tornado Disc Harrow	Nutmeg.	4 feet.	8	20 inch.	400 lbs.	48 00
No. 6, Imp. Tornado Disc Harrow	Nuzzle.	5 feet.	10	20 inch.	450 lbs.	50 00
No. 7, Imp. Tornado Disc Harrow	Oakling.	6 feet.	12	20 inch.	511 lbs.	52 00
No. 8, Imp. Tornado Disc Harrow	Obconic.	7 feet.	14	20 inch.	550 lbs.	56 00
No. 9, Imp. Tornado Disc Harrow	Obelisk.	8 feet.	16	20 inch.	600 lbs.	60 00

Spring Trip Center Tooth Attachment....Code Word—Obiter.........Each, $4 00.

HALF SEEDERS.

Right Hand.	Code Word.	Price.	Left Hand.	Code Word.	Price.
Nos. 1 or 7	Objector.	$11 00	Nos. 1 or 7	Obrogate.	$11 00
Nos. 2 or 8	Obliger.	12 00	Nos. 2 or 8	Obscurer.	12 00
Nos. 3 or 9	Oblocutor.	13 25	Nos. 3 or 9	Observer.	13 25

B. F. AVERY & SONS.   LOUISVILLE, KY.

Avery's Improved "Tornado" Sectional Disc Harrow.

WITH SECTIONAL DISCS AND ANTI-FRICTION END WASHERS.

Has two levers.
No side draft whatever.
Perfect working cleaners.
Perfect two or three-horse center hitch. No neck weight.
Both gangs can be set at any angle while the team is in motion.
Tongue rigid or flexible; easily changed for either two or three horses.

It is flexible, with improved couplings, permitting each gang to vibrate and revolve independently.

Anti-friction end washers that revolve independent of gangs receiving the end pressure and preventing riding or locking of gangs and removing all strain from bearings and reducing the draft.

Seeders can be furnished to be attached to all Nos. 1 and 2.
Spring trip center tooth attachment can be furnished when desired.
Can furnish the 6 and 7 feet Improved Tornado Sectional Disc Harrow with 20-inch disc blades when specially ordered.

PRICE LIST.

With Two, Three, or Four-Horse Hitch as ordered, excepting on No. ½, which has Two-Horse Hitch only.

Number and Name.	Code Word.	Width of Cut.	No. of Disc.	Size of Disc.	Weight.	Price.
No. ½, Improved Tornado Sectional Disc	Obstructer.	4 feet.	8	16 in.	330 lbs.	$44 00
No. 0, Improved Tornado Sectional Disc	Obstrude.	5 feet.	10	16 in.	378 lbs.	46 50
No. 1, Improved Tornado Sectional Disc	Obversant.	6 feet.	12	16 in.	415 lbs.	49 00
No. 2, Improved Tornado Sectional Disc	Occasive.	7 feet.	14	16 in.	500 lbs.	53 50

Spring Trip Center Tooth Attachment.. Code Word—Occursion .... Each, $4 00

HALF SEEDERS.

Right Hand.	Code Word.	Price.	Left Hand.	Code Word.	Price.
No. 1......	Octave.	$11 00	No. 1......	Odorous.	$11 00
No. 2......	Octuple.	12 00	No. 2......	Offender.	12 00

B. F. AVERY & SONS.   LOUISVILLE, KY.

Avery's "Eureka" Reversible Disc Harrow.

WITH SOLID DISCS.

Iron and steel throughout.
Has perfect working cleaners.
Adjustable in width and range.
Both gangs can be set at any angle while the team is in motion.
Both levers are under perfect control of the operator while in the seat, and each gang can be worked independently of the other.

    Can be changed from "out-throw," as shown in above cut, to "in-throw" in two minutes; change can be made while in the field without taking the harrow apart to do so. To reverse, loosen the nuts on top of pivot stems and reverse the section.

    Scrapers should always be in the rear, so, when reversing, be sure and shift the scrapers by placing the right scraper on the left side and the left scraper on the right side, which is done by simply removing two bolts on each section.

PRICE LIST.

Furnished with Two-Horse Hitch only.

Number and Name.	Code Word.	Width of Cut.	No. of Discs.	Size of Disc.	Weight.	Price.
No. 25, Eureka Disc Harrow	Officinal.	4 feet	8	16 in.	345 lbs.	$45 00
No. 26, Eureka Disc Harrow	Ogee.	5 feet	10	16 in.	380 lbs.	47 00
No. 27, Eureka Disc Harrow	Oiler.	4 feet	8	20 in.	400 lbs.	53 00
No. 28, Eureka Disc Harrow	Oleander.	5 feet	10	20 in.	450 lbs.	55 00

B. F. AVERY & SONS. LOUISVILLE, KY.

Avery's "Eureka" Reversible Disc Harrow.

WITH SECTIONAL DISCS.

The Eureka is by far the best Reversible and Adjustable Disc Harrow on the Market.

For general description see preceding page.

When to be used for cultivating, the gangs can be closed up in the center.

When wanted to straddle a row, a clearance of twenty inches between the sets of Discs can be given; the adjusting is done by removing one bolt on each section, sliding the section in or out on the frame as desired.

PRICE LIST.

Furnished with Two-Horse Hitch only.

Number and Name.	Code Word.	Width of Cut.	No. of Discs.	Size of Disc.	Weight.	Price.
No. 35, Eureka Disc Harrow	Olidous.	4 feet	8	16 in.	348 lbs.	$47 00
No. 36, Eureka Disc Harrow	Olivin.	5 feet	10	16 in.	381 lbs.	49 50
No. 37, Eureka Disc Harrow	Omer.	4 feet	8	20 in.	379 lbs.	55 00
No. 38, Eureka Disc Harrow	Omnibus.	5 feet	10	20 in.	419 lbs.	57 50

B. F. AVERY & SONS. LOUISVILLE, KY.

Avery's "U" Bar Steel Frame Lever Harrow.

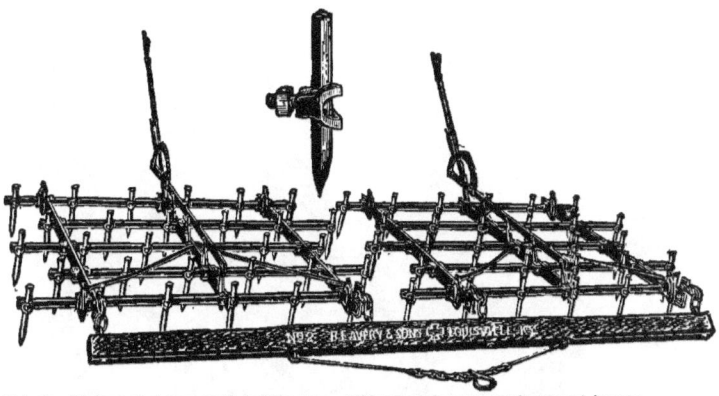

Painted black. Distance between teeth is 10 inches. All harrows have extra front or A braces.
The bars are made of U-shape wrought steel, and the main cross or connecting bars are 2-inch steel channels.
Malleable runners are attached to each corner of each section, turned down when teeth are thrown out of the ground for transportation over unplowed ground.
Headed steel teeth which are held firmly in place by a simple, strong malleable clamp, easily releasing tooth for adjustment of depth, or to be taken out to be sharpened.
A lever is attached to each section by which the teeth can be given any desired slant, either for the purpose of releasing trash, for pulverizing the soil, or for smoothing.
For repairs see page 141.

PRICE LIST.

Square Steel Teeth, 1-2 x 1-2 or 5-8 x 5-8 x 9 inches. In Ordering State Size of Teeth Wanted. Furnished with Draw Bar.

Order Number.	Number of Teeth.	Cut.	With 1/2 x 9 Inch Teeth.			With 5/8 x 9 Inch Teeth.		
			Code Word.	Weight.	Price.	Code Word.	Weight.	Price.
No. 1	30-Tooth.	5 feet.	Omoplate.	122 lbs.	$9 75	Oppone.	134 lbs.	$10 00
No. 2	60-Tooth.	10 feet.	Onerate.	249 lbs.	19 50	Opposer.	269 lbs.	20 00
No. 3	90-Tooth.	15 feet.	Ontology.	372 lbs.	29 25	Oppressor.	407 lbs.	30 00
No. 4	120-Tooth.	20 feet.	Opacous.	501 lbs.	39 00	Optic.	541 lbs.	40 00
No. 5	25-Tooth.	4 feet.	Opera.	109 lbs.	9 25	Opulent.	119 lbs.	9 50
No. 6	50-Tooth.	8 feet.	Operculum.	226 lbs.	18 50	Oraison.	242 lbs.	19 00
No. 7	75-Tooth.	12 feet.	Ophite.	332 lbs.	28 00	Oratoris.	362 lbs.	28 50
No. 8	100-Tooth.	16 feet.	Opium.	441 lbs.	37 25	Orbital.	481 lbs.	38 00

AVERY'S "COMMON SENSE" HARROW.

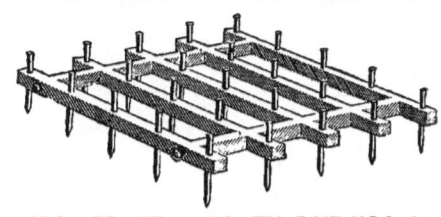

WOOD FRAME.   TWENTY-FIVE TOOTH.

Painted red. Distance between teeth 11 1/4 inches. Headed steel teeth 5/8 x 12 inch.
The five parallel oak bars are held rigid by two strong iron bars running through oak braces.
By changing the hitch from one corner to the other you always have sharp teeth on line of draft.
Hitch to the ring on either corner, which draws the harrow so that no tooth follows the track of the other, thoroughly harrowing the ground passed over.
For repairs see page 141.

PRICE LIST.

Size and Name.	Cut.	Code Word.	Weight.	Price.
25-Tooth Common Sense Harrow	5 feet 9 inches.	Ordainer.	97 lbs.	$9 00

B. F. AVERY & SONS. LOUISVILLE, KY.

"Cherokee" Corn Planter and Check Rower.
(Patented.)

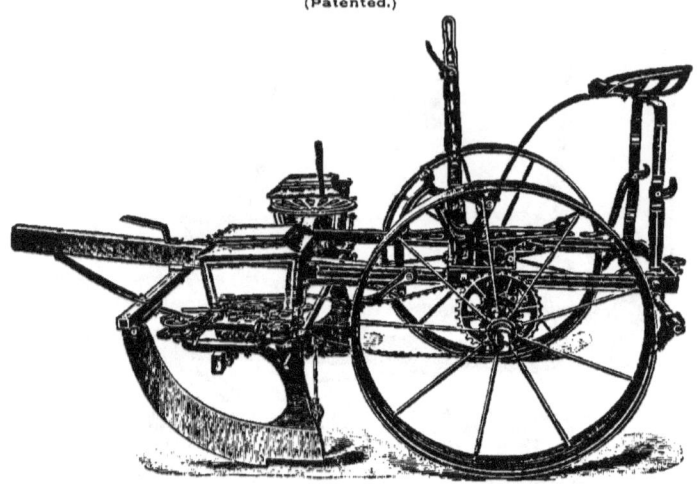

Force drop feed.
Perfect self drill planter.
Perfect hand drop planter.
Perfect check rower planter.

Metal frame.
Adjustable in width.
Wheels run on or off rows.
High concave or open wheels.

THE DROP. The principle of the combined drop is well known, and has become very popular. It is a planter that has a revolving feed shaft which operates the rotary plates, and is driven by a sprocket chain from the **center** of main axle, and drops one kernel at a time into the heel, until a full hill is dropped, at which time the hill is deposited from the heel to the ground by the operation of the check rower, or by hand. The corn being carried low in the heel, and having only **a short distance to drop, insures accurate checking.** It is a very simple device and will give the best results.

    THE DRILL. The machine can be quickly converted into a self drill planter by simply hooking the valve back, allowing the corn to drop from the hopper to the ground, any distance apart you may like. Full directions in top of seed box.

    THE PLATES. Each planter is supplied with six sets of plates suitable for average size corn, which is a sufficient number to plant any distance apart you are likely to require. Plates for sorghum, broom-corn, peas, etc., may be had at slight extra cost.

    THE CHECK ROWER. Our check rower is known as the low-down style, and allows the wire to run **close to the ground** and near a straight line. This relieves the friction on both wire and machine, insures light draft, and **less wear and breakage.**

    CENTER LEVER. Our combination center lever may be used to force the planter into hard ground, or may, by a slight movement of the foot, be thrown out of use, leaving the planter to be controlled by the foot treadles, thus allowing the runner-frame to run independent in rough ground—**a valuable feature.**

    POINTS. Automatically thrown out of gear when runners are raised. Spring pressure to hold in or out of ground. Furnished with or without covering blades. Adjustable in width 42, 44, 46, and 48 inches between runners. When leaving the factory all planters are set at 44 inches. Has simple foot-brake to control reel in laying out wire. High, strong wheels—light draft.

    FERTILIZER ATTACHMENT, which will fit any width planter, can be furnished if desired.

    CLOD FENDERS can be supplied if wanted.

PRICE LIST.

Number, Name, and Style.	Code Word.	Weight.	Price.
No. 1, Cherokee Planter with Check Rower, six sets of plates and 80 rods of wire.	Ordinate.	534 lbs.	$68 00
No. 2, Cherokee Planter without Check Rower and with six sets of plates	Organ.	424 lbs.	56 00
Fertilizer Attachment	Organon.	140 lbs.	21 00
Covering Shovels, with Clod Fenders, per set	Orignu.	60 lbs.	5 50
Covering Shovels, without Clod Fenders, per set	Orilton.	40 lbs.	3 50
Extra Wire (in 10-rod lengths), per rod	Ornithon.	5 lbs.	12
Steel Doubletrees, per set	Orrery.		2 00
Steel Neckyoke, each	Orthogon.		1 00

B. F. AVERY & SONS.  LOUISVILLE, KY.

Avery's Union Corn Drill.

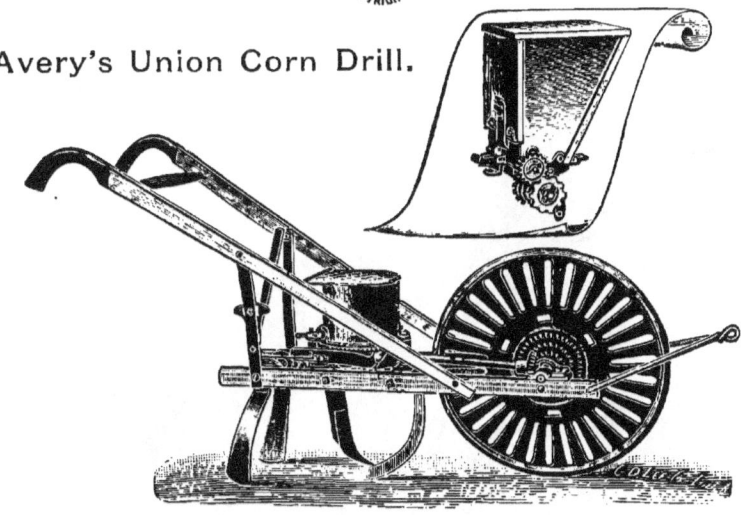

No. 14. WITH HOE AND COVERING SHARES.

Steel frame. Furnished with or without Fertilizer attachment, which is easily attached or taken off without interfering with the balance of the drill. It will distribute regularly any and all kinds of commercial fertilizer.

Corn can be dropped several different distances apart without changing the feed plates. This change can be made while the drill is in motion, with the lever used for throwing drill in and out of gear.

Furnished with one ten-hole plate, which can be adjusted to drop 7, 9, 11, 12, 14, 16, 18, and 25 inches apart. We can furnish, at a small additional cost, plates for planting beans, sorghum broom corn, garden seed, and other special purposes.

No. 16. WITH SHOE AND CONCAVE WHEEL FOR COVERING.

Furnished with one ten-hole plate, which can be adjusted to drop 8, 11, 13, 15, 19, and 24 inches apart. The general description given above will also apply to this drill.

Number and Name.	Code Word.	Weight.	Price.
No. 14, Union Corn Drill	Orval.	104 lbs.	$19 00
No. 14, Union Corn Drill and Fertilizer	Osoule.	133 lbs.	26 00
No. 16, Union Corn Drill	Ossnary.	103 lbs.	19 00
No. 16, Union Corn Drill and Fertilizer	Osteocope.	129 lbs.	26 00

B. F. AVERY & SONS. LOUISVILLE, KY.

Avery's "Modern" Cotton and Corn Planter.

The cut-off is metal, no brush being used.
Covering standards are friction break-back.
The flow of seed is regulated by a cut-off slide.
Plants delinted cotton seed out of the corn plate any distance or quantity.
As a cotton planter it will plant a continuous drill in any quantity wanted.
The opener standard can be made rigid with a bolt or to break-back with a wooden pin.
Plants corn three different distances apart, viz: 7, 15, and 23 inches, one grain in each hill.
Feed is driven by cog wheels, which are incased so that trash can not be wound into them or clog them.
Blades have reversible ends, and are also adjustable up or down to regulate the depth of planting and covering.
Regularly furnished with shovel blade coverers (unless otherwise ordered), which can be set to any side angle desired.
Distributes cottonseed meal and all commercial fertilizers perfectly, from the smallest to the largest flow desired.
A new feature of the covering blades is that they can be set upward or downward, and inward or outward, to throw more or less dirt on the seed.

The Modern Planter is designed especially to plant cotton and corn, but will also plant perfectly sorghum, beans, peas, or any seed, for which special plates will be supplied.
The planter is constructed entirely of iron and steel; is light, durable, well-balanced, well-proportioned, simple and easy to operate, and the strongest combined planter in the field.
Fertilizer attachment which requires no changes to attach can be furnished. Costs extra.
Wood dragboard coverer, or a concave roller, can be furnished. Costs extra.
Special plates, to plant more and other distances apart than those regularly sent, can be furnished on application.
Directions for setting up and operating on page 156.
For prices on repairs, see page 156.

PRICE LIST.

Each Planter is regularly furnished with one Cotton and three Corn Plates.

Number, Name, and Style.	Code Word.	Weight.	Price.
No. 1, Modern Cotton and Corn Planter, with Diamond Point Blade Coverers	Ottar.	103 lbs.	$18 50
No. 2, Modern Cotton and Corn Planter, with Spoon Blade Coverers	Ousel.	103 lbs.	18 50
Fertilizer Attachment	Outcast.	14 lbs.	7 50
Wood Dragboard Coverer, with Steel Springs	Ovarious.	7 lbs.	1 50
Concave Roller	Ovicular.	18 lbs.	2 25

B. F. AVERY & SONS. LOUISVILLE, KY.

Avery's "Louisville" Planter.

Perfect combined planter and drill.
Has a cut-off lever by which operator regulates flow of seed.
Constructed of iron and steel ; is light, yet strong and durable.
The reversible opener blade is adjustable to regulate the depth of planting.
Plants cotton, corn, beans, peas, or any seed perfectly, either in hills or drills.
Will plant corn, from one to three grains, 4½, 6, 9, 12, 18, 24, 36, and 72 inches apart.
Patent break-backs on opener blade standard, and also on covering blade standards.
As a cotton planter it will plant a continuous drill in any quantity that may be desired.
We supply five (5) planting plates for dropping corn, and can supply special plates for special distances or particular seeds, from the smallest to the largest.
Planter has the rotary movement, driven by a sprocket wheel and chain, the chain being attached outside of frame, thus avoiding all liability to clog or load with trash from the driver wheel.
Directions for setting up and operating on page 154.
For prices on repairs, see pages 154 and 155.

PRICE LIST.

Number, Name, and Style.	Code Word.	Weight.	Price.
No. 1, Louisville Planter, with Blade Coverers	Orulum.	110 lbs.	$19 00
No. 2, Louisville Planter, with Spoon Blade Coverers	Owser.	121 lbs.	19 00
Spring Board Coverer, for either Nos. 1 or 2	Oxygen.	9 lbs.	1 25

Avery's "Dow-Law" Cotton Planter.

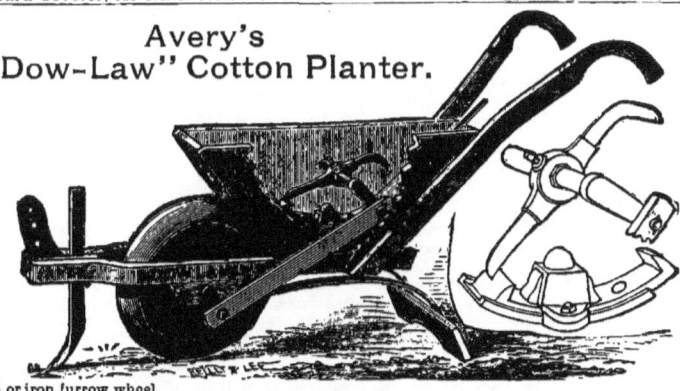

With wood or iron furrow wheel.
The springboard coverer has the best of spring-steel springs.
Made of seasoned wood, first-class material, and well finished.
Corn planting attachment (as shown at right of planter) is only sent when specially ordered, and will cost extra.
Nos. 3 and 4 have our new cut-off feed lever (see it between the handles), by which operator can regulate easily and certainly the flow of seed, or stop the flow entirely while in motion, thus preventing wasting of seed while turning around. For prices on repairs, see page 149.

PRICE LIST.

Number and Name.	Style.	Code Word.	Weight.	Price.	Corn Attachment.
No. 1, Dow-Law Cotton Planter	Old, with Wood Wheel.	Pacifier.	64 lbs.	$6 00	$2 00
No. 2, Dow-Law Cotton Planter	Old, with Iron Wheel	Pacos.	72 lbs.	6 50	2 00
No. 3, Dow-Law Cotton Planter	New, with Wood Wheel.	Paddock.	63 lbs.	6 00	2 00
No. 4, Dow-Law Cotton Planter	New with Iron Wheel	Pageant.	72 lbs.	6 50	2 00

B. F. AVERY & SONS.  LOUISVILLE, KY.

AVERY'S "REVOLUTION" DISC CULTIVATOR.
(Patented.)

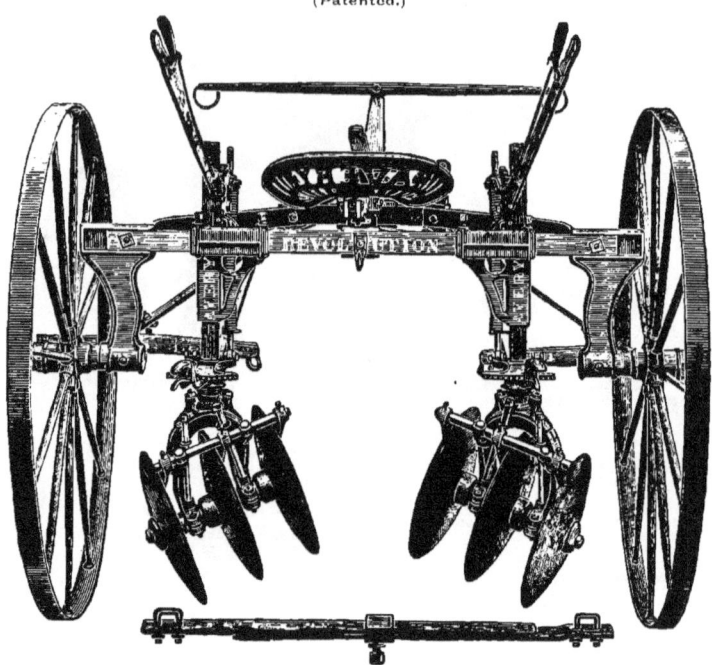

Avery's "Revolution" Disc Cultivator has scored unqualified, sweeping success in all parts of the country, and is admittedly far in the lead of all other machines. Reports received from all dealers and farmers who handled them during the past several seasons are that they have given universal satisfaction.

The simplicity of the various adjustments is not embodied or equaled in any other, and is sure to be appreciated by those who are aware that it takes from twenty to forty-five minutes to accomplish the same changes on all other disc cultivators that are made in ours in a very few moments.

Avery's "Revolution" Disc Cultivator will do perfect work and be under perfect control while the operator walks. No other will.

CONSTRUCTION:

The wheels are of steel, with removable boxes.
The wheel spindles are made of cold-rolled steel.
The fenders are adjustable for either large or small corn.
The seat can be raised or lowered as desired, to suit either man or boy.
Covered oil holes are at the top of the disc yoke, convenient to get at and preventing dirt from getting into the boxes.
The "Revolution" is constructed almost entirely of steel, and is perfect in point of strength and durability.

Ball Bearings. The discs revolve on hardened steel balls of the very finest kind, which lightens the draft materially and adds years to the life of the machine.

The arch is from four to eight inches higher than that of any other disc cultivator, and, as will be seen from the cut, is entirely free from obstructions, having no connecting yoke to interfere with the crop being cultivated; thus any crop may be "laid by" with the "Revolution."

Swivel Frame. By means of a swivel frame the operator guides the machine perfectly with the hand lever. The "Revolution" is more readily guided by means of either the hand lever or the team than any other disc cultivator, because the discs are connected directly with the frame and the action is therefore instantaneous, and with the Crescent Ratchet attachment the guiding lever can be set at any angle desired, which will be of special advantage when working in circular rows or on hillsides.

B. F. AVERY & SONS.  LOUISVILLE, KY.

Avery's "Revolution" Disc Cultivator—Continued.
(Patented.)

The Discs can be set to different angles by a hand lever. This is a very important feature, especially on hillsides.

To adjust the discs to the angle or slant of the corn or cotton rows it is only necessary to loosen two nuts, which can be done in a moment.

The penetration of the discs is regulated by the levers, and the bottom edge of the discs can be lowered seven inches below the wheels or raised six inches above them or the ground.

The soil can be thrown to or from the plants by removing one bolt from the adjusting lever, when the discs can be completely reversed without being removed from the spindle.

Each set of discs is entirely independent of the other, and is governed by its own lifting lever. In cultivating in rough or uneven ground, any movement or position given one gang does not in any way affect the other.

To widen or narrow the distance between the two sets of discs it is only necessary to loosen two set-screws, when the entire gang, lever, spindle, and all slide on the frame, and can be placed at any point desired. When straight the two inner discs can be narrowed to a four-inch space, or widened to twenty-six inches.

We can furnish two extra discs to be bolted on by hubs, which convert the cultivator into a first class Disc Harrow. When using as a harrow, the discs can be arranged to throw in one direction only, doing much better work than can be done with a regular disc harrow. (Always use bedding bar when bedding or harrowing.)

A disc cultivator pulverizes the soil around drill or row crops better than any other implement.

The Hitch. The eveners are so arranged that the horses always walk exactly in the middle of the furrows.

The distance between the hitches of our eveners can be adjusted from three feet eight inches to four feet two inches.

The Draft is direct from the steel eveners to the discs, not on the pole, thus relieving the frame and pole of all strain, and necessarily making the life of the cultivator triple that of any other made. The "gather" of the wheels is as accurate as that of any buggy, which makes the cultivator run very light.

The Tread. While we have a wider range between the discs than any other disc cultivator, the "tread" or distance between the wheels is less than any other; the narrowest tread being 52½ inches, and the widest 57½ inches. This advantage prevents the wheels from running on sides of the adjoining rows, for which other disc cultivators are now being condemned. This change may be made by loosening one nut.

Attachments. We make the following implements complete, or as attachments to the Revolution frame or carriage.

Many combination tools are failures because attempting too much. Each and every one of the following "Revolution" line, however, is absolutely perfect as a single, separate tool, or as an attachment, and in combinations:

Six Shovel Cultivator, see cut and description on page 66.
Spring Tooth Cultivator, see cut and description on page 67.
Stalk Cutter with Spiral Knives, see cut and description on page 68.
Stalk Cutter with Straight Knives, see cut and description on page 68.
Disc Harrow. We can furnish two extra discs to be bolted on by hubs, which convert the cultivator into a first class disc harrow.

For sugar land and other special work we build extra big machines, known as Revolution No. 2, No. 3, No. 4, and No. 5, on special orders. No. 1 has been found strong and big enough for heaviest work in corn, cotton, etc.

Directions for setting up and operating on page 157.

For prices on repairs, see pages 158 and 159.

PRICE LIST.

With Steel Singletrees and Neckyoke, Adjustable Fenders, Bedding Bar, and Six 16-Inch Discs.

Number and Name.	Code Word.	Weight.	Price.
No. 1. Revolution Disc Cultivator	Palace.	650 lbs.	$57 50
Pair 16-inch Discs, with Attachments to make an 8 Disc Cultivator or Harrow	Palatine.	38 lbs.	6 00

B. F. AVERY & SONS. LOUISVILLE, KY.

Avery's "Revolution" Six-Shovel Cultivator.

WITH BOLTED OR BREAK PIN FOOT. EXTRA STRONG.

The above shows our Revolution Disc Cultivator Frame with Six-shovel Cultivator Attachment. It is built extra strong; ignorant labor can not hurt it, and it will "stall" any two-horse or two-mule team before breaking or bending. Adapted to the cultivation of all drill or row crops, at all stages of growth. A small boy can work it.

The gangs used are those of our celebrated No. 104 X Comet Cultivator, which cultivator is so popular in the cotton districts.

The gangs may be moved or operated independently, and steadily held to the work, and maintain any depth from two inches to eight inches deep without varying or shying, no matter what the condition of soil.

The standards are made of such strength that the wood break pins are unnecessary, but the cultivator can be used as a break pin by removing lower bolt in malleable foot and inserting wood pin; they are adjustable in every way, up or down, and are held steadily to the work, maintaining any depth uniformly, from two to eight inches, no matter what the condition of the soil, and without any extra exertion on part of the driver.

One, two, or three shovels may be used on each side or gang, and any of the different style blades as shown on pages 135 to 139, or any other styles of blades using ⅜-inch bolt up to ⅞-inch heel bolt may be used.

The pitch of the shovels may be varied by adjustment of beams at eveners.

The Revolution Disc Cultivator is fully described on pages 64 and 65.

Directions for setting up and operating on page 157.

For special blades, see pages 135 to 139.

For prices on repairs, see page 160.

PRICE LIST.
With Steel Singletrees and Neckyoke.

Furnished with the following blades unless otherwise ordered:

```
One No. 47 Wallis Combination Shovel..................2    -3 x 10 x ¼.
One No. 47 Wallis Combination Shovel..................2½-4 x 10 x ¼.
One No. 47 Wallis Combination Shovel..................3    -5 x 10 x ¼.
One No. 48 Wallis Combination Shovel..................2    -3 x 10 x ¼.
One No. 48 Wallis Combination Shovel..................2½-4 x 10 x ¼.
One No. 48 Wallis Combination Shovel..................3    -5 x 10 x ¼.
```

Number and Name.	Code Word.	Weight.	Price.
No. 1, Revolution Six-Shovel Cultivator Complete	Palendar.	697 lbs.	$57 50
No. 1, Revolution Six-Shovel Attachment only	Palilogy.	165 lbs.	23 00

B. F. AVERY & SONS.   LOUISVILLE, KY.

Avery's "Revolution" Spring Tooth Cultivator.

Above cut shows our Revolution Disc Cultivator Frame with Spring Tooth Cultivator Attachment, which is especially adapted for use in rough or stony ground and for shallow cultivation. A perfect cultivator for all drill or row crops, at all stages of growth.

The springs are flexible, and allow the teeth to pass around or over any ordinary obstruction.

The diamond point blades are reversible, and, being small, they do not penetrate far enough to injure the crop roots, while at the same time they destroy all weeds and surface growth between the rows and permit proper absorption of moisture by the growing plant.

Each set of gangs is entirely independent of the other; is governed by its own lifting lever. In cultivating in rough or uneven ground, any movement or position given one gang does not in any way affect the other.

To widen or narrow the distance between the two sets of shovels it is only necessary to loosen two set-screws, when the entire gang, lever, spindle, and all slide on the frame, and can be placed at any point desired.

Each set of blades can be adjusted in any way desired, to fit the sides of beds. The blades can be set at different angles by means of a hand lever in easy reach of the operator. This is a very important feature, especially on hillsides.

The penetration of the blades is regulated by the lifting levers.

Reversible for in or out-throw. The soil can be thrown to or from the plants by simply loosening two nuts on yoke swivel J X 97 and shifting the gangs to position desired.

The Revolution Disc Cultivator is fully described on pages 64 and 65.

Directions for setting up and operating on page 157.

For prices on repairs, see page 160.

PRICE LIST.
With Steel Singletrees and Neckyoke.

Number and Name.	Code Word.	Weight.	Price.
No. 1, Revolution Spring Tooth Cultivator Complete	Pallial.	612 lbs.	$50 00
No. 1, Revolution Spring Tooth Attachment only	Palmar.	80 lbs.	14 00

B. F. AVERY & SONS. LOUISVILLE, KY.

AVERY'S "REVOLUTION" STALK CUTTER.

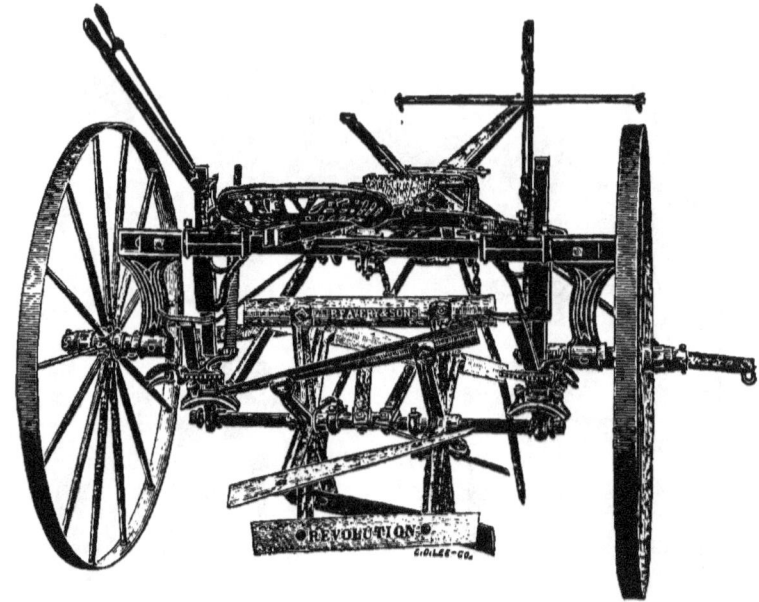

WITH EITHER SPIRAL OR STRAIGHT KNIVES.

Above cut represents our "Revolution" Disc Cultivator Carriage with Stalk Cutter Attachment.

An extra high grade machine in principle, construction, and execution. *Without question the strongest and best stalk cutter made.* Has all the pressure and cutting capacity you wish to get. Cuts the heaviest cotton or cornstalks, no matter what their condition, green or wet, *and it will cut stalks where no other machine will.*

The only stalk cutter that satisfactorily and easily cuts the big, heavy stalks of the Brazos bottoms in Texas, and of the Delta and other bottoms.

Cuts the stalks into twelve-inch pieces.

Has seven (7) double-edged and reversible spiral knives.

Wheels and cylinder spider; both have removable boxes.

With the easy motion of the spiral knives there is no jolting.

The drag hooks are raised or lowered by means of a lever within easy reach of the operator.

Cylinder revolves on the axle, and the axle itself does not revolve, hence there is no danger of vines or trash winding about the axle; it is non-cloggable.

Any degree of penetration can be given the knives by means of the levers, by which the entire weight of machine and driver can be forced on the knives.

STRAIGHT KNIFE STALK CUTTER. We can furnish same to any one preferring them.

The Revolution Disc Cultivator is fully described on pages 64 and 65.

Directions for attaching stalk cutter attachment on page 161.

For prices on repairs, see pages 160 and 161.

PRICE LIST.

Number and Name.	Style.	Weight.	Code Word.	Price.
No. 1, Revolution Stalk Cutter, complete, with Steel Singletrees and Neckyoke..	Spiral Knives	713 lbs.	Palsical.	$63 00
No. 2, Revolution Stalk Cutter, complete, with Steel Singletrees and Neckyoke..	Straight Knives....	713 lbs.	Pampre.	63 00
No. 1, Revolution Stalk Cutter Attachment only.............................	Spiral Knives	211 lbs.	Pandora.	27 00
No. 2, Revolution Stalk Cutter Attachment only.............................	Straight Knives....	211 lbs.	Panicle.	27 00

B. F. AVERY & SONS.      LOUISVILLE, KY.

AVERY'S RIDING CULTIVATORS.
(Patented.)

**No. 175. "New South" Combined Riding and Walking Cultivator.
With Rigid Pipe Beams and Break-Back Standards.**

This cultivator is especially adapted to the black, waxy land of Texas and the rich delta of the Mississippi and similar stiff or sticky soils.

Has rigid pipe beams of extra length.

The frame used is the same as the Western.

The space between the beams can be narrowed or widened as desired.

The standards are made of $1\frac{3}{8}$ inch round spring steel, and can be adjusted up or down and given any pitch desired.

The friction break-back attachment used on this cultivator relieves any excessive strain which may be thrown on the shovels or standards, and does away with the annoyance of the wooden break pin.

The shovels are securely bolted to the solid round steel standards, with the foot extending well under and toward the point, which supports the shovel in the weakest part.

We make this cultivator with Spring Trip Foot, see No. 177.

For prices on repairs, see pages 162, 163, and 164.

For special blades, see pages 135 to 139.

Directions for setting up on page 165.

PRICE LIST.

With Steel Singletrees and Neckyoke, Fenders, Two Plain Shovels, No. 36, Two Corn Shovels, No. 35, and Two Drane-Dixon Sweeps, No. 46.

Number and Name.	With	Code Word.	Weight.	Price.
No. 175, New South Cultivator.	Friction Break-Back.	Pantheon.	460 lbs.	$47 00
No. 177, New South Cultivator.	Spring Trip.	Pantry.	476 lbs.	51 50

B. F. AVERY & SONS.   LOUISVILLE, KY.

AVERY'S RIDING CULTIVATORS.
(Patented.)

No. 160. "Western" Combined Riding and Walking Cultivator, with Parallel Beams and Break Pin Foot.

The Western Cultivator has the strongest frame of any cultivator offered to the trade, and possesses every feature essential to perfect and easy operation.

The wheels are adjustable to different width of rows.

The arch is extra high and adapted to the tallest corn or cotton.

The handles can be adjusted to any desired height or distance apart.

The depth of cultivating is regulated by lengthening or shortening the chain.

Adjustable foot, by which the shovel can be given any desired degree of penetration or pitch.

The gangs are balanced with springs, which enables the operator to lift and operate the gangs with perfect ease.

Adjustable standards, which can be raised or lowered to suit depth of cultivation, specially adapting cultivator for ridge cultivating.

Adjustable shovels. By means of the shovel block the shovels can be set at any desired angle, to throw the ground to or from the cotton or corn.

The seat is adjustable forward or backward or to any height desired, and when cultivator is used as a walker the seat can be thrown forward.

With parallel square pipe beams. In the parallel movement each shovel stands square with the work or at right angle to the line of draft, and remains in the same position when the gangs are shifted to the right or left.

Spring tooth gangs can be attached to any of our Western Cultivators. See cut, page 76.

For prices on repairs, see pages 162, 163, and 164.

For special blades, see pages 135 to 139.   Directions for setting up on page 165.

PRICE LIST.
With Steel Singletrees and Neckyoke, Fenders, Two Plain Shovels, No. 25, and Two Twisted Shovels, Nos. 26 and 27.

No.	Name.	With	Style Foot.	Code Word.	Weight.	Price.
160	Western Cultivator	Four Shovel Standards.	Break Pin.	Papescent.	475 lbs.	$45 00
160	Spring Tooth Cultivator Gangs, per set			Pappous.	105 lbs.	14 00

| B. F. AVERY & SONS. | | LOUISVILLE, KY. |

AVERY'S RIDING CULTIVATORS.
(Patented.)

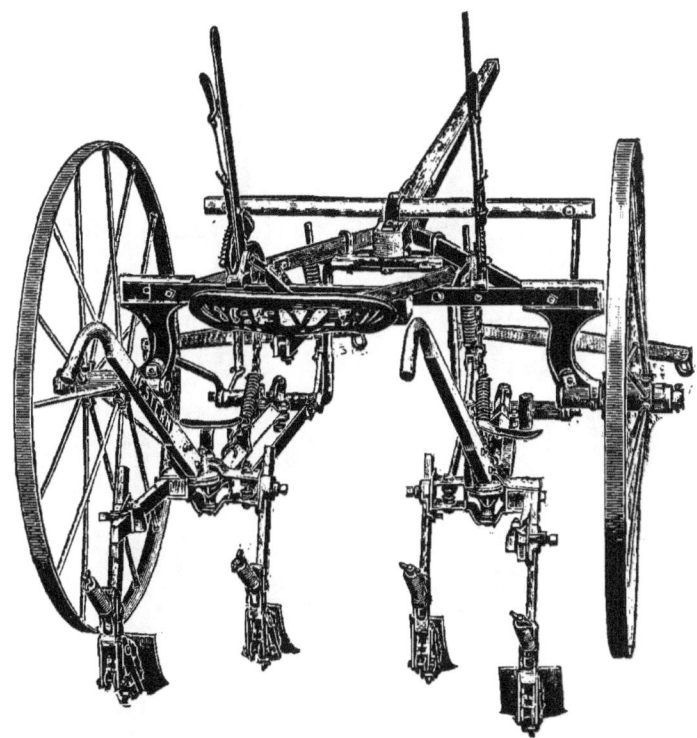

No. 161. "Western" Combined Riding and Walking Cultivator, with Parallel Beams and Spring Trip Foot.

With the exception of the foot, this cultivator is the same as the No. 112 described on previous page. Our spring trips will be found to give entire satisfaction; are strong, durable, and effective, and not liable to get out of order. Great care is taken that our spring trips leave the factory properly adjusted, and no adjustment is necessary by the user.

The Western cultivators are strictly first-class in every particular—material, construction, strength, and workmanship.

They have a greater number of adjustments, which can be more quickly and easily made, than any other cultivator offered to the trade.

Spring Tooth Gangs can be attached to any of our Western cultivators. See cut on page 76.
For prices on repairs, see pages 162, 163, and 164.
For special blades, see pages 135 to 139.
Directions for setting up on page 165.

PRICE LIST.
With Steel Singletrees and Neckyoke, Fenders, Two Plain Shovels, No. 25, and Two Twisted Shovels, Nos. 26 and 27.

No.	Name.	With	Style Foot.	Code Word.	Weight.	Price.
161	Western Cultivator	Four Shovel Standards	Spring Trip	Parachute.	483 lbs.	$49 50
160	Spring Tooth Cultivator Gangs, per set			Pappous.	105 lbs.	14 00

B. F. AVERY & SONS.   LOUISVILLE, KY.

AVERY'S WALKING CULTIVATORS.
(Patented.)

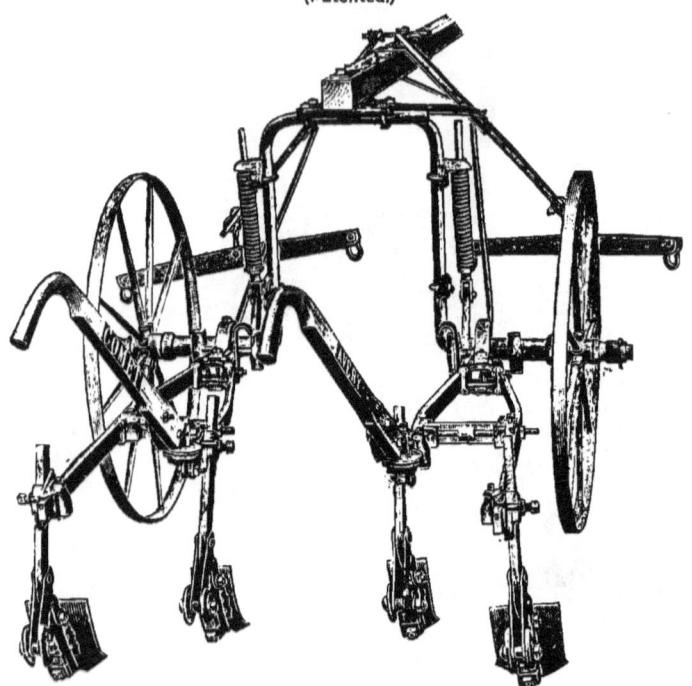

No. 107. "COMET" WALKING CULTIVATOR. WITH BREAK PIN FOOT.

This cultivator can be more quickly and easily adapted for different classes of work than any other cultivator offered to the trade, and is equaled by none as to strength and freeness from weak points.

The general finish and appearance is bright and light; the frame and gangs are painted a bright red and striped, and the wheels yellow.

The arch is high and adjustable, and can be easily widened out or narrowed in.

The steel wheels are high, have removable boxing, and move with the arch, which leaves plenty of room to work the gangs laterally.

The draft is direct from the end of the gangs, preventing racking or straining the frame.

The distance between the standards can be narrowed or widened to suit different width of shovels, and are adjustable up or down for deep or shallow cultivation.

The foot can be adjusted so as to change the penetration of the shovels, and with the shovel block the shovels can be set at any angle desired, to throw the dirt to or from the cotton or corn; any style of shovel that fastens with a common heel bolt can be attached.

The handles can be adjusted to any height or distance apart.

Special blades can be furnished for scraping up both sides of a cotton or corn row at once, and for barring off or laying by cotton or corn. For special blades see pages 135 to 139.

Spring tooth gangs can be attached to any of our Comet Cultivators. See cut on page 76.

For prices on repairs see pages 166, 167, and 168.

Directions for setting up on page 169.

PRICE LIST.
With Steel Eveners, Singletrees, and Neckyoke, Fenders, Two Plain Shovels, No. 25, and Two Twisted Shovels, Nos. 26 and 27.

No.	Name.	With	Style Foot.	Code Word.	Weight.	Price.
107	Comet Cultivator	Four Shovel Standards.	Break Pin.	Paradisea.	329 lbs.	$29 00
107	Spring Tooth Cultivator Gangs, per set	....		Paragraph	105 lbs.	14 00

B. F. AVERY & SONS.  LOUISVILLE, KY.

AVERY'S WALKING CULTIVATORS.
(Patented.)

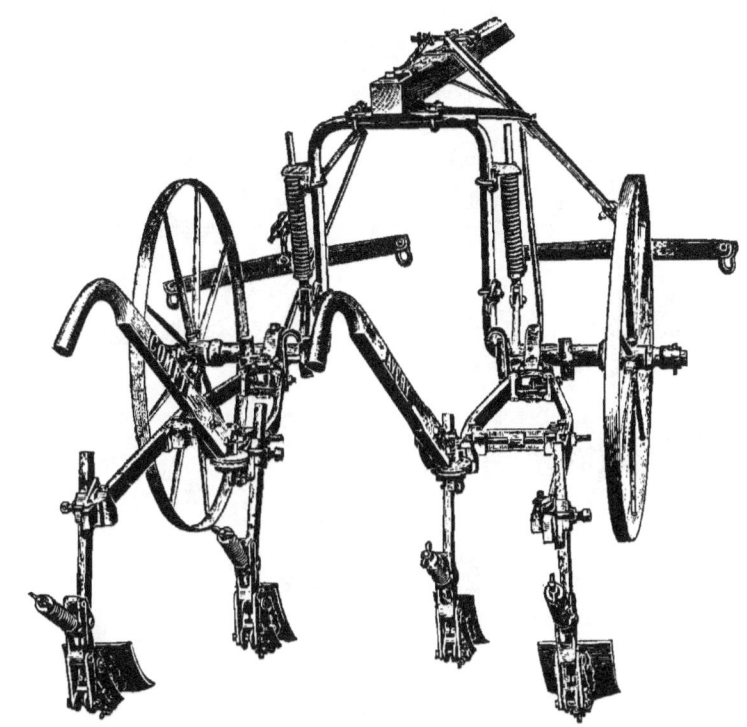

No. 108. "COMET" WALKING CULTIVATOR. WITH SPRING TRIP FOOT.

With the exception of the foot this cultivator is the same as the No. 107, described on previous page. Our spring trips will be found to give entire satisfaction; are strong, durable, and effective, and not liable to get out of order. Great care is taken that our spring trips leave the factory properly adjusted, and no adjustment is necessary by the user.

With the adjustable arch, adjustable gangs, adjustable standards, adjustable foot, adjustable handles, and the shovels adjustable on foot, we offer a cultivator that can be adapted for any crop or soil. The Comet Cultivators are noted for their strength. They are not light, flimsy-built cultivators, but are strongly constructed and free from weak points.

The draft is direct from the end of the gangs, preventing racking or straining the frame.

Spring tooth gangs can be attached to any of our Comet Cultivators. See cut on page 76.

For prices on repairs, see pages 166, 167, and 168.

For special blades, see pages 135 to 139.

Directions for setting up on page 169.

PRICE LIST.

With Steel Eveners, Singletrees, and Neckyoke, Fenders, Two Plain Shovels, No. 25, and Two Twisted Shovels, Nos. 26 and 27.

No.	Name.	With	Style Foot.	Code Word.	Weight.	Price.
108	Comet Cultivator	Four Shovel Standards	Spring Trip	Paralogy.	331 lbs.	$32 50
107	Spring Tooth Cultivator Gangs, per set		----------	Paragraph.	105 lbs.	14 00

B. F. AVERY & SONS.      LOUISVILLE, KY.

AVERY'S WALKING CULTIVATORS.
(Patented.)

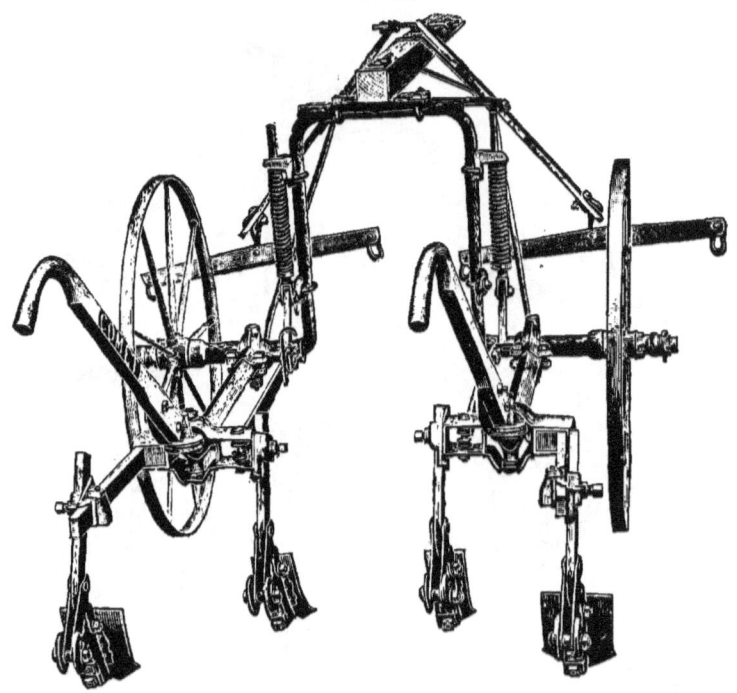

No. 112. "Comet" Walking Cultivator. With Break Pin Foot.
With Parallel Beams.

With the parallel movement embraced in this cultivator, all the shovels stand in the same relative position to the line of draft at all times, and the front and rear shovels have precisely the same amount of lateral movement. The square pipe beams are light, yet strong and durable.

SOME OF THE DESIRABLE FEATURES OF THE COMET CULTIVATOR ARE:

Adjustable High Arch,   High Steel Wheels (with removable boxes),
Adjustable Standards,   Steel Eveners (do not wear pole),
Adjustable Handles,   Steel Singletrees and Neckyoke,
Adjustable Foot,   Strong Lifting Springs,
Shovels can be set at any desired angle on the Foot.

The draft is direct from the end of the gangs, which makes it impossible to rack or strain the frame.

Spring tooth gangs can be attached to any of our Comet Cultivators. See cut on page 76.
For prices on repairs, see pages 166, 167, and 168.
For special blades, see pages 135 to 139.
Directions for setting up on page 169.

PRICE LIST.
With Steel Eveners, Singletrees, and Neckyoke, Fenders, Two Plain Shovels, No. 25, and Two Twisted Shovels, Nos. 26 and 27.

No.	Name.	With	Style Foot.	Code Word.	Weight.	Price.
112	Comet Cultivator Four Shovel Standards,		Break Pin.	Paraquet.	325 lbs.	$31 00
112	Spring Tooth Cultivator Gangs, per set	----------		Paravail.	105 lbs.	14 00

B. F. AVERY & SONS. LOUISVILLE, KY.

AVERY'S WALKING CULTIVATORS.
(Patented.)

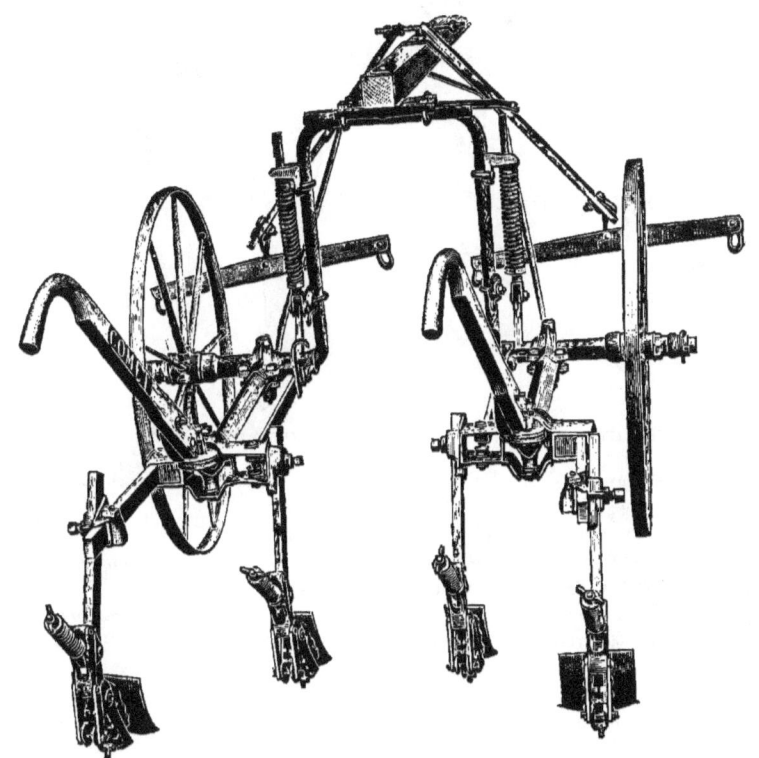

No. 113. "Comet" Walking Cultivator with Spring Trip Foot.
With Parallel Beams.

With exception of the foot, the general construction is the same as the No. 112 described on previous page.

The spring trips are strong, durable, and effective.

A spring trip cultivator to successfully stand the jarring and racking in rooty and rocky land should be strongly constructed and free from weak points. This cultivator will be found to wear longer and necessitate less expense for repairs than any other offered to the trade.

The number of different adjustments in this cultivator makes it the most desirable cultivator on the market.

Spring Tooth Gangs can be attached to any of our Comet Cultivators. See cut on page 76.
For prices on repairs, see pages 166, 167, and 168.
For special blades, see pages 135 to 139.
Directions for setting up on page 169.

PRICE LIST.

With Steel Eveners, Singletrees, and Neckyoke, Fenders, Two Plain Shovels,
No. 25, and Two Twisted Shovels. Nos. 26 and 27.

Number.	Name.	With	Style Foot.	Code Word.	Weight.	Price.
113	Comet Cultivator	Four Shovel Standards	Spring Trip	Parcener.	335 lbs.	$34 50
112	Spring Tooth Cultivator Gangs, per set	....		Paravail.	105 lbs.	14 00

AVERY'S SPRING TOOTH CULTIVATORS.

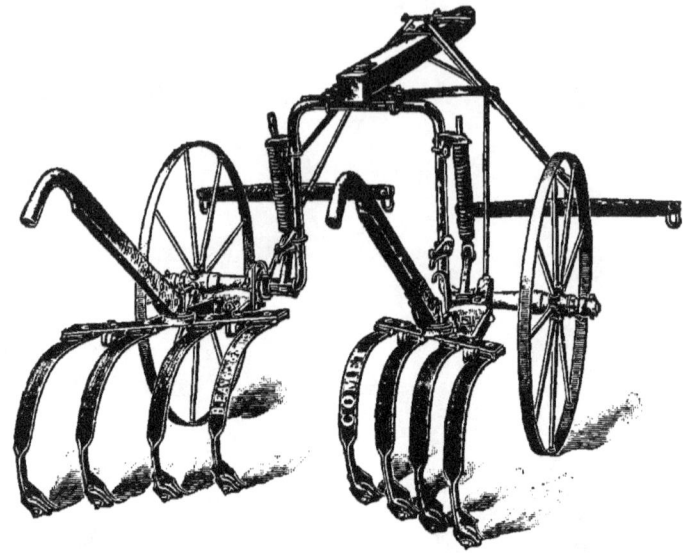

No. 10. "COMET" WALKING CULTIVATOR. WITH SPRING TOOTH GANGS.

The above shows our Comet Cultivator Frame with Spring Tooth Gangs. These Gangs can be attached to any of our Comet or Western Cultivators.

This cultivator is especially adapted for shallow cultivation.

The springs are flexible and allow the teeth to pass around or over any ordinary obstruction, thus adapting it particularly for use in rough or stony ground.

The diamond point blades are reversible, and, being small, they do not penetrate far enough to injure the crop roots, while at the same time they destroy all weeds and surface growth between the rows and permit proper absorption of moisture by the growing plants.

The Spring Tooth Gangs can be adjusted so that the blades will throw the ground to or from the plant by simply loosening the bolt on coupling head B117 and shifting the gangs to position desired.

The handles can be adjusted to any desired height or distance apart.

For prices on repairs, see pages 166, 167, and 168.

Directions for setting up on page 169.

PRICE LIST.
With Steel Eveners, Singletrees, and Neckyoke.

Number and Name.	Style.	Code Word.	Weight.	Price.
No. 10, Comet Spring Tooth Cultivator, complete	Walking	Pargasite.	190 lbs.	$24 50
No. 20, Western Spring Tooth Cultivator, complete.	Riding	Parisian.	320 lbs.	40 00
No. 160, Spring Tooth Cultivator Gangs, per set		Pappous.	105 lbs.	14 00
No. 107, Spring Tooth Cultivator Gangs, per set		Paragraph	105 lbs.	14 00
No. 112, Spring Tooth Cultivator Gangs, per set		Paravail.	105 lbs.	14 00

B. F. AVERY & SONS.   LOUISVILLE, KY.

AVERY'S WALKING CULTIVATORS.
(Patented.)

☞ This cultivator is built so strong that no ground is stiff or rooty enough to bend or break any part. Used with perfect success in new ground.

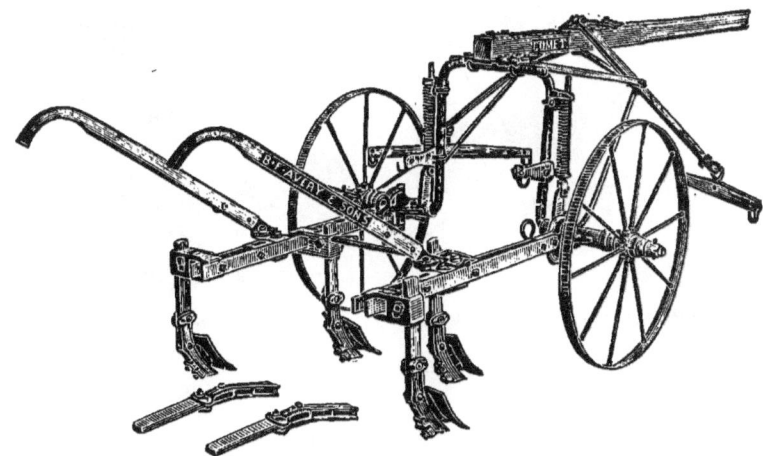

No. 104. "Comet" Walking Cultivator. Extra strong. With Rigid Beams and Bolted or Break Pin Foot.

No. 104 with four shovel standards. No. 104X with six shovel standards.

This cultivator frame and gangs make the most complete cultivator on the market, as well as the strongest, and can be used in new ground with perfect safety, as this cultivator will stall any ordinary team of horses without breakage.

The frame is constructed on the same principle as our other styles of Comet Cultivators, except that it is made extra heavy, and with wide hitch, especially adapted to the cultivation of cotton and corn.

The standards are made of such strength that the wood break pins are unnecessary, but the cultivator can be used as a break pin by removing lower bolt in malleable foot and inserting wood pin. They are adjustable in every way, up and down, and forward or backward, and to either side, so as to suit all work, and will work with any kind of blade found on a plantation.

Every operation from the first cultivation until the cotton is laid by is done with this cultivator, and can be operated by any one that can handle a double shovel plow.

With this cultivator (and the attachments we make for it described on pages 135 to 139) we have demonstrated to the satisfaction of the largest cotton and corn planters in the Mississippi Delta that it will save over two dollars every day the cultivator is at work.

No. 104X. WITH SIX SHOVEL STANDARDS.

We make this cultivator with six shovel standards. In ordering, be careful to give the correct number.

For prices on repairs, see pages 166, 167, and 168.
For special blades, see pages 135 to 139.
Directions for setting up on page 169.

PRICE LIST.

With Steel Eveners, Singletrees, and Neckyoke, Fenders, No. 104 with Two Plain Shovels, No. 25, and Two Twisted Shovels, Nos. 26 and 27, No. 104X with Three each Nos. 47 and 48 Walls Combination Shovels.

Number and Name.	With	Code Word.	Weight.	Price.
No. 104 Comet Cultivator	Four Shovel Standards.	Parlor.	390 lbs.	$40 00
No. 104X Comet Cultivator	Six Shovel Standards.	Paroquet.	408 lbs.	46 00

B. F. AVERY & SONS. LOUISVILLE, KY.

AVERY'S "STEEL FIELD ROLLER" WITH SEASONED OAK WEIGHT BOX.

AVERY'S "STEEL FIELD ROLLER" WITH HEAVY ANGLE STEEL WEIGHT BOX.

Adjustable self-oiling boxing.
Steel axle, 1¾ inches in diameter.
Steel drums, 24 inches in diameter.
Wood weight boxes are built with adjustable truss rods, that will carry any weight without allowing the frame to sag.

PRICE LIST.

No.	Name.	With	Length.	Code Word.	Weight.	Price.
1	Steel Field Roller	Wood Weight Box	6 feet	Parrotry.	685 lbs.	$45 00
2	Steel Field Roller	Wood Weight Box	7 feet	Parterre.	735 lbs.	48 50
3	Steel Field Roller	Wood Weight Box	7½ feet	Partisan.	765 lbs.	50 50
4	Steel Field Roller	Wood Weight Box	8 feet	Partridge.	797 lbs.	53 00
5	Steel Field Roller	Steel Weight Box	6 feet	Paschal.	710 lbs.	45 00
6	Steel Field Roller	Steel Weight Box	7 feet	Pastel.	758 lbs.	48 50
7	Steel Field Roller	Steel Weight Box	7½ feet	Pasture.	765 lbs.	50 50
8	Steel Field Roller	Steel Weight Box	8 feet	Patella.	797 lbs.	53 00

B. F. AVERY & SONS.   LOUISVILLE, KY.

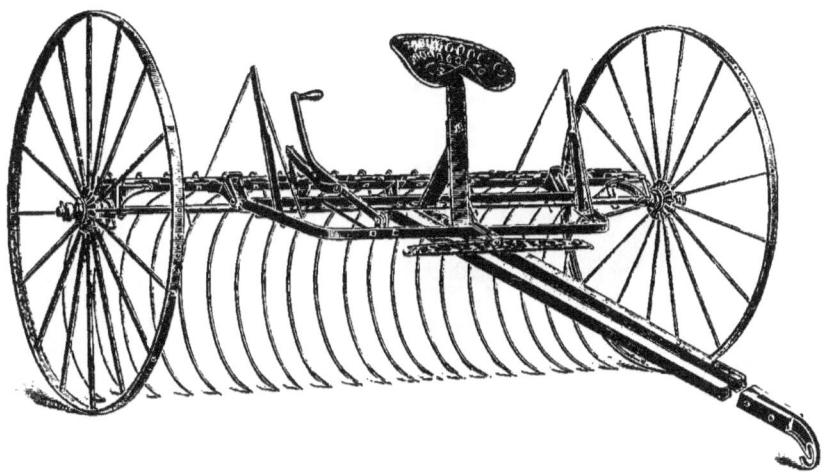

"PROGRESS" HAND-DUMP HAY RAKE—ALL STEEL.

Coiled teeth with flat points, oil tempered and thoroughly tested; angle steel head, steel axle 1¼ inches diameter; lock lever, which holds the teeth to their work automatically; raising the lever slightly releases the lock and dumps the load, the operation being aided by the weight of the driver. The 8 and 10 foot rakes have combination pole and shaft; the 12 foot rake has pole only.

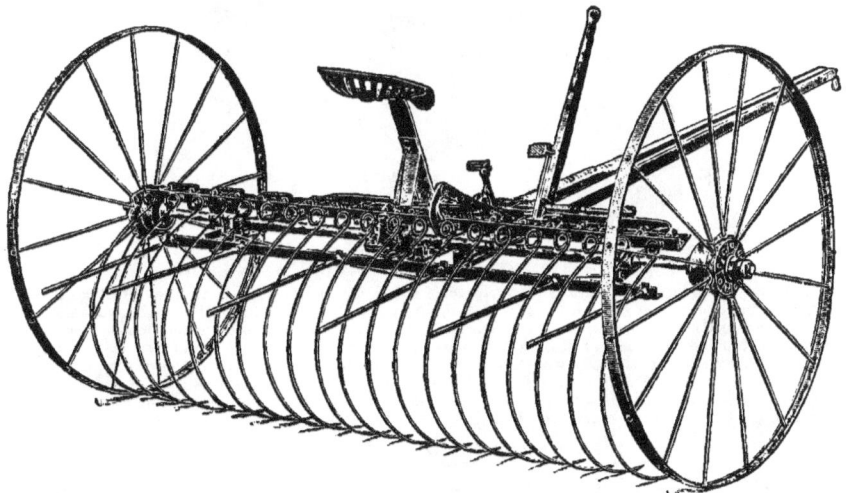

"PROGRESS" SELF-DUMP HAY RAKE—ALL STEEL.

The dumping device is simple but positive in its operation, and is operated by means of a convenient foot trip lever, a touch of the foot throwing it into action. The description given above applies also to the self-dump.

Number and Name.	Style.	Size.	No. of Teeth.	Code Word.	Weight.	Price.
No. 7, Progress Hay Rake	Hand-Dump	8 foot	20	Pathic.	337 lbs.	$29 00
No. 8, Progress Hay Rake	Hand-Dump	10 foot	26	Patina.	385 lbs.	32 00
No. 9, Progress Hay Rake	Hand-Dump	12 foot	32	Patroe.	437 lbs.	36 00
No. 10, Progress Hay Rake	Self-Dump	8 foot	20	Patroon.	397 lbs.	34 50
No. 11, Progress Hay Rake	Self-Dump	10 foot	26	Pauser.	483 lbs.	37 50
No. 12, Progress Hay Rake	Self-Dump	12 foot	32	Pavilion.	500 lbs.	42 00

B. F. AVERY & SONS. LOUISVILLE, KY.

AVERY'S SORGHUM AND SUGAR-CANE MILL.

THE IMPROVED THREE-ROLL AVERY CANE MILL.

With crucible steel shafts, reversible feed guide, brass boxes, and all the latest and best improvements, made of the very best material, and the lightest running mills on the market.

These mills have the gears cast separate from the rolls, so that when a cog-wheel wears out it can be replaced at small cost by a new one. In other mills, where the gear and rolls are cast together, the breaking of a cog-wheel, or even one tooth, involves a heavy expense to repair them. The main shaft is heavy and strong, and just long enough to enable the mill to be set near the ground without any liability to twisting or bending it. A high quality mill, hence very little breakage. Costs more to start with, but cheapest in the end.

SIZE, CAPACITY, WEIGHT, AND PRICE.

Number	0	1	2	3	4
Size	One Horse.	Regular One Horse.	Two Horse.	Regular Two Horse.	Heavy Two Horse.
Estimated capacity, per hour	40 gallons.	60 gallons.	80 gallons.	100 gallons.	120 gallons.
Height of Rolls	5½ inches.	6 3-16 inches.	7½ inches.	9¼ inches.	12 inches.
Diameter Large Rolls	10½ inches.	11⅜ inches.	13½ inches.	14 13-16 inches.	16 inches.
Diameter Small Rolls	6½ inches.	6¾ inches.	7½ inches.	8 inches.	9 11-16 inches.
Weight	400 pounds.	500 pounds.	725 pounds.	900 pounds.	1,200 pounds.
Code Word	Peacock.	Peasant.	Peccavi.	Pectoral.	Pedarian.
Price, with wrench and bolts	$30 00	$40 00	$60 00	$80 00	$100 00

B. F. AVERY & SONS. LOUISVILLE, KY.

AVERY'S IMPROVED COOK'S EVAPORATOR.

Our pans are made of the very best quality of **galvanized steel** or hard rolled copper. In our **Improved Cook's Pans** the bottoms are absolutely tight. By a recent invention we do away with all punching of holes and riveting of bolts to the bottom. These bolt-holes (and there are from twenty to forty in all other makes of pans) cause leaks and no end of trouble. By our device our pans are much stronger, can not leak or pull apart.

Our furnaces are made of strong and heavy sheet iron of best quality (we consider selected wrought iron for this purpose better than steel), and are well braced. There is no question about the superiority of the **Rocker Furnace** for the Cook's Pan.

An Evaporator means Pan, Furnace, Chimney, and Grate Complete. In ordering **Evaporators** to go with Avery Mills always order one or two numbers higher than the **Mills.**

COOK'S IMPROVED EVAPORATORS—Complete, Pan and Furnace.

No.	Size.	Capacity per day in galls. syrup.	GALVANIZED STEEL.			COPPER.			FURNACE ONLY.	
			Code Word.	Weight	Price.	Code Word.	Weight	Price.	Code Word.	Price.
2	44x 72 in.	35 to 50	Pedireme.	250 lbs.	$45 00	Pemmican.	270 lbs.	$75 00	Pension.	$25 00
3	44x 90 in.	50 to 70	Peeress.	275 lbs.	55 00	Pendant.	285 lbs.	90 00	Pentecost.	30 00
4	44x108 in.	65 to 100	Pekoe.	300 lbs.	65 00	Penguin.	315 lbs.	105 00	Pepastic.	35 00
5	44x126 in.	75 to 125	Pellocid.	350 lbs.	75 00	Pennate.	365 lbs.	125 00	Perceiver.	40 00

COOK'S IMPROVED PANS.—Without Furnaces.

Same pan used for either portable or stationary furnaces.

No.	Size.	Capacity per day in gallons syrup.	GALVANIZED STEEL.			COPPER.		
			Code Word.	Weight.	Price.	Code Word.	Weight.	Price.
2	44x 72 in.	35 to 50	Percolate.	80 lbs.	$20 00	Periwig.	100 lbs.	$50 00
3	44x 90 in.	50 to 70	Perennial.	100 lbs.	25 00	Permitter.	110 lbs.	60 00
4	44x108 in.	65 to 100	Perfidy.	120 lbs.	30 00	Perroquet.	135 lbs.	70 00
5	44x126 in.	75 to 125	Perianth.	135 lbs.	40 00	Personal.	150 lbs.	85 00
6	44x144 in.	125 to 175	Perilous.	150 lbs.	50 00	Perspire.	175 lbs.	100 00
7	44x180 in.	150 to 200	Periplus.	175 lbs.	60 00	Perturber.	200 lbs.	125 00

FURNACE FRONTS AND DOOR, GRATES, ETC., FOR BRICK ARCHES.

No.	Name.	Extreme Size.	Size of Door.	Code Word.	Price.
1	Light Furnace Front and Door	31 x13½ in.	12½x 9 in.	Perverter.	$4 00
2	Grate for same	30 x18 in.		Pestle.	3 00
3	Heavy Furnace Front and Door	28½x14½ in.	18 x10 in.	Petiole.	6 00
4	Grates, per set (6), with Bearing Bar	32 x18 in.		Petrific.	8 00
5	Cast Plate for Chimney	31½x 7 in.		Pettycoy.	1 25

For the convenience of our customers we have gotten up the above castings for brick or stone arches. They will be found very essential and convenient in erecting stationary furnaces.

B. F. AVERY & SONS.   LOUISVILLE, KY.

Avery's "Luckey" Pea and Bean Thresher.

This is a moderate-priced hand-power machine that separates peas and beans from the pods, and cleans them perfectly without breaking same. Is substantially made, has an attractive appearance, and is simple in construction and operation. Threshes from five to seven bushels per hour. Is easy running, strong, and durable, and has gone through its campaign for the public favor with an untarnished record. Does away with the old tiresome way of hulling peas and beans by hand, and will in a short time save its cost many times over.

PRICE LIST.

Name.	Code Word.	Weight.	Price.
Luckey Pea and Bean Thresher	Phalanx.	200 lbs.	$40 00

"Dixie" Pea Huller and Bean Separator.

It pays for itself in a short while.

Cleans eight to ten bushels per hour, and does not break or injure the peas—runs light.

It is cheap, and the peas which are now flayed out by hand at a great expense can, with the Dixie, be separated at very small cost.

PRICE LIST.

Name.	Code Word.	Weight.	Price.
Dixie Pea Huller and Bean Separator	Pharmacy.	300 lbs.	$40 00

B. F. AVERY & SONS.   LOUISVILLE, KY.

"DEWEY" LAWN MOWER.
Five Sizes—10, 12, 14, 16, and 18 inch.

8½-inch wheels. 5½-inch cutting reel. Three cutting blades. Continuous shear. Solid steel tree guard. Brass bearings. Well made and accurately adjusted.

"PRINCESS" HIGH WHEEL LAWN MOWER.
Four Sizes—14, 16, 18, and 20 inch.

The best high wheel lawn mower on the market.
10½-inch wheels made with an extra rim, raising the gearing away from the ground, thus preventing dirt from collecting therein.
6-inch cutting reel mounted on ⅝-inch steel shaft, which runs in self-aligning high grade brass bearings. Four cutting blades.
Wheel axles are solid steel. Continuous shear. Accurate adjustments.

PRICE LIST.

Size and Name.	Code Word.	Weight.	Price.
10-inch Dewey Lawn Mower	Pheon.	32 lbs.	$3 90
12-inch Dewey Lawn Mower	Philomot.	35 lbs.	4 00
14-inch Dewey Lawn Mower	Philter.	37 lbs.	4 10
16-inch Dewey Lawn Mower	Phoca.	38 lbs.	4 20
18-inch Dewey Lawn Mower	Phosphor.	41 lbs.	4 40
14-inch Princess Lawn Mower	Phrenic.	52 lbs.	6 50
16-inch Princess Lawn Mower	Phylarch.	55 lbs.	7 00
18-inch Princess Lawn Mower	Phytozoa.	59 lbs.	7 75
20-inch Princess Lawn Mower	Picage.	61 lbs.	8 25

AVERY'S "TRUCKER'S" CULTIVATORS.

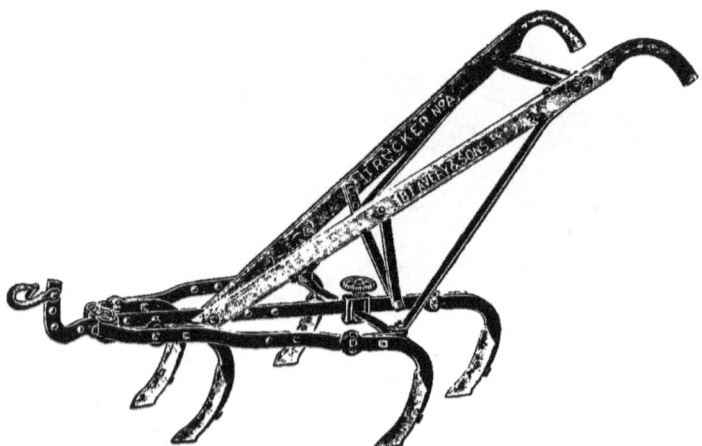

No. A—FIVE TOOTH—WITH WHEEL SET-SCREW.

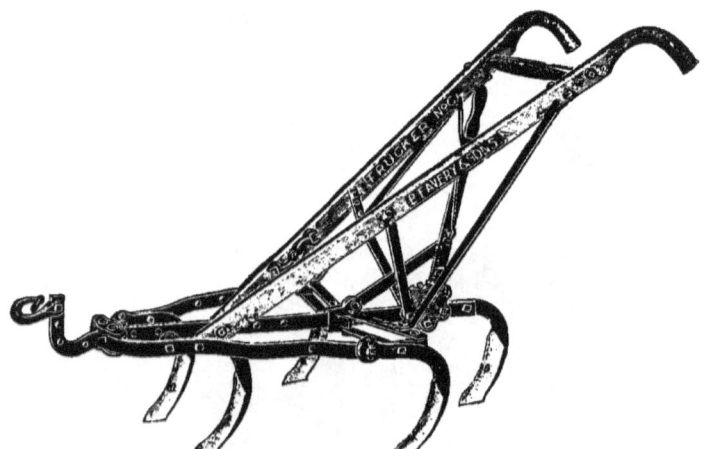

No. C—FIVE TOOTH—WITH EXPANDING LEVER.

Frame painted green, striped red, and handles varnished.
Standards are adjustable, so as to give the blades different degrees of pitch or slant.
Have two sets of handle braces, which hold the handles rigid and stiffen the entire cultivator.
All five-tooth cultivators have extra holes in frame, to admit attaching additional standards, converting it into a seven-tooth cultivator.
Frames are made extra long to avoid clogging in narrow rows, and the standards are of extra height. This makes the cultivators of very light draft.

Permit of very numerous adjustments, hence are particularly well adapted to use where variation in the width or distance between the rows being cultivated exists. Especially valuable for work in gardens, orchards, truck patches, as well as in general field work.

Each cultivator is furnished with the blades mentioned in price list unless otherwise specified.
Gauge wheel and billing blades, as described on following page, can be attached to either style.

B. F. AVERY & SONS.   LOUISVILLE, KY.

AVERY'S "TRUCKER'S" CULTIVATORS.

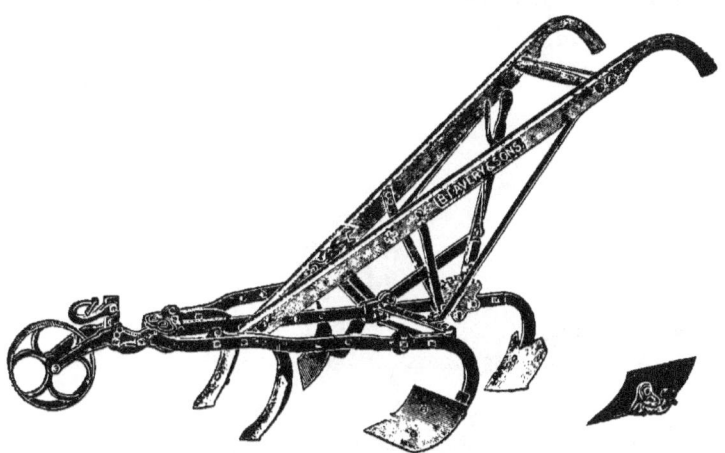

Showing with Expanding Lever, Gauge Wheel, and Rear and Side Hilling Blades.

The Gauge Wheel is a great convenience for transporting the cultivator to and from the field, steadies the running, regulates depth of blades, and assists greatly to turn easily at the end of each row. The wheel arm has four holes by which the depth of cut can be varied by shifting the position of wheel arm.

Hillers or horse hoe blades are valuable to make the cultivator serviceable for a wider range of work.

The side hilling blades attachment can be adjusted to give blades any angle desired, including in-throw or out-throw.

For regular and special blades, see page 140.

For prices on repairs, see page 141.

PRICE LIST—WITH WHEEL SET-SCREW.

Number and Name.	Blades.	Code Word.	Weight.	Price.
No. A, Trucker's Cultivator	With 5 No. 3A, 3x6 in.	Picnic.	52 lbs.	$4 50
No. B, Trucker's Cultivator	With 7 No. 2A, 2x8 in.	Picul.	58 lbs.	5 50

PRICE LIST—WITH EXPANDING LEVER.

Number and Name.	Blades.	Code Word.	Weight.	Price.
No. C, Trucker's Cultivator	With 5 No. 3A, 3x8 in.	Pierage.	60 lbs.	$6 00
No. D, Trucker's Cultivator	With 7 No. 2A, 2x8 in.	Piggin.	65 lbs.	7 00

PRICE LIST OF ATTACHMENTS.

Can be attached to any of the above styles or sizes.

Name.	Code Word.	Weight.	Price.
Gauge Wheel, with Arm and Bolt	Pilcher.	7 lbs.	$0 70
Rear and Side Hilling Blades, consisting of one each Nos. 10A, 11A, and 12A Blades	Pilgrim.	10 lbs.	1 20

B. F. AVERY & SONS. LOUISVILLE, KY.

Avery's Steel Frame "Orchard" Harrows.

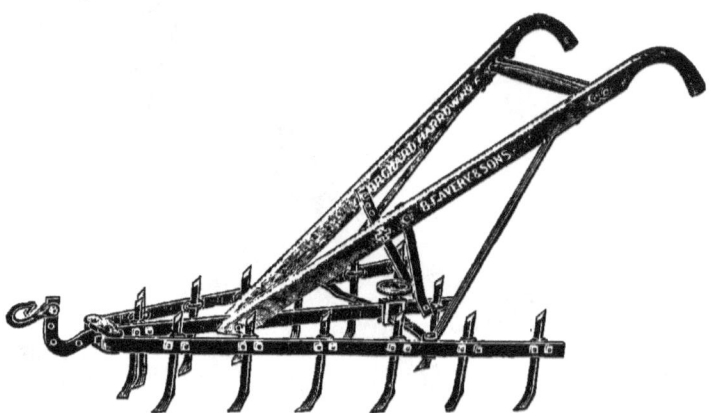

No. F. FOURTEEN TEETH. WITH WHEEL SET-SCREW.

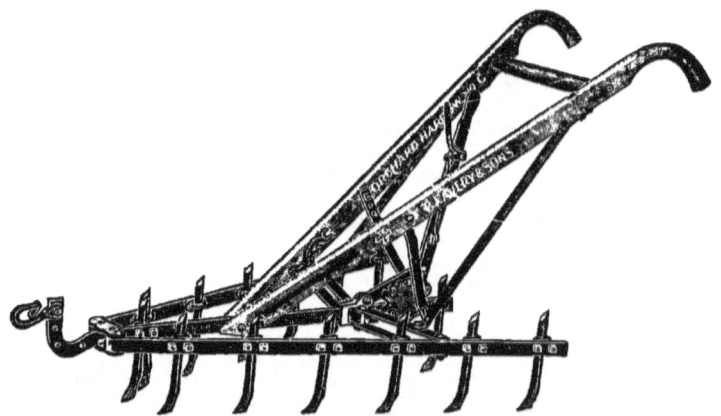

No. G. FOURTEEN TEETH. WITH EXPANDING LEVER.

Frame painted green, handles varnished.
Have two sets of handle braces, which hold the handles rigid and stiffen the entire harrow.
The clamp attachment for each tooth permits setting teeth at any angle or vertical position desired.
Have reversible steel diamond-shaped teeth $\frac{5}{8} \times \frac{7}{8} \times 9\frac{1}{2}$ inches, drawn to a cutting edge on one end and beveled on the other.

The above tools are especially adapted for truckers, gardeners, and general field harrowing and cultivating. The great variety of range and adjustments makes them quite a universal and handy tool on every farm, large or small.

Gauge wheel can be furnished when desired, which will cost extra.

For prices on repairs, see page 141.

PRICE LIST.

Number and Name.	Code Word.	Weight.	Price.	Gauge Wheel Complete.	Teeth, per doz.
No. F, Orchard Harrow	Pillau.	56 lbs.	$6 00	$0 70	$2 00
No. G, Orchard Harrow	Pilser.	64 lbs.	7 00	70	2 00

Avery's "Wallis" Steel Frame Side Harrow.

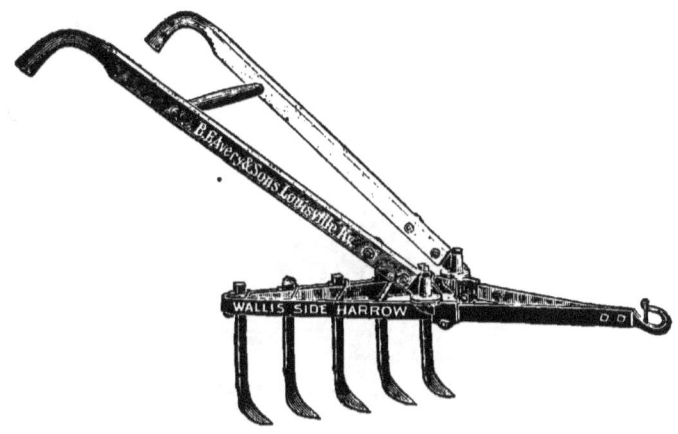

Frame painted red, handles varnished.

Has every adjustment possible of any side harrow.

Built very strong and entirely of steel, except the handles.

Handles can be raised or lowered, or moved to the right or left.

Teeth can be adjusted up or down, or moved closer together or further apart.

Furnished with duck teeth ⅞ inch square; they are securely clamped between the two rear ends of frame and held firmly in place by grooved plates and bands with no danger of working loose.

The Wallis Side Harrow is always shipped righthand. Any one wishing to change to lefthand can easily do so simply by loosening the handle clips from frame, turn frame upside down, reverse hook clevis and teeth, and reclamp handle clips to opposite side of frame from the position they originally occupied.

A most useful implement for loosening up around drill or row crops, and for tearing down and cleaning ridges.

PRICE LIST.

Name.	With	Code Word.	Weight.	Price.
Wallis Steel Frame Side Harrow ..	Duck-foot Teeth	Pindaric.	51 lbs.	$6 00

B. F. AVERY & SONS. LOUISVILLE, KY.

AVERY'S "DELTA" CULTIVATOR.

Beam and handles varnished.
Diamond point shovels, reversible, 2¼ x 9 inches.
Sent with four different braces, with which it can be converted into six different implements, viz: "A" shaped cultivator, "V" shaped cultivator, square cultivator, right hand side harrow, left hand side harrow, and a four-tooth harrow, for straddling a row.

One of the most popular and complete light cultivators made on account of its many adjustments, adapting it to almost any kind of cultivation.

AVERY'S SIDE HARROW.

WITH DUCK-FOOT TEETH.

Frame and handles varnished.
Strongly constructed with wrought iron brace from beam to cross-bar.
Duck teeth are ⅞ inch square, threaded and fastened to frame by nuts, and headed.

A very useful implement for cleaning ridges and stirring middles.

PRICE LIST.

Name.	Code Word.	Weight.	Price.
Delta Cultivator	Pinnace.	48 lbs.	$8 50
Side Harrow with Duck-foot Teeth	Piony.	40 lbs.	5 00

B. F. AVERY & SONS. LOUISVILLE, KY.

No. 8X. GARDEN DRILL.

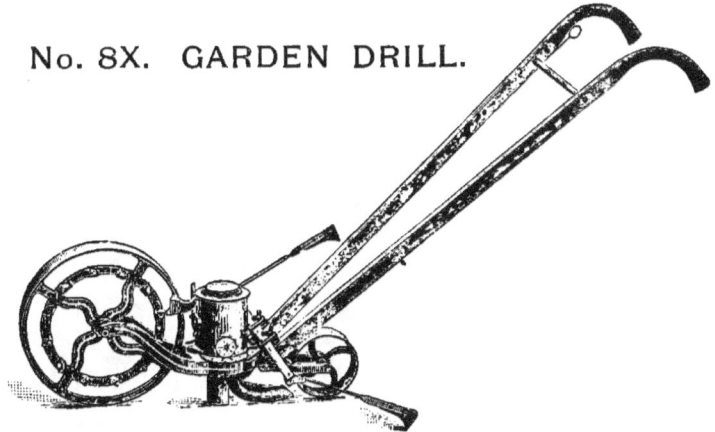

This Drill is designed to be used in field or garden. It works on the agitator principle, which is certain in its action.

Opens the furrow, drops the seed accurately at the desired depth, covers it and lightly rolls the earth down over it, and at the same time marks the next row, all of which is done with mechanical precision by simply propelling the drill forward. In this way it sows, with an evenness and rapidity impossible for the most skillful hand to do, all the different varieties of **Beet, Carrot, Onion, Turnip, Parsnip, Sage, Spinach, Sorghum, Peas, Beans, Broom Corn, Fodder Corn**, etc.

Has an instantaneously acting seed cut-off by which the flow of seed can be stopped while turning at the ends of rows. **Accurately gauges the uniform deposit of the seed to any required depth**, thus avoiding the risk of planting at irregular depths. The improved markers are made adjustable for the purpose of marking the rows at any desired distance apart, and distinctly, whether the ground is even or uneven.

For prices, see page 92.

No. 9X. "HILL AND DRILL" SEEDER.

This Seeder is the same as the Garden Drill already described, with the modification here illustrated, and described below:

PINS IN THE WHEEL serve as a means for securing the various dropping distances of 4, 6, 8, 12, 16, 24, and 48 inches apart, as well as for sowing continuously in drills.

HILL DROPPING. The distance apart is varied by the number of pins in the driving wheel, against which the agitator strikes. The seed can not drop except as the hole in the bottom of seed box is opened by the **agitator** raising the "**cut-off**," as it strikes a pin in the wheel, and the **spring** immediately closes it again when the agitator clears the pin. This **saves seed**, as no more can drop at a time than passes in the short space of raising and dropping the agitator.

DRILLING. The change to the ordinary drill is made by one thumbscrew in detaching the "cut-off" from the agitator and fastening it back on the frame.

ADVANTAGES. Corn and beans are generally planted in hills, but the same idea may be carried out with root crops, such as Beets, Carrots, Turnips, Parsnips, etc., by making use of the shorter drops, thus also saving considerable labor in thinning.

For prices, see page 92.

No. 10X. COMBINATION DRILL.

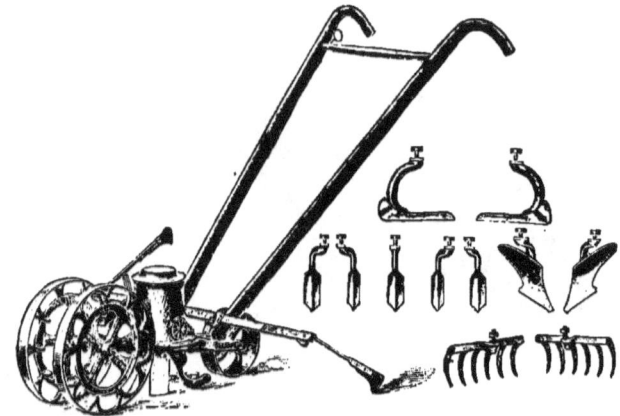

Double Wheel Seeder, with Hoe, Cultivator, Plow, and Rake Attachments.

Combination Drill with **One** Wheel for Seeding.

Combination Drill with Two Wheels and Rake Attachments for Cultivating.

This drill has the advantage of being either a double wheel or single wheel implement at will, the change from the one to the other being readily made. Can be used either astride or between the rows.

It is a conceded fact that by far the nicer work can be done by a one-wheel seed drill.

The two wheels are desirable, however, when used as a cultivator or wheel hoe, as in this way the rows of **young** plants may be straddled, and the cultivating done on both sides of the row at one passing. There are three adjustments for regulating depth when used as a cultivator, and five when used as a seeder. It is a perfect combination.

The attachments are: 1 pair hoes, 5 cultivator teeth, 1 pair rakes, and 1 pair plows.

For prices, see page 92.

No. 5X. DOUBLE WHEEL HOE.
WITH HOE BLADES ONLY.

The ease with which a great amount of work may be accomplished by the use of **wheel hoes** leads many to buy several of these tools. In such cases it is not always necessary to have them all fitted out with complete sets of attachments.

The **hoe blades** are the attachments most generally used.

For prices, see page 92.

B. F. AVERY & SONS. LOUISVILLE, KY.

No. 4X. Double Wheel Hoe, Cultivator, Plow, and Rake.

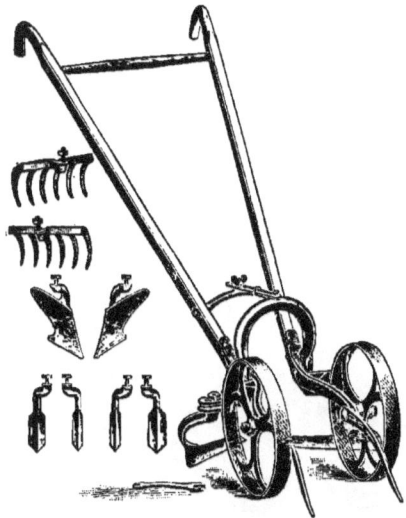

Specially designed for working both sides of the row at one passing.

The special recommendation is the **adjustable arch**, by which not only the **depth of** work can be gauged, but which, by an ingenious device, enables the teeth to be pitched at any angle desired.

It can be pushed straight ahead, but better results are obtained by using it same as a scuffle hoe with successive strokes of length to suit the nature of soil and crop.

It can be used either astride of or between rows.

It is so symmetrically constructed that in passing astride rows of large plants the foliage once raised by the vine guards meets no obstruction between the wheel arms and the arch, and is, therefore, dropped by the implement without unnecessary damage and without delaying the operator.

There are nine adjustments of depth.

The attachments are: 1 pair hoes, 1 pair plows, 1 pair rakes, 4 cultivator teeth, and 1 pair vine or leaf guards.

For prices, see page 92.

No. 1X. Single Wheel Hoe, Cultivator, Plow, and Rake.

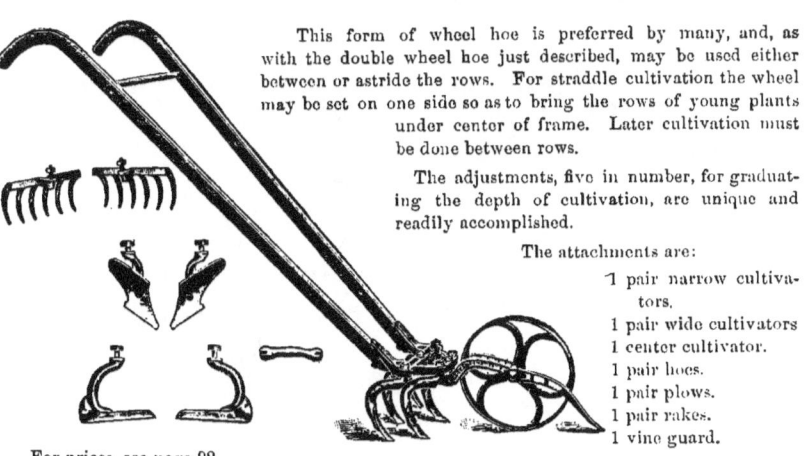

This form of wheel hoe is preferred by many, and, as with the double wheel hoe just described, may be used either between or astride the rows. For straddle cultivation the wheel may be set on one side so as to bring the rows of young plants under center of frame. Later cultivation must be done between rows.

The adjustments, five in number, for graduating the depth of cultivation, are unique and readily accomplished.

The attachments are:

1 pair narrow cultivators.
1 pair wide cultivators
1 center cultivator.
1 pair hoes.
1 pair plows.
1 pair rakes.
1 vine guard.

For prices, see page 92.

B. F. AVERY & SONS. LOUISVILLE, KY.

No. 2X.—Single Wheel Hoe, Cultivator, and Plow.

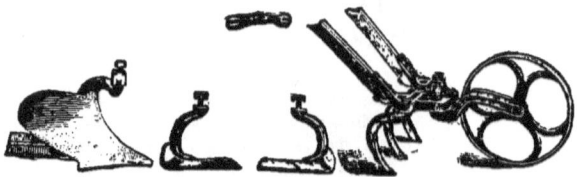

This implement is same as our regular Single Wheel Hoe, except in the variety of attachments, which are:

1 pair hoes.
1 large plow.
1 pair cultivators.
1 center cultivator.

No. 7X.—Garden Seed Drill.

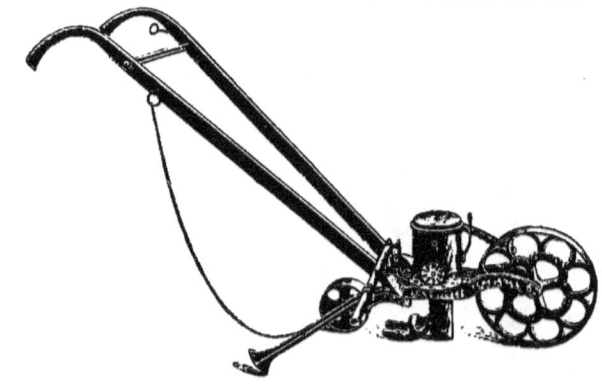

Has been perfected to meet the demand for a low-priced seeder. We have not only accomplished this, but here offer a drill with all the essential qualities even to embodying **Seed Drill, Indicator,** and **Regulator** from exactly same patterns as those used in our larger and more expensive drills. We do not recommend this drill for use **instead** of the larger size, but we are sure that all in want of such a drill as we represent this to be, will find it to their advantage to buy the No. 7X.

No. 6X.–Hand Wheel Plow.

This little labor-saving implement is one that commends itself to all gardeners. It can be used to prepare the ground, to furrow out, to cover, and to cultivate. The moldboard is of steel, polished and tempered.

PRICE LIST.
(Boxed.)

Number and Name.	Code Word.	Weight.	Price.
No. 1X, Single Wheel Hoe, Cultivator, Plow, and Rake	Piquet.	24 lbs.	$6 50
No. 2X, Single Wheel Hoe, Cultivator and Plow	Pisophalt.	26 lbs.	5 50
No. 3X, Single Wheel Hoe (not illustrated)	Pitahaya.	18 lbs.	3 50
No. 4X, Double Wheel Hoe, Cultivator, Plow, and Rake	Pitchy.	38 lbs.	7 50
No. 5X, Double Wheel Hoe	Pittacal.	30 lbs.	4 50
No. 6X, Hand Wheel Plow	Placard.	19 lbs.	2 50
No. 7X, Garden Seed Drill	Plagal.	38 lbs.	7 00
No. 8X, Garden Drill	Plaintiff.	50 lbs.	9 00
No. 9X, Hill and Drill Seeder	Planet.	55 lbs.	10 00
No. 10X, Combination Drill	Planorbis.	67 lbs.	12 50

B. F. AVERY & SONS. LOUISVILLE, KY.

AVERY'S NEW GARDEN PLOW.

Painted red.
The attachments are:
Steel turning shovel.
Malleable iron rake.
Malleable iron wrench.
Steel sweep or weeding blade.
Steel reversible furrow opener.
Has steel wheel 24 inches in diameter.
Handles are adjustable to suit the height of a small child or a man.

It is the perfection of labor-saving implements for working all kinds of garden beds.
For pleasure or profit in gardening, this tool is unrivaled. The high wheel causes easy work, and every user is delighted.

PRICE LIST.

Name.	Code Word.	Weight.	Price.
Avery's New Garden Plow	Plasma.	18 lbs.	$3 00

Turning Plow	$0 25	Wheel	$1 25
Bull and Calf Tongue	25	Wrench	15
Sweep	25	Standard	60
Rake	25	Finished Handles, per pair	80

AVERY'S WOOD BEAM SINGLE SHOVEL.

Beam, standard, and handles varnished, black tipped.
Extra thick shovel attached to standard by one large bolt.
Regularly supplied with a 7x14 shovel, but if specially ordered we will furnish with an 8x14 shovel without extra charge.
Jumping or straight knife coulter can be furnished (cost extra); if either is desired, mention in ordering which is wanted.

PRICE LIST.

Number and Name.	Code Word.	Weight.	Price.	No. 59, Straight Knife Coulter.	No. 60, Jumping Coulter.	Stock without Blade.
No. 1, Single Shovel	Platinum.	31 lbs.	$3 50	$1 00	$1 25	$3 00

REPAIR PRICE LIST.

No. 1.	Price.	No. 1.	Price.
Blade No. 130, 7 x 14 x 5-16, with one Bolt.	$0 60	Finished Handles, per pair	$0 75
Finished Beam, 3⅜ x 2½ x 52½ inches	1 00	Standard Brace	25
Finished Standard, 3¼ x 3 inches	75	Clevis	15

B. F. AVERY & SONS.   LOUISVILLE, KY.

AVERY'S "WING" SHOVEL PLOW.

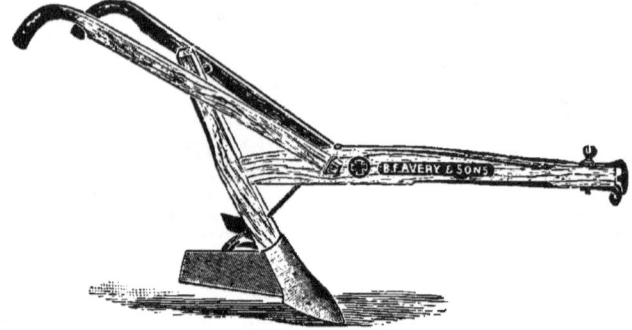

Full width of spread 30 inches.
A splendid tool for hilling potatoes.
Beam, standard, and handles varnished.
Adjustable wings, which can be used together or separately, and can be set at different angles by means of spreader rods. The wings are hinged to blade, and can be removed entirely when not wanted.

AVERY'S DOUBLE SHOVELS.

No. 2. "UNIVERSAL." WOOD BEAM, WITH WOOD STANDARDS.

Well made in every respect, and strongly braced.
Beam, standards, and handles painted blue, black tipped.
Blades No. 122, 6 x 11 x ¼ inches, attached by two bolts.

PRICE LIST.

Number and Name.	Code Word.	Weight.	Price.	Stock without Blade.
Wing Shovel	Plausive.	36 lbs.	$4 25	$2 25
No. 2, Universal, Double Shovel	Pleach.	32 lbs.	4 00	

REPAIR PRICE LIST.

No. 2, Universal, Double Shovel.	Price.	Wing Shovel.	Price.
Blades No. 122, 6 x 11 x ¼, with two Bolts, each.	$0 35	Blade No. 132, with Wings and Spreader Rods.	$1 75
Finished Wood Beam, 2⅞ x 2⅝ x 4 ft. 4 in. long.	75	Finished Beam	1 00
Finished Wood Long Standard, 3 x 2¼	60	Finished Standard	75
Finished Wood Short Standard, 3 x 2¼	40	Finished Handles, per pair	75
Finished Handles, per pair	75	Standard Brace	25
Standard Braces, each	20	Clevis	15
Clevis	15		

B. F. AVERY & SONS.      LOUISVILLE, KY.

AVERY'S DOUBLE SHOVELS.

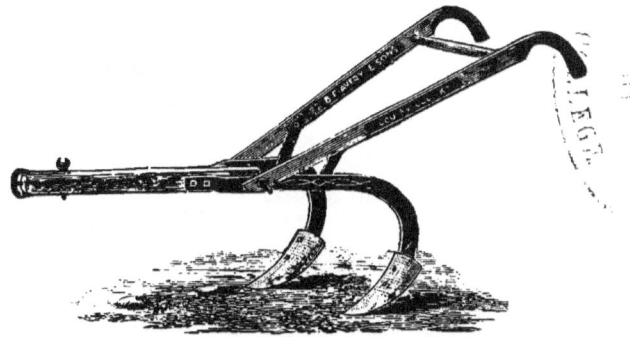

No. 3. WOOD BEAM, STEEL STANDARDS.

Heavy steel standards 1⅝ x 1 1/16 inches.
Blades No. 120, 5 x 11 x ⅛ inches, fastened with two bolts.
Beam and handles painted red, black tipped, and standards painted black.
The standards are bolted to the beam with two bolts passing through iron wedges, which permit of adjustment for widening or narrowing the plow.

No. 3X. WITH REGULATING RUNNER.

The regulating runner attached only to our No. 3 Wood Beam, Iron Standard, Double Shovel Plow regulates the depth of the shovels, causes it to run steadily, and prevents the unpleasant jumping and twisting motions found more or less in double shovel plows.

PRICE LIST.

Number and Name.	Code Word.	Weight.	Price.	HeelSlides, per pair.
No. 3, Double Shovel	Plebeian.	40 lbs.	$3 50	$0 60
No. 3X, Double Shovel, with Regulating Runner	Plenist.	50 lbs.	5 00	60
Regulating Runner only	Plethora.		1 50	

REPAIR PRICE LIST.

No. 3, Double Shovel.	Price.	No. 3, Double Shovel.	Price.
Blades No. 120, 5 x 11 x ¼, with two Bolts, each.	$0 35	Handle Braces, each	$0 20
Finished Long Standard, 1⅝ x 11-16	1 00	Spreader Rod	20
Finished Short Standard, 1⅝ x 11-16	75	Wedges, each	10
Finished Wood Beam	50	Clevis	15
Finished Handles, per pair	75		

B. F. AVERY & SONS. LOUISVILLE, KY.

AVERY'S DOUBLE SHOVELS.

No. 5—LOUISVILLE.

Steel beams painted black, handles varnished. The old reliable, famous for correct set, ample strength, and uniform quality. The No. 10 has extra heavy strong beams and blades, and is especially adapted for rocky ground.
No. 5, Louisville—Steel beams 1½ x ¾ inches; blades No. 120, 5 x 11 x ¼ inches, attached with two Bolts.
No. 10, Hoosier—Steel beams 1¾ x ¾ inches; blades 6 x 11 x 5-16 inches, attached with two bolts.

No. 6—"SUPERIOR."

Beams painted red, handles varnished, red tipped.
Has malleable spreader wedges and malleable handle braces.
Steel beams 1⅝ x 11-16 inches, blades No. 120, 5 x 11 x ¼ inches, attached with one Bolt.
Standard feet have two holes in each, and a teat at end; one-hole blades fitted on are slotted in back and can be lowered to bottom hole as they wear down.
In every way a superior cultivator and of beautiful finish.

PRICE LIST.

Number and Name.	Code Word.	Weight.	Price.	Heel Slides, per pair.	Fenders, each.
No. 5, Louisville Double Shovel	Plinth.	39 lbs.	$3 25	$0 60	$0 60
No. 10, Hoosier Double Shovel	Plucker.	46 lbs.	4 25	60	60
No. 6, Superior Double Shovel	Plumelet.	41 lbs.	3 75	60	60

REPAIR PRICE LIST.

No. 5.	Price.	No. 10.	Price.	No. 6.	Price.
Blades, with two Bolts, each.	$0 35	Blades, with two Bolts, each.	$0 40	Blades, with one Bolt, each.	$0 35
Finished Long Beam	1 00	Finished Long Beam	1 25	Finished Long Beam	1 00
Finished Short Beam	75	Finished Short Beam	1 00	Finished Short Beam	75
Finished Handles, per pair.	60	Finished Handles, per pair.	75	Finished Handles, per pair.	75
Handle Braces, each	20	Handle Braces, each	20	Handle Braces, each	20
Spreader Rod	20	Spreader Rod	20	Spreader Wedge	20

B. F. AVERY & SONS.   LOUISVILLE, KY.

AVERY'S DOUBLE SHOVELS.

No. 4—"BLACKLAND." WOOD BEAM. STEEL STANDARDS.

Beam and handles varnished, standards painted black.
Malleable iron handle braces, by which the handles can be raised or lowered.
Hardened soft center steel blades, No. 121, 5½ x 11 x ¼ inches, attached with two bolts.
Heavy steel standards 1⅝ x ¾ inches, adjustable so as to narrow or widen the distance between blades.
Break pin foot (which can be bolted to standard or fastened by a wood pin) is adjustable so as to give different degrees of pitch or slant to blades.
    This double shovel plow has met fully the demands of the black, waxy lands of Texas and other Southern States.

No. 7—"BREAK PIN."

Extra heavy steel beams 1¾ x ¾ inches.
Beams painted black, handles varnished.
A five-hole clevis is used instead of style shown in cut.
Blades, No. 47, one 2-3 x 10 x ¼ and one 2¼-4 x 10 x ¼ or two No. 120, 5 x 11 x ¼ inches, attached with two bolts. In ordering state which blades are wanted.
Break pin foot (which can be bolted to standard or fastened by a wood pin) has an open or loop foot so that any style of blade can be attached by means of a heel bolt; is also adjustable so as to give different degrees of pitch or slant to blades. Is unsurpassed for stumpy or rocky country.

PRICE LIST.

Number and Name.	Code Word.	Weight.	Price.	Fenders, each.
No. 4, Blackland Double Shovel	Plunger.	52 lbs.	$5 25	
No. 7, Break Pin Double Shovel	Pocoson.	42 lbs.	4 25	$0 60

B. F. AVERY & SONS.      LOUISVILLE, KY.

AVERY'S DOUBLE SHOVEL CULTIVATOR.

No. 47.   No. 47.

Heel Slide.

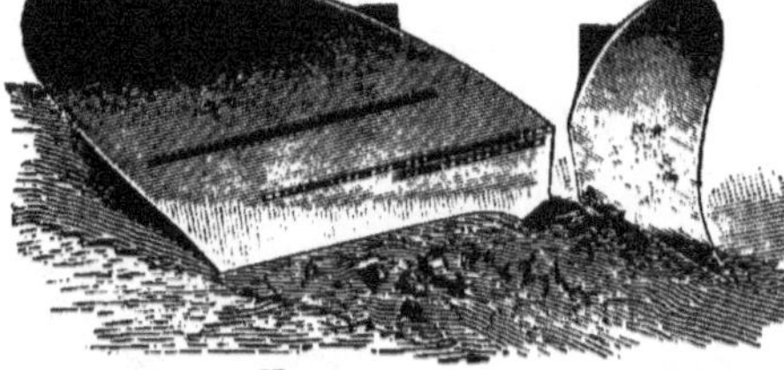

No. 31.   No. 32.

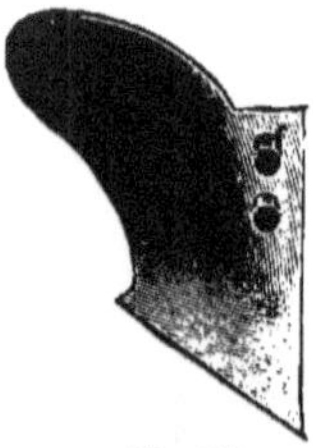

No. 33. 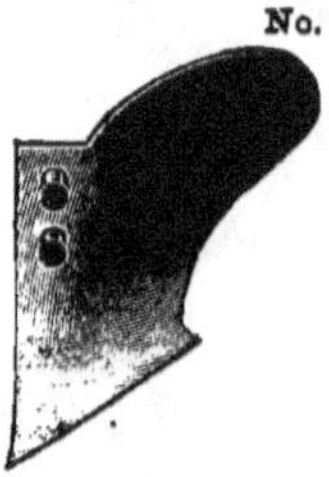   No. 34. 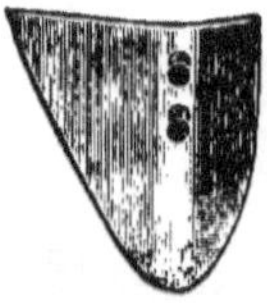   No. 44. 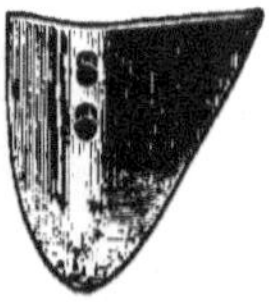   No. 45.

The prominent features of this splendid tool are strength, simplicity, and great variety of work to which it can be adapted.

Cut shows No. 33 right-hand turning shovel, and No. 44 right-hand shovel sweep on Cultivator.

Aside from blades shown in above cut, viz., Nos. 47, 33, and 44, also right or left scraper blades Nos. 31 or 32 can be used to great advantage in combination with Nos. 33 or 44. By adding left turning Shovel No. 34 you have a first class middle splitter at small cost.

Unless otherwise ordered, the No. 7 is shipped with one No. 47 blade, 2-3x10x¼, and one No. 47, 2½-4x10x¼; all other blades shown in cut are extras, and must be specially ordered if wanted. These blades are made in various sizes.

Universal open loop foot, to which any style sweep, shovel, or scooter blade can be attached with two small bolts or heel bolt, and allowing any pitch to shovels.

The heel-slide, when attached to either foot, makes the tool run steady and prevents drifting.

For a general description of the construction, see Avery's Break Pin Double Shovel No. 7, on preceding page.

For Regular and Special Blades, see pages 135 to 139.

PRICE LIST.

Number and Name.	Code Word.	Weight.	Price.
No. 7, Double Shovel Cultivator, with one blade No. 47, 2-3x10x¼, and one No. 47, 2½-4x10x¼	Poetics.	45 lbs.	$4 25

AVERY'S SINGLE PLOW STOCKS.

B.F.AVERY & SONS
UNIVERSAL SINGLE STOCK

No. 5. "UNIVERSAL."

Beam and handles varnished. With extra strong adjustable standard, bent or loop foot, made in one piece. Handle clips, heel bolt, and "T" washer are furnished with each stock.

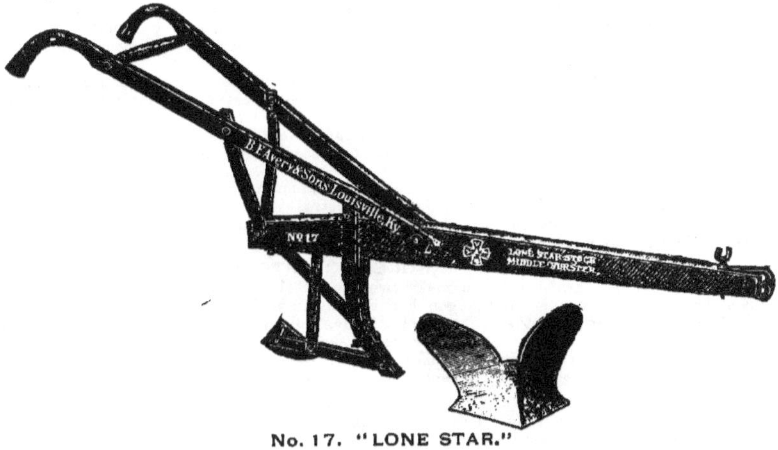
B.F.Avery&Sons Louisville Ky.
No 17

No. 17. "LONE STAR."

Beam and handles painted red. Heel bolt and "T" washer are furnished with each stock.
The landslide or center bars at the bottom follow in the wake of any blade used on the standard.
A steel rudder is attached to the rear end of the landside, which may be adjusted up or down, giving the blade such pitch or suck as desired, and making the sweep run steady.
Our double-wing or middle burster blade for bursting out "middles," old stalk rows, ditching, etc., may be attached by means of heel bolt.

PRICE LIST.

Number and Name.	Code Word.	Weight.	Stock Complete, no Blade.	Knife Coulter.
No. 5, Universal Single Stock	Pointel.	22 lbs.	$2 00	$1 00
No. 17, Lone Star Single Stock	Polacca.	36 lbs.	4 60	1 00
No. 18, Lone Star Single Stock	Polemic.	45 lbs.	5 10	1 00

REPAIR PRICE LIST.

No. 5, Universal Plow Stock.	Price.	Lone Star Plow Stock.	Price No. 17.	Price No. 18.
Standard, 1¾ x ½ inches	$0 75	Standard, No. 17, 1¾ x ⅜ inches. No. 18, 1¾ x 7-16 inches	$1 50	$1 75
Finished Beam, 1¾ x 3½ x 46 inches	50	Finished Beam, No. 17, 2⅛x4⅜x56½ inches. No. 18, 2½ x 4¾ x 58 inches	1 25	1 40
Finished Handles, per pair	50	Finished Handles, per pair	75	75
Clevis	15	Clevis, each	15	25

AVERY'S SINGLE PLOW STOCKS.

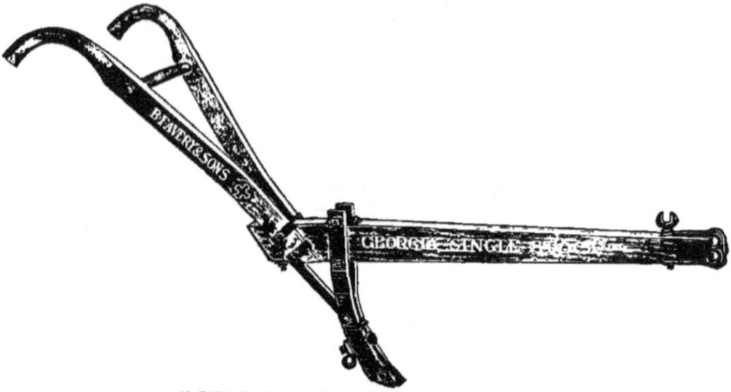

"GEORGIA" SINGLE PLOW STOCK.

Beam and handles varnished. A simple stock with ratchet, heel bolt, T washer, and patented malleable handle clips. These clips are of value to the planter, avoiding trouble with split handles, and will be sent with all of our single stocks (excepting Carolina and Lone Star Stocks) unless ordered otherwise.

The standard moves on a pivot which passes through it and the brace, and can be set at any angle by loosening the two bolts by which standard is fastened to beam, and moving standard forward or backward as desired.

Any kind or style of blade that takes a heel bolt can be used on these stocks.

All our plow stocks are made of good material, oak beams and handles, and justly command the top of the market.

Special knife coulter, which is fastened to beam with a clamp, and is a splendid attachment to use in trashy land, can be furnished if desired. Costs extra.

No. 1 (Georgia stock), beam $1\frac{3}{4}$x$3\frac{3}{8}$x46 inches, standard wrought iron $1\frac{3}{4}$x$\frac{5}{16}$ inches.

No. 2 (Georgia stock), beam $1\frac{3}{4}$x$3\frac{3}{8}$x46 inches, standard wrought iron $1\frac{3}{4}$x$\frac{1}{4}$ inches.

"TEXAS" SINGLE PLOW STOCK.

Beam and handles varnished. We make two sizes of this series, heavy and medium. The beams of both sizes are heavier and longer than the No. 1 and No. 2 stocks, and the standard of the No. 7 is heavier than any other offered to the trade, making this series considerably stronger and more durable. In every other respect they are the same as the Georgia stocks described above.

No. 6 (Texas stock), beam $1\frac{3}{4}$x$3\frac{1}{2}$x54 inches, standard wrought iron $1\frac{3}{4}$x$\frac{5}{16}$ inches.

No. 7 (Texas stock), beam $2\frac{1}{4}$x$4\frac{3}{8}$x55 inches, standard wrought iron $1\frac{3}{4}$x$\frac{3}{8}$ inches.

"CAROLINA" SINGLE PLOW STOCK.

Beam and handles painted red. Has straight handles extending out on the beam in front of standard, supported by two wrought iron braces by which handles can be adjusted up or down to suit the operator. In every other respect it is the same as the regular Georgia stock.

No. 10 (Carolina stock), beam $1\frac{3}{4}$x$3\frac{3}{8}$x46 inches, standard wrought iron $1\frac{3}{4}$x$\frac{5}{16}$ inches.

PRICE LIST.

Number and Name.	Code Word.	Weight.	Price.	Straight Knife Coulter.
No. 1, Georgia Single Stock........	Polisher.	20 lbs.	$1 60	$1 00
No. 2, Georgia Single Stock........	Polity.	19 lbs.	1 60	1 00
No. 6, Texas Single Stock..........	Polliwig.	21 lbs.	2 00	1 00
No. 7, Texas Single Stock	Poltroon.	26 lbs.	2 30	1 00
No. 10, Carolina Single Stock	Polygar.	24 lbs.	2 10	1 00

REPAIR PRICE LIST.

	No. 1.	No. 2.	No. 6.	No. 7.	No. 10.
Standard....................................	$0 60	$0 50	$0 60	$0 85	$0 60
Finished Beam................................	50	50	75	90	50
Finished Handles, per pair	40	40	50	50	60
Handle Clips, per set........................	10	10	10	10	....
Handle Braces, each..........................	....	....	....	....	20
Clevis	15	15	15	15	15
Stock, without Standard	75	75	....	....	....

B. F. AVERY & SONS.   LOUISVILLE, KY.

AVERY'S DOUBLE PLOW STOCKS.

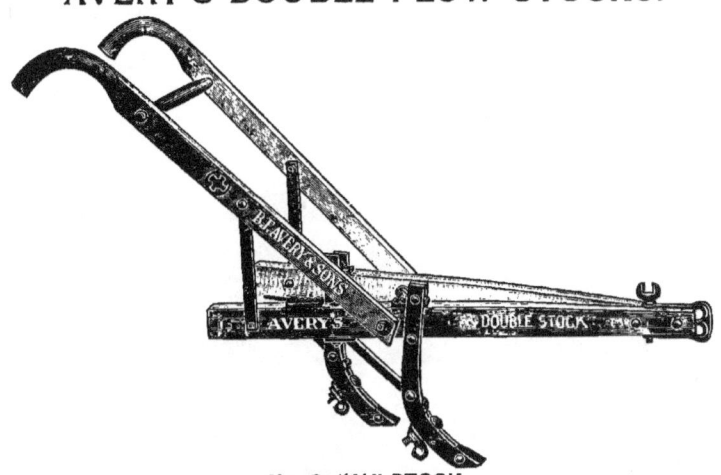

No. 8—"V" STOCK.

Beams and handles varnished. Standards with ratchets. Heel bolts and T washers with each stock. Beams 1¼ x 2⅝ x 41 inches long. Has same adjustability and utility of single stocks previously described, but with double the capacity.

No. 9—"PLANTER'S FRIEND."

Beams and handles varnished. Above known also as the "parallel" beam double stock. Heel bolts and T washers with each stock. Beams 1½ x 2⅝ x 33 inches long. Standards, with ratchets, are adjustable, and distance between them may be widened or narrowed as desired.

PRICE LIST.

Number and Name.	Code Word.	Weight.	Stock Complete, No Blades.
No. 8, "V" Stock	Polymorph.	32 lbs.	$3 30
No. 9, Planter's Friend	Polypus.	35 lbs.	3 60

REPAIR PRICE LIST.

	No. 8.	No. 9.		No. 8.	No. 9.
Standards, 1¾ x 5-16 inches, each	$0 60	$0 60	Handle Braces, per pair	$0 25	$0 25
Finished Beams, per set	1 00	1 50	Clevis	15	
Finished Handles, per pair	50	50	Wrought Hitch with shackle complete		75

B. F. AVERY & SONS. LOUISVILLE, KY.

AVERY'S COMBINATION SCRAPER AND SWEEP
WITH ATTACHMENTS.

Beam and handles varnished. Beam 2⅜ x 3¾ x 53 inches long.
The gauge wheel on the rear end of standard guides the plow so that it is easily handled.
Unless otherwise specified, the following blades are regularly sent, viz: 18-inch Magnolia Sweep, 8-inch Narrow Point Shovel, 3½-inch Bull Tongue, and No. 19A Scraper Blade.
With one stock and standard you can change the blade in a moment for any sort of work.
Besides being a useful plow on a farm, it is superior for gardening and truck farming.

PRICE LIST.

Number and Name.	Code Word.	Weight.	Price.
No. 1, Combination Scraper and Sweep, complete, with extras, as shown in cut	Pomeroy.	74 lbs.	$6 50
No. 2, Combination Scraper, complete, with Blade	Pomposo.	42 lbs.	4 60
No. 4, Combination Scraper, without Blade	Pongo.	36 lbs.	4 00
No. 3, Combination Sweep, complete, with Blade	Pontoon.	40 lbs.	4 50
No. 6, Combination Sweep, without Blade	Poplar.	33 lbs.	4 00
No. 7, Combination Stock and Clevis only	Populin.	13 lbs.	2 80
No. 8, Combination Standard and two Beam Bolts	Porgee.	17 lbs.	1 70
No. 5, Combination Steel Turning Plow Bottom, with extra Point.	Porret.	44 lbs.	2 25

AVERY'S COTTON SWEEP.
PLAIN STANDARD.

Sent with Magnolia Sweep No. 1, 18 x 12 x 3-16 inches.
Beam and handles varnished. Beam 2⅜ x 3⅜ x 53 inches long.
We make all sizes and kinds of Sweeps, but invariably send above when size is not specified.

PRICE LIST.

Number and Name.	Code Word.	Weight.	Price.
No. 8, Plain Sweep, complete, with Blade	Portend.	36 lbs.	$4 30
No. 9, Plain Sweep, without Blade	Portoise.	30 lbs.	3 80
No. 10, Plain Sweep, Stock and Clevis only	Poser.	13 lbs.	2 80

REPAIR PRICE LIST.

Number and Name.	Blade.	Cast Standard with (2) Bolts.	Clevis.	Finished Beam.	Fin. Handles, per pair.
No. 8, Avery Cotton Sweep	$0 75	$1 25	$0 15	$0 60	$0 50

B. F. AVERY & SONS. LOUISVILLE, KY.

AVERY'S COTTON SCRAPERS.

No. 5—"MITCHELL."

Beam and handles varnished.
Sent with Mitchell Scraper Blade No. 119, 11 x 10 x 3-16 inches.

A cotton scraper having strong advocates in some sections of the country, and holding its sway in favor with the planter.

PRICE LIST.

Number and Name.	Code Word.	Weight.	Price.
No. 5, Mitchell Cotton Scraper, complete	Posset.	46 lbs.	$4 90
No. 5½, Mitchell Cotton Scraper, less Blade	Postea.	39 lbs.	4 20

No. 6—AVERY, WITH PLAIN STANDARD.

Beam and handles varnished.
Sent with Avery Scraper Blade No. 19A, 14 x 10 x 3-16 inches.
Improved Scraper Blade No. 19 can be used and is sent when specially ordered.

The above scraper has given perfect satisfaction for many years.

PRICE LIST.

Number and Name.	Code Word.	Weight.	Price.
No. 6, Avery's Cotton Scraper, complete	Postil.	39 lbs.	$4 40
No. 7, Avery's Cotton Scraper, less Blade	Postulant.	32 lbs.	3 70
No. 7½, Avery's Cotton Scraper, Stock and Clevis only	Potagro.	13 lbs.	2 80

REPAIR PRICE LIST.

No. 5, Mitchell Cotton Scraper.	Price.	No. 6, Avery Cotton Scraper.	Price.
Blade No. 119, 14 x 10 x 3-16 inches	$1 00	Blade No. 19A, 14 x 10 x 3-16 inches	$1 00
Standard (cast) with two Bolts	1 50	Standard (cast) with two Bolts	1 25
Finished Beam, 2⅜ x 3¼ x 53 inches long	60	Finished Beam, 2⅜ x 3¼ x 53 inches long	60
Finished Handles, per pair	50	Finished Handles, per pair	50
Clevis	15	Clevis	15

B. F. AVERY & SONS.  LOUISVILLE, KY.

AVERY'S "MOON" ROLLING COULTER.
(Patented.)

This coulter enables an ordinary walking plow to turn easily perfectly any growth of mammoth clover, pea, strawberry, or other vines, stalks, weeds, or Johnson grass, or matted and tangled growths of any kind, no matter how high or dense, without clogging or choking the plow or coulter, because of the patented shoe or gauge in the center of which the coulter revolves. This shoe presses down all weeds and trash, and holds same firmly while being cut by the coulter, and prevents tough grass from doubling over its edge and clogging it in soft soil. The center of disc runs within one inch of the surface of the ground, consequently the cutting point is on a horizontal line with its center, or nearly so, thus overcoming the tendency to roll over trash and throw the plow out of the ground as is the case with other coulters. It is a perfect gauge as to depth (adjustable up or down), and no wheel or jointer is needed with coulter in use.

They are now in successful and general use in every State in the Union.

1st. Their use will save 20 per cent in draft in stiff land where there is no grass, and from 30 to 40 per cent in Bermuda or crab grass sod, and fully as much in labor for the plowman.

2d. Attached to any turn plow, from 6 inch cut up, a perfect furrow can be turned without clogging in any growth of pea-vines, crab or Bermuda grass, clover, cornstalks, etc.

3d. We have the only **sand proof** boxing and journal **ever made**, requiring oil but once a year.

4th. With the adjustable clamp used the coulter can be adjusted up or down, or placed in any position desired, without being unfastened from the beam, and is guaranteed not to work loose. As the bolts in clamp for wood beam are longer than those for steel beam, in ordering state whether coulters are wanted for wood or steel beam plows.

5th. By the use of small discs, such as we use in combination with our shoe for riding down and holding the rubbish, a greater depth will be cut, and the tendency to roll over rubbish without cutting is almost entirely overcome.

6th. As the shoe slides on the ground and regulates the depth of plowing, all weight should be removed from the animal's back by lengthening backbands of harness, which will prevent back galls.

7th. Our coulter is a **grand success** in plowing soft marsh lands.

CAUTION IN ORDERING.

Remember this: Do not order these coulters according to size of other rolling coulters you may have used. Order them by the numbers below, namely, No. 1, No. 2, No. 3.

Because, while the ordinary rolling coulter cuts only within two or three inches of the center, the "Moon" coulter cuts within one inch of the center of the disc, cutting into and through the weeds and trash, where the ordinary coulter rides on top of it.

The No. 1 "Moon" Coulter (8 inches) is equal and superior in capacity to the ordinary 10-inch coulter (use it on plows 6 to 8 inch cut, inclusive).

The No. 2 "Moon" (10 inches) does the work of an ordinary 13-inch coulter (use it on plows 9 to 12 inch cut, inclusive).

The No. 3 "Moon" (12 inches) equals an ordinary 15-inch coulter in capacity (use it on **plows 13 to 16 inch cut, inclusive**).

B. F. AVERY & SONS.   LOUISVILLE, KY.

ROLLING COULTERS.

Moon Coulter.

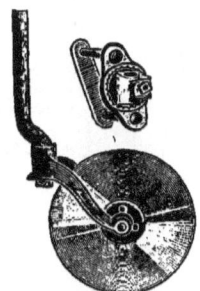
Caster Rolling Coulter.

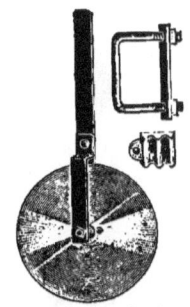
Stiff Shank Rolling Coulter.

We furnish with our Moon and Caster Rolling Coulters an adjustable beam clamp, by which the coulters can be adjusted up or down, or placed in any position desired without being unfastened from beam.

Order Moon Coulter by number, and state whether for wood or steel beam, as the bolts in clamp for wood beam are longer than those for steel beam.

See preceding page for general description of our Moon Coulter.

For prices on repairs, see page 141.

MOON ROLLING COULTER.

Number and Size.	Diameter of Blade.	Code Word.	Weight.	Price.
No. 1, for Plows of 6 to 8 in. cut, inclusive	8 in.	Pothecary.	17 lbs.	$2 50
No. 2, for Plows of 9 to 12 in. cut, inclusive	10 in.	Pouch.	20 lbs.	3 00
No. 3, for Plows of 13 to 16 in. cut, inclusive	12 in.	Pounder.	23 lbs.	3 50

CASTER ROLLING COULTER, WITH ROUND SHANK.

	Diameter	Code Word.	Weight.	Price.
10-inch	10 in.	Poverty.	18 lbs.	$3 00
12-inch	12 in.	Powldron.	20 lbs.	3 50
14-inch	14 in.	Practisant	23 lbs.	4 25

STIFF SHANK ROLLING COULTER.

	Diameter	Code Word.	Weight.	Price.
9-inch	9 in.	Prance.	8 lbs.	$1 75

FIN CUTTERS, WITH BOLTS.

New Clipper	Number	10	12	14	16			
	Code Word	Predacean.	Predial.	Preen.	Prefix.			
	Price, each	$0 70	$0 70	$0 70	$0 70			
Pony Series	Number	Pony.	A.O.	B.O.	C.O.	D.O.	E.O.	
	Code Word	Prejudice.	Prelude.	Premise.	Premorse	Preparer.	Presage.	
	Price, each	$0 60	$0 60	$0 70	$0 70	$0 70	$0 70	
Tiny Tim	Code Word	Prescious.						
	Price, each	$0 60						
Western	Number	Pony.	A.O.	B.O.	C.O.	D.O.	E.O.	
	Code Word	Presenter.	President	Presser.	Prestige.	Pretence.	Preterit.	
	Price, each	$0 60	$0 60	$0 70	$0 70	$0 70	$0 70	

B. F. AVERY & SONS.  LOUISVILLE, KY.

KNIFE COULTERS, JOINTERS, AND GAUGE WHEELS.

50 51  52 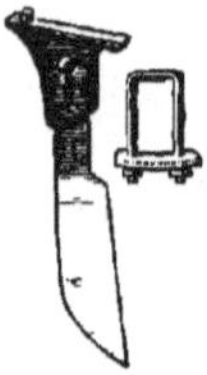 53 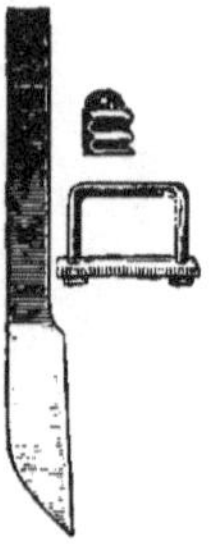 54 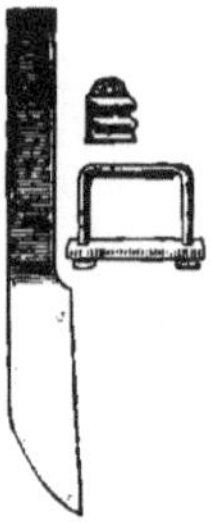 55

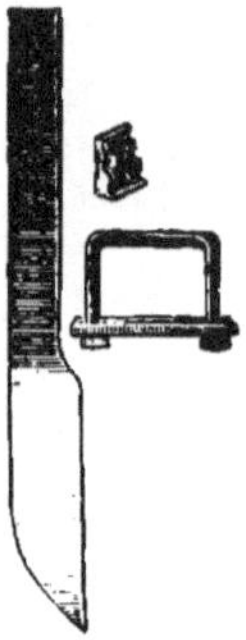

56

Straight.  Jumping.  Reversible.  Clamp and Cast Wedge.

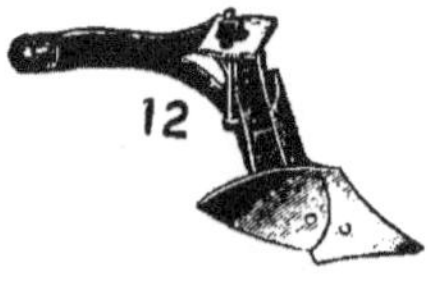

12

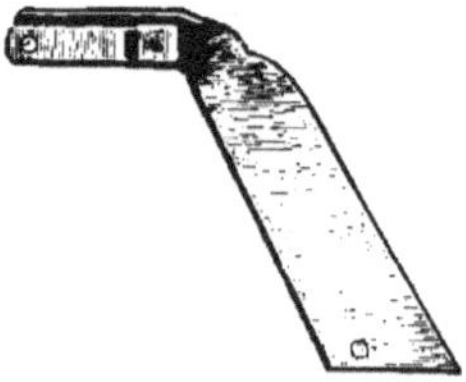

90

No. A. 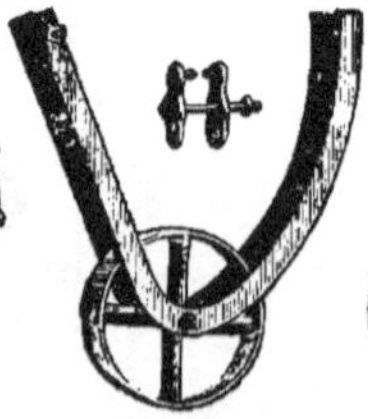 No. B.  No. C.  No. D.

☞ See price list next page.

PRICE LIST.

Order by number and state whether for Wood or Steel Beam Plow.

STRAIGHT KNIFE COULTERS (Steel).	Plows Used On.	Code Word.	Approximate Wt.	Price Each.
No. 50. 1½ x ⅜ x 14 in., with malleable bracket, same as shown in Cut No. 12	14-14½-15—Granite	Pretty.	6.00 lbs.	$0 75
No. 51. 1¾ x ½ x 17 in., with malleable bracket, same as shown in Cut No. 12		Preventer.	7.05 lbs.	1 00
No. 52 (old style). 1½ x ⅜ x 15 in., with bracket and clamp	½-1—Advance; Single plow stocks	Preying.	5.12 lbs.	75
No. 52X. 1¾ x ½ x 25 in., with clamp and cast wedge	½-1—Advance; Single plow stocks	Pricket.	7.06 lbs.	1 00
No. 53. 1¾ x ½ x 25 in., with clamp and cast wedge	Pony-A. O.—Pony Series; Pony-A. O.—Western; 6½-7—Dandy	Prier.	7.06 lbs.	1 00
No. 54. 2 x ½ x 26 in., with clamp and cast wedge	B. O.—Pony Series; B. O.—Western; 8-9—Dandy; 61X-20-O.—Blackland	Primary.	8.07 lbs.	1 00
No. 55. 2¼ x ⅝ x 28 in., with clamp and cast wedge	C. O.-D. O.—Pony Series; C. O.-D. O.—Western; 62½X-63X-40-O-Blackland; 409-410—Rainbow; 10—New Clipper; 9-10—Imp. Blackland; 8-9-10—Ohio Valley; 10—Dandy	Primero.	14.05 lbs.	1 50
No. 56. 2½ x ⅝ x 30 in., with clamp and cast wedge	E. O.—Pony Series; E. O.—Western; 64X 65X—Blackland; 11-12—Improved Blackland; 12-14-16—New Clipper; 11-12—Ohio Valley	Primo.	16.05 lbs.	1 75
No. 57. 2 x ⅝ x 26 in., with clamp and cast wedge	62X-30-O—Blackland; 7-8—Improved Blackland	Principate.	12.03 lbs.	1 25
No. 58. 2 x ⅝ x 24 in., with clamp and plate	1-2—Improved New Ground	Priorate.	12.03 lbs.	1 25
No. 59. With off set 1¾ x ½ x 25 in., with band and key wedge	1—Single Shovel	Privacy.	7.06 lbs.	1 00
JUMPING COULTERS (Steel).				
No. 60. 1¾ x ½ x 25 in., with band and key wedge	1—Single Shovel	Prizer.	8.00 lbs.	1 25
No. 61. 2 x ⅝ x 24 in., with band, plate, and bolts	1—Old Style New Ground	Probator.	12.07 lbs.	2 00
No. 62. 2 x ⅝ x 24 in., with band and plate		Prochein.	13.00 lbs.	2 00
No. 63. 2 x ⅝ x 26 in., with two wedge keys	15 16—Jumping Shovel	Procreant.	8.08 lbs.	1 25
No. 64. 2 x ⅝ x 24 in., with band, plate, and bolts	1-2—Improved New Ground	Procurer.	12.07 lbs.	2 00
REVERSIBLE COULTERS (Steel).				
No. 70. 2¼ x ⅝ x 28 in., with band, plate, and bolts	8—Samson New Ground	Produce.	12.05 lbs.	2 00
No. 71. 2½ x ⅝ x 30 in., with band, plate, and bolts	9—Samson New Ground	Proface.	13.05 lbs.	2 00
QUINCY COULTERS (Steel).				
No. 80. 4¾ x ¼ x 22½ in., with bolts	1—Railroad	Profert.	6.07 lbs.	1 75
KNEE CUTTERS (Steel).				
No. 90. For one-horse plows		Profile.	4.12 lbs.	1 25
No. 91. For two-horse plows		Profligate.	5.00 lbs.	1 50
JOINTERS.				
No. 12. With malleable bracket and standard	For all sizes Granite Plows	Profusion.	8.00 lbs.	1 75
No. A6 Gauge Wheels, with cast shank, plate, and 6-inch wheel, used on 14-14½-15—Granite. Pony-A. O—Pony Series, steel beam. Pony-A. O—Western, steel beam. 7—Improved Blackland. 61X—Blackland, steel beam. 20-O—Blackland, steel beam		Progress.	11.00 lbs.	$1 10
No. A7 Gauge Wheels, with cast shank, plate, and 7-inch wheel, used on B. O.-C. O.-D. O.-E. O.—Pony Series, steel beam. B. O.-C. O.-D. O.-E. O.—Western, steel beam. 8-9-10-11-12—Ohio Valley, steel beam. 10-12-14-16—New Clipper, steel beam. 8-9-10-11-12—Improved Blackland, 62X-62½X-63X-64X-65X—Blackland, steel beam. 30 O-40 O—Blackland, steel beam		Proin.	12.00 lbs.	1 20
No. B6 Gauge Wheels, with wrought quadrant, plate, and 6-inch wheel, used on Pony A. O.-B. O.—Pony Series, wood beam. Pony A. O.-B. O.—Western, wood beam. Tiny Tim. 8-9—Ohio Valley, wood beam. 61X—Blackland, wood beam. 20 O-30 O—Blackland, wood beam		Proleptic.	10.00 lbs.	1 50
No. B8 Gauge Wheels, with wrought quadrant, plate, and 8-inch wheel, used on C. O.-D. O.-E. O.—Pony Series, wood beam. C. O.-D. O.-E. O.—Western, wood beam. 10-11-12—Ohio Valley, wood beam. 62X-62½X-63X-64X—Blackland, wood beam. 40 O-50 O—Blackland, wood beam		Prolong.	10.08 lbs.	1 50
No. C9 Gauge Wheels, with wrought stiff shank, band, and 9-inch wheel, used on 10-12-14-16—New Clipper, wood beam. 65X—Blackland, wood beam. 409-410—Rainbow		Promiser.	15.00 lbs.	1 50
No. D12 Gauge Wheels, with wrought stiff shank, adjustable spindle, and 12-inch wheel, used on No. 1 Railroad or Grading plow		Prompter.	18.08 lbs.	4 00

Right or left hand.

B. F. AVERY & SONS.   LOUISVILLE, KY.

AVERY'S PATENT "U" STEEL TREES.

Avery's Patent Steel Trees are " U "-shaped wrought steel, and have our famous patent self-locking end hooks, which prevent the traces from becoming loose accidentally. They are the best ever invented for general or special work; have great strength, are practicably indestructible, and have malleable hooks and center eye; all metal, not a particle of wood. There is no wearing out, except the hooks after long service, and which can be replaced at a mere nominal expense by any blacksmith. Clips or hooks are riveted and do not get loose from shrinkage, as on all kinds of wood trees. Especial favorites in dry climates.

SINGLETREES. FOR UNIVERSAL USE.

Size.	Code Word.	Weight per doz.	Price per doz.
22-inch Singletrees	Pronoun.	47 lbs.	$5 50
24-inch Singletrees	Prop.	51 lbs.	5 75
26-inch Singletrees	Propel.	54 lbs.	6 00
28-inch Singletrees	Prophesy.	59 lbs.	6 75
30-inch Singletrees	Propolis.	61 lbs.	8 25
32-inch Singletrees	Proposer.	77 lbs.	9 00

DOUBLETREES. FOR PLOWS AND WAGONS.

Size.	Code Word.	Weight per doz.	Price per doz.
32-inch Doubletrees	Prosaic.	77 lbs.	$9 00
36-inch Doubletrees	Proselyte.	86 lbs.	10 50
41-inch Doubletrees	Prosper.	154 lbs.	14 50
44-inch Doubletrees	Prostrate.	160 lbs.	16 50
48-inch Doubletrees	Protector.	175 lbs.	18 00

When not specified otherwise, Doubletrees for Plows will always be sent.

DOUBLETREES. IN SETS. FOR PLOWS.

Number and Size.	Code Word.	Weight per set	Price per set.
No. 1, Two 24-inch and one 36-inch	Protocol.	16 lbs.	$1 83
No. 2, Two 26-inch and one 36-inch	Protractor.	17 lbs.	1 87
No. 3, Two 28-inch and one 36-inch	Provent.	18 lbs.	2 00
No. 4, Two 30-inch and one 36-inch	Provider.	18 lbs.	2 25

DOUBLETREES. IN SETS. FOR WAGONS, WITH HOOKS IN DOUBLETREES FOR STAY-CHAINS.

Number and Size.	Code Word.	Weight per set.	Price per set.
No. 5, Two 30-inch and one 41-inch	Provision.	23 lbs.	$2 58
No. 6, Two 32-inch and one 41-inch	Provoker.	26 lbs.	2 70
No. 7, Two 32-inch and one 44-inch	Proximate.	27 lbs.	2 87
No. 8, Two 36-inch and one 44-inch	Prudish.	29 lbs.	3 12
No. 9, Two 36-inch and one 48-inch	Prussic.	30 lbs.	3 25

B. F. AVERY & SONS.   LOUISVILLE, KY.

AVERY'S PATENT "U" STEEL TREES.

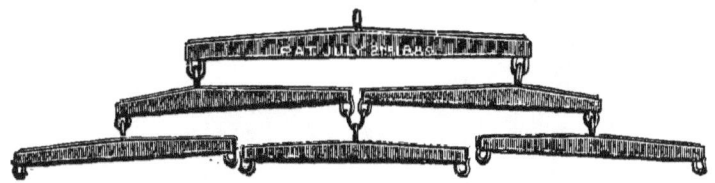

TRIPLETREES. REGULAR. FOR WALKING AND SULKY PLOWS.

Number and Size.	Code Word.	Weight per set.	Price per set.
No. 1, One 42-inch, two 28½-inch, and three 26-inch	Puberal.	37 lbs.	$4 40
No. 2, One 42-inch, two 28½-inch, and three 28-inch	Publicist.	39 lbs.	4 60
No. 3, One 48-inch, two 33½-inch, and three 30-inch	Puceron.	43 lbs.	5 00
No. 4, One 48-inch, two 33½-inch, and three 32-inch	Puddler.	48 lbs.	5 20

FOUR-HORSE EVENERS. FOR SULKY OR GANG PLOWS.

Number and Size.	Code Word.	Weight per set.	Price per set.
No. 1, One 62-inch wood, and two 28-inch steel, and four 26-inch steel	Puffer.	55 lbs.	$6 00
No. 2, One 62-inch wood, and two 30-inch steel, and four 28-inch steel	Puissant.	57 lbs.	6 50

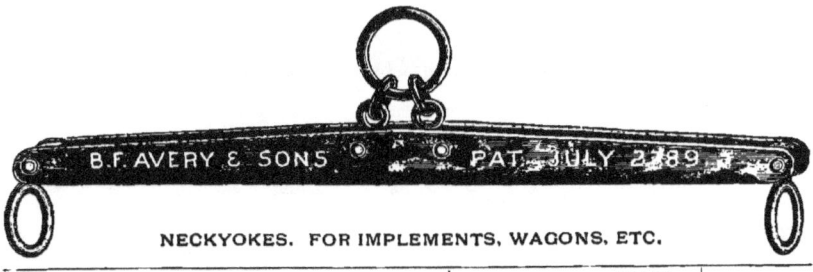

NECKYOKES. FOR IMPLEMENTS, WAGONS, ETC.

Size and Style.	Code Word.	Weight per dozen.	Price per doz.
36 inches, Light	Pullet.	91 lbs.	$12 00
36 inches, Heavy	Pulsator.	103 lbs.	14 00

REPAIRS FOR AVERY'S PATENT "U" STEEL TREES.
Rivets included in prices.

No. 228. End Hook for 22, 24, 26, 28, 30, and 32-inch Singletrees	per dozen,	$1 00
No. 225. End Hook for 32 and 36-inch Doubletrees	per dozen,	1 00
No. 224. End Hook for 40, 44, and 48-inch street-car and wagon Doubletrees	per dozen,	1 50
No. 229. Center Eye for 22, 24, 26, 28, 30, and 32-inch Singletrees	per dozen,	1 50
No. 226. Center Eye for 32 and 36-inch Doubletrees	per dozen,	2 00
No. 227. Center Eye for 40, 44, and 48-inch wagon Doubletrees	per dozen,	3 00
No. 222. Center Eye for 40, 44, and 48-inch street-car Doubletrees	per dozen,	5 00
No. K48. Center Eye for Tripletrees	per dozen,	3 00
No. 228. Stay Chain Hooks for 40, 44, and 48-inch wagon Doubletrees	per dozen,	1 00
No. 221. Rub Plate for 40, 44, and 48-inch street-car and wagon Doubletrees	per dozen,	4 50
No. 223. Lifting Hook for 40, 44, and 48-inch street-car Doubletrees	per dozen,	1 00
Wrought Connecting Loop for Tripletrees	per dozen,	1 10

PLOW SINGLETREES.
Length 20, 22, 24, 26, 28, and 30 inches.

Number and Style.	Center Clip.	End Clip.	Hook.	Code Word.	Average Weight.	Price per doz. 20-26-inch	Price per doz. 28, 30-in.
No. 1, Light...Varnished	7/16	3/8	5/16	Pummel.	35 lbs.	$2 40	$2 70
No. 2, Medium..Painted Red	7/16	7/16	5/16	Puncheon.	40 lbs.	3 00	3 30
No. 3, Extra...Painted Red	1/2	1/2	3/8	Punctuist.	57 lbs.	4 20	4 50

PLOW SINGLE AND DOUBLETREES—MALLEABLE IRONS.

Number and Style.	Length.	Code Word.	Average Weight.	Price per doz. 22-26-in.	Price per doz. 28, 30-in.
No. 200, Singletrees..Varnished	22, 24, 26, 28, and 30 in.	Punisher.	38 lbs.	$3 00	$3 30
No. 202, Doubletrees..Varnished	36 inches.	Pupil.	87 lbs.		6 00

PLOW SINGLETREES.
Malleable End Ferrules with 3/8-inch Hooks, 9/16-inch Center Clip with 1/2-inch Ring.

Number and Style.	Length.	Code Word.	Average Weight.	Price per doz. 26-in.	Price per doz. 28, 30-in.
No. 4, Varnished	26, 28, and 30 inches.	Purchaser.	60 lbs.	$4 00	$4 30
No. 4, Painted Red	26, 28, and 30 inches.	Purifier.	60 lbs.	4 25	4 55

PLOW DOUBLETREES.
Length 36 inches.

Number and Style.	Center Clip.	End Clip.	Hook.	Code Word.	Average Weight.	Price per doz.
No. 13, Light........Varnished	9/16	1/16	7/16	Purlin.	77 lbs.	$4 80
No. 14, Medium......Painted Red	5/8	5/8	1/2	Purprise.	84 lbs.	6 00
No. 15, Extra Heavy..Painted Red	5/8	5/8	1/2	Pursue.	110 lbs.	9 60

PLOW DOUBLETREES.
Length 36 inches.

Number and Style.	Center Clip.	End Clip.	Code Word.	Average Weight.	Price per doz.
No. 18, Light ....Varnished	$\frac{9}{16}$	$\frac{7}{16}$	Puseyite.	60 lbs.	$4 40
No. 19, Medium......Painted Red ...	$\frac{5}{8}$	$\frac{1}{2}$	Puttock.	70 lbs.	5 50
No. 20, Extra Heavy.Painted Red ...	$\frac{3}{4}$	$\frac{5}{8}$	Pyramid.	100 lbs.	9 00

WAGON SINGLETREES.

$\frac{1}{2}$ inch Strap End, $\frac{3}{8}$ inch Hook, $\frac{5}{8}$ inch Center Clip, $\frac{1}{2}$ inch Ring, 2 Rivets in Wear Irons.

Number and Style.	Length.	Code Word.	Average Weight.	Price per doz.
No. 9, Painted Red	36 in.	Pyro.	86 lbs.	$7 20

WAGON SINGLETREES.

Malleable Strap Ends, $\frac{3}{4}$ inch Wrought Hooks, $\frac{5}{8}$ inch Center Clip, $\frac{1}{2}$ inch Ring.

Number and Style.	Length.	Code Word.	Average Weight.	Price per doz.
No. 9½, Painted Red and Striped	34 and 36 in.	Pyrosis.	90 lbs.	$7 80

WAGON SINGLETREES.

Malleable End Ferrules, $\frac{3}{4}$ inch Wrought Hook, $\frac{5}{8}$ inch Center Clip, $\frac{1}{2}$ inch Ring.

Number and Style.	Length.	Code Word.	Average Weight.	Price per doz.
No. 10, Varnished	26 in.	Python.	74 lbs.	$5 40

B. F. AVERY & SONS. LOUISVILLE, KY.

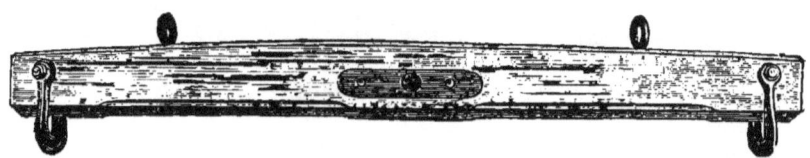

WAGON DOUBLETREES.

Size of Wood 4 x 2 x 48 inches.

Number and Style.	Code Word.	Average Weight.	Price per doz.
No. 12, Self-Colored	Quadra.	166 lbs.	$9 60

WAGON NECKYOKES.

Number and Style.	Length.	Code Word.	Average Weight.	Price per doz. 40 inch.	Price per doz. 48 inch.
No. 45, Varnished	40 and 48 in.	Quadrel.	98 lbs.	$7 50	$12 00
No. 45, Painted Red	40 and 48 in.	Quadroon.	98 lbs.	8 25	12 75

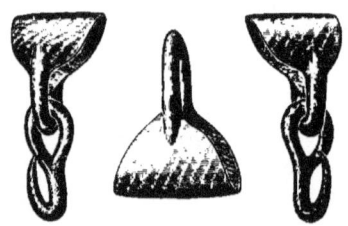

SINGLETREE IRONS—WELDED.

Number and Style.	Center Clip.	End Clip.	Hook.	Code Word.	Average Weight.	Price per doz.
No. 48, Light	7/16	3/8	5/16	Quaffer.	15 lbs.	$1 90
No. 49, Medium	1/2	7/16	3/8	Quaker.	20 lbs.	2 10
No. 50, Extra	9/16	1/2	3/8	Quamoclit.	25 lbs.	2 80

DOUBLETREE IRONS—WELDED.

Number and Style.	Center Clip.	End Clip.	Hook.	Code Word.	Average Weight.	Price per doz.
No. 51, Light	9/16	7/16	7/16	Quarreler.	25 lbs.	$2 90
No. 52, Medium	5/8	1/2	1/2	Quartern.	30 lbs.	3 40
No. 53, Extra	3/4	5/8	5/8	Quassia.	35 lbs.	4 90

B. F. AVERY & SONS.  LOUISVILLE, KY.

PLOW HANDLES.

Extra First-Class, Thorough Seasoned Handles of White Clear Oak.

IN ROUGH WITH VARNISHED HAND HOLDS.

Size.	Used For	Code Word.	Weight per doz.	Price per doz.
1⅜ x 2⅜ x 3 feet 6 inches	Georgia Stocks	Queach.	36 lbs.	$1 50
1⅜ x 2⅜ x 3 feet 9 inches	Scrapers, Sweeps, and Dow-Law Cotton Planters	Queller.	37 lbs.	1 85
1⅜ x 2⅜ x 4 feet 6 inches	One-Horse Cast Plows and Double Shovels	Querpo.	45 lbs.	2 10
1⅜ x 2⅜ x 5 feet 0 inches	One-Horse Steel Plows	Questor.	50 lbs.	2 30
1½ x 2½ x 5 feet 2 inches	Two-Horse Cast and Steel Plows	Quickener.	52 lbs.	2 60

NOTE—The 3-foot 6-inch Handles are only used on Georgia Stocks, and are shipped side bent. When not specified, we ship one half right hand and one half left hand bent.

Extra for side Bending .... per dozen, $0 40
All edge-bent handles are machine dressed. Extra for same .... per dozen, 75

POLISHED LAP RINGS AND LINKS.

Round.   End Open.   Side Open.

LAP LINKS—END OPEN.

Number and Size.	Code Word.	Weight per doz.	Price per doz.
No. 21, ⅜ x 1¼ inches inside	Quiddle.	2.6 lbs.	$0 25
No. 22, ⁷⁄₁₆ x 2 inches inside	Quilt.	3.6 lbs.	30
No. 23, ½ x 2 inches inside	Quintain.	5.0 lbs.	45
No. 24, ⁹⁄₁₆ x 2⅛ inches inside	Quippa.	6.3 lbs.	60
No. 25, ⅝ x 2¼ inches inside	Quittal.	7.5 lbs.	70

LAP LINKS—SIDE OPEN.

No. 26, ⁷⁄₁₆ x 2 inches inside	Quizzer.	3.4 lbs.	$0 30
No. 27, ½ x 2⅛ inches inside	Quoter.	5.0 lbs.	45
No. 28, ⁹⁄₁₆ x 2¼ inches inside	Rabbit.	6.3 lbs.	60
No. 29, ⅝ x 2¼ inches inside	Racer.	7.5 lbs.	70

ROUND LAP RINGS.

No. 30, ⅜ x 1½ inches inside	Racker.	2.5 lbs.	$0 25
No. 31, ⁷⁄₁₆ x 1¾ inches inside	Raddock.	3.5 lbs.	30
No. 32, ½ x 1¾ inches inside	Radiator.	5.0 lbs.	45
No. 33, ⁹⁄₁₆ x 2 inches inside	Radius.	6.3 lbs.	60
No. 34, ⅝ x 2⅛ inches inside	Rafty.	8.0 lbs.	70

B. F. AVERY & SONS. LOUISVILLE, KY.

PLAIN FENDER, WITH CLAMP.
For Steel Beam Double Shovel Plows.

Code Word.	Weight, each.	Price, each.
Ragout.	5¼ lbs.	$0 60

MISSISSIPPI SCRAPER.

The best Scraper made for cotton; saves labor and largely increases the yield; fits all our one-horse plows.

Code Word.	Weight.	Price, each.
Raiment.	10 lbs.	$1 50

HEEL SLIDE, WITH BOLTS.

For regulating the depth of cultivating and making the plow run steady. Can be attached to any of our Steel Beam or Steel Standard Double Shovels.

Code Word.	Weight, per pair.	Price, per pair.
Raker.	3 lbs.	$0 60

GRASS RODS.

Size.	Code Word.	Approximate Weight per dozen.	Price per doz.
16x¼ square.	Ramage.	20.05 lbs.	$1 00
17x9-16 square.	Rammer.	22.00 lbs.	1 25
17x9-16 round.	Rampier.	21.00 lbs.	1 00
19x9-16 round.	Rancor.	22.05 lbs.	1 25

T WASHER.

Malleable, for Single and Double Plow Stocks.

Number.	Code Word.	Price, each.
No. 266. For Single Stocks Nos. 1, 2, 5, 6, 7, 10, 17, 18...	Ranger.	$0 06
No. 267. For Double Stocks Nos. 8 and 9.................	Ransom.	06

STEEL HARROW TEETH—HEADED.

Size.	Code Word.	Weight per 100.	Price per pound.
½ inch square x 10 inches long	Rapacious.	70 lbs.	
⅝ inch square x 10 inches long	Rapier.	110 lbs.	
¾ inch square x 10 inches long	Rarefy.	160 lbs.	
⅝ inch square x 12 inches long	Rasher.	120 lbs.	
¾ inch square x 12 inches long	Ratany.	175 lbs.	5 cents.
⅞ inch square x 12 inches long	Ratifier.	260 lbs.	
1 inch square x 12 inches long	Ratlin.	340 lbs.	
1 inch square x 14 inches long	Rattoon.	395 lbs.	

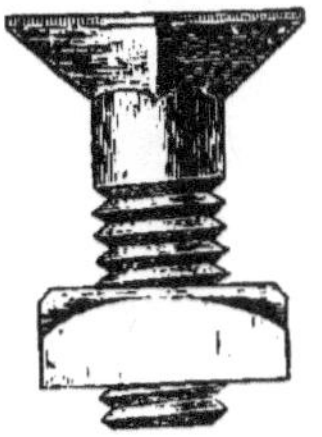

SQUARE HEAD PLOW BOLTS.

No.	Size.	Code Word.	Weight per 100.	Price per 100.
1	3/8 x 1 1/8 in.	Raven.	7½ lbs.	$2 00
2	3/8 x 1½ in.	Rawish.	9½ lbs.	2 10
3	3/8 x 2 in.	Razure.	10¼ lbs.	2 30
4	7-16 x 1¼ in.	Reader.	12 lbs.	2 60
5	7-16 x 1½ in.	Reagent.	12¾ lbs.	2 75
6	½ x 1½ in.	Realty.	17 lbs.	3 70

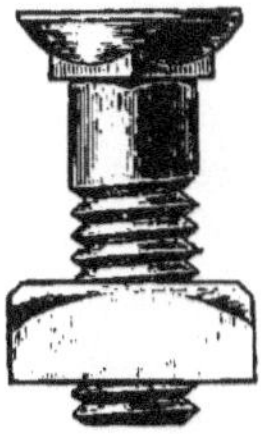

ROUND HEAD PLOW BOLTS.

No.	Size.	Code Word.	Weight per 100.	Price per 100.
7	3/8 x 1 in.	Reasoner.	7½ lbs.	$2 00
8	3/8 x 1¼ in.	Rebec.	8 lbs.	2 00
9	3/8 x 1 3/8 in.	Rebuff.	8½ lbs.	2 10
10	3/8 x 1 5/8 in. lg.sq.	Rebutter.	8½ lbs.	2 10
11	3/8 x 1½ in. lg.sq.	Recast.	9 lbs.	2 10
12	7-16 x 1 3/8 in.	Recense.	11½ lbs.	2 60
13	7-16 x 1½ in.	Recheat.	12¾ lbs.	2 75
14	7-16 x 1½ in. lg.sq.	Recite.	13 lbs.	2 75
15	7-16 x 2½ in.	Recline.	16¾ lbs.	3 35
16	½ x 1 in.	Recoil.	14 lbs.	3 50
17	½ x 1¼ in.	Recompact.	15 lbs.	3 50
18	½ x 1 3/8 in.	Reconciler.	16¾ lbs.	3 70
19	½ x 1½ in.	Recorder.	17½ lbs.	3 70
20	3/8 x 1½ in. sp'l.	Recreant.	.... lbs.	2 10

BOLTS USED FOR PLOW POINTS.

Name and Number of Plow.	Take Bolt No.	For
Advance, Nos. ½, 1	7	Point
American, Nos. A, B..........	4	Point
American, Nos. 10, 13, 19, 20, 40	6	Point
Big Bolt, Nos. 107, 108, 109....	17	Point
Cadet, Nos. 6, 7...............	8	Point
Cast Plows, Nos. 8, 12	5	Point
Cast Plows, Nos. 8, 12	3	Han'les
Cast Plows, Nos. ½, 1	4	Point
Cast Plows, Nos. ½, 1	2	Lan'sid
Cast Plows, Nos. ½, 1	3	Han'les
Cast Plows, No. 2..............	4	Point
Cast Plows, No. 3..............	4	Point
Chilled Plows, Nos. 8, 12.....	5	Point
Dandy, Nos. 6½, 7, 8X	17	Point
Dandy, Nos. 9, 10.............	17 and 18	Point
Granite, Nos. 14, 14½, 15	4	Point
Granite, Vineyard, No. 15....	4	Point
Hard Pan, Nos. 6, 8	16 face 19 side	Point

BOLTS USED FOR PLOW POINTS—CONTINUED.

Name and Number of Plow.	Take Bolt No.	For
Hillside Plow, No. 7...........	7	Point
Ideal, No. 26..................	4	Point
Ideal, No. 28..................	6	Point
Imp'ved Black Land, Nos. 7, 8	7 face 7 side	Point
Imp'ved Black Land, Nos. 9, 10	7 face 8 side	Point
Imp'ved Black Land, Nos. 11, 12	7 face 8 side	Point
Middle Burster, Nos. 9, 10, 12.	7 and 12	Point
Middle Burster, Nos. 14, 16, 18, 20	12	Point
New Clipper, Nos. 10, 12, 14, 16,	7 face 11 side	Point
Ohio Valley, No. 8............	7 and 18	Point
Ohio Valley, Nos. 9, 10, 11, 12.	7 and 19	Point
Orange Plow, No. 11..........	7	Point
"O" Series, Black Land, No. 20 O	7 face 10 side	Point
"O" Series, Black Land, Nos. 30 O, 40 O	12 face 14 side	Point
Pony Series Plows, Nos. Pony, A.O., B.O.	7 face 10 side	Point
Pony Series Plows, Nos. C.O. D.O., E.O.	12 face 14 side	Point
Railroad Plow, No. 1..........	12 face 15 side	Point
Rainbow, Nos. 407, 408, 409, 410	17 face 18 side	Point
Red Pony......................	7 face 9 side	Point
Tiny Tim......................	7 face 10 side	Point
Veteran, Nos. 6½, 7	4	Point
Western, No. B.O.............	7 face 9 side	Point
Western, Nos. C.O., D.O., E.O.	12 face 13 side	Point
X Series, Black Land, No. 61X	7 face 20 side	Point
X Series, Black Land, No. 62X	7 face 11 side	Point
X Series, Black Land, Nos. 62½X, 63X, 64X..............	7 face 14 side	Point
X Series, Black Land, No. 65X	12 face 14 side	Point

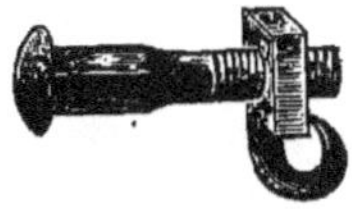

HEEL BOLTS.

Size.	Code Word.	Approximate Weight per doz.	Price per doz.
3¼ x 5/8	Recruit.	8.03 lbs.	$0 70
3¾ x 5/8	Rector.	8.08 lbs.	75
4½ x 5/8	Recurrent.	9.06 lbs.	80

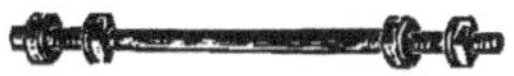

SPREADER RODS.

(With four Nuts and four Washers.)

Size.	Used For	Code Word.	Wt. per Doz.	Pr. per Doz.
½x11	Nos. 5 & 6 D'ble Sh'ls	Redden.	9 lbs.	$1 80
½x14	No. 3 Double Shovels	Redemise.	11 lbs.	2 20
7-16x13½	No. 4 Double Shovels	Redolent.	9 lbs.	1 80
9-16x12	No. 10 Double Sh'ls..	Redress.	16 lbs.	2 00
5/8x10½	No. 7 Double Shovels	Reductive	13 lbs.	2 20
½x14	No. 8 Double Stock..	Reedy.	11 lbs.	2 20
9-16x15	No. 9 Planter's Friend	Reeming.	17 lbs.	2 40

B. F. AVERY & SONS. LOUISVILLE, KY.

PLOW HAMES.

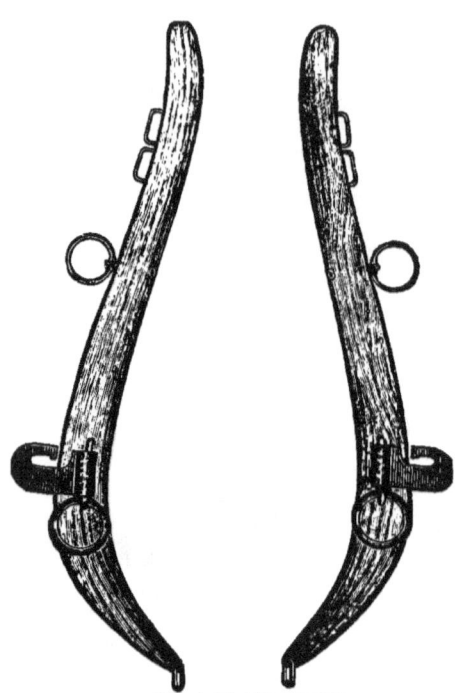

No. 1 PLOW HAME.

THE "MOCK" STEEL HAME.

Made entirely of steel. Hooks are forged steel.

We carry in stock a general line of different styles and sizes of Plow Hames, the quality and finish of which are first-class in every respect.

PRICE LIST.

No.	Style.	Finish.	Sizes.	Code Word.	Weight per doz. Pairs.	Price per doz. Pairs.
46	Single Cut Hooks	Varnished, Red Top	All sizes	Reeve.	35 lbs.	$4 50
40½	Single Cut Hooks	Varnished, Red Top	Horse & Mule	Refiner.	30 lbs.	5 10
30	Single Cut Hooks, Full Iron Bound	Varnished	Horse & Mule	Reflex.	45 lbs.	5 50
1	Single Cut Hooks	Varnished	Horse & Mule	Reformer.	45 lbs.	5 20
2	Single Cut Hooks	Varnished	Horse & Mule	Refresher.	45 lbs.	5 50
155	Double Cut Hooks	Varnished	One size	Refunder.	50 lbs.	6 20
100	Double Cut Hooks, Half-Strapped	Red, Bronzed Top	All sizes	Refuter.	45 lbs.	7 80
12	Double Cut Hooks, Brass over Top	Red, Bronzed Top	One size	Regally.	45 lbs.	11 00
166	Double Cut Hooks, Ball Top	Red, Bronzed Top	One size	Regatta.	60 lbs.	9 50
10	Solid Malleable Hooks, Brass over Top	Red, Bronzed Top	One size	Regicide.	50 lbs.	12 00
75	Double Cut Hooks	Varnished	All sizes	Registry.	40 lbs.	11 20
85	Double Cut Hooks	Red	All sizes	Regress.	45 lbs	12 20
120	Solid Malleable Hooks	Red, Bronzed Top	All sizes	Regulator.	65 lbs.	13 00
750	Double Cut Hooks, Brass Globe Ball	Red, Bronzed Top	One size	Rehearser.	50 lbs.	12 20
755	Staple and Ring Tug, Brass Globe Ball	Red, Bronzed Top	One size	Rein.	50 lbs.	14 50
850	Solid Malleable Hooks	Varnished, Red Top	All sizes	Reiter.	75 lbs.	20 00
	Mock Steel Hames	Red, Black Tipped	18 to 23 inches.	Rejoindure.	80 lbs.	16 20
Extra per dozen pairs for painted instead of varnished Hames				Relapser.		1 00

MALLEABLE WRENCHES.

No.	Style.	Length.	Weight.	For Square Nuts. Openings.	For Hexagon Nuts. Openings.	Code Word.	Price each.	Used on
64	Straight.	7 in.	7 oz.	1, ¾ in.	....	Releaser.	$0 15	Nos. A, B, Z, 10 American Plows.
65	Straight.	9½ in.	12 oz.	1 1-16, 15-16, ¾ in.	....	Relic.	20	Nos. 14, 14½, 15 Granite Plows.
66	Straight.	9¼ in.	12½ oz.	1⅛, 14-16 in.	1 3-16-in.	Reliquary.	20	Invincible Sulkies, Invincible Disc Plows.
J97	Straight.	10 in.	1 lb.	13-16, 15-16, ⅞, ¾, ⅝ in.	15-16 in.	Relume.	25	New South and Western Cultivators, Louisville Stalk Cutters.
38	Straight.	6¾ in.	9 oz.	1¼, 1⅛, ⅞, ¾ in.	....	Remanence	20	Perfection Harrows, Tornado Harrows, Eureka Harrows.
E54	Straight.	12½ in.	1½ lb.	1½, 1¼, 1 1-16 in.	....	Remedy.	50	Simple Sulky, Sugarland Cultivators, Stubble Shaver, Stubble Digger.
K189	S	6¼ in.	7 oz.	¾, 9-16 in.	....	Remiges.	10	Truckers' Cultivators, Orchard Harrows.
60	S	7¾ in.	8 oz.	⅞, ⅝ in.	....	Remitter.	25	General purposes.
93	S	7½ in.	7 oz.	⅞, ¾, ½ in.	....	Remorse.	10	Louisville Planter, Modern Planter.
67	S	8½ in.	12 oz.	1¼, 1, ⅞ in.	....	Remover.	20	Nos. 13, 19, 20, 40 American Plows.
T52	Socket.	4¼ in.	5 oz.	7-16 in.	....	Renderer.	20	Fertilizer Distributor.
AA34	Socket.	11¼ in.	1 lb. 2 oz.	....	1 3-16 in.	Renewer.	40	Fertilizer Distributor.
JX62	Socket.	11¼ in.	1½ lb.	....	1 7-16 in.	Renowned.	30	Revolution Disc Cultivator.

TRACE CHAINS.

Wire Number	0	1	2	3
Inch	5-16	9-32	¼	7-32

STRAIGHT LINK WITH RING.

Length Feet.	Links to Foot.	Wire No.	Code Word.	Weight per pair.	Price per pair.	Length Feet.	Links to Foot.	Wire No.	Code Word.	Weight per pair.	Price per pair.
6½	6	3	Repacify.	4¼ lbs.	....	7	10	2	Reprobate.	6¾ lbs.	....
6½	6	2	Repartee.	5½ lbs.	....	7	8	1	Reprover.	8¼ lbs.	....
6½	8	2	Repeater.	6 lbs.	....	7	10	1	Repudiator.	9¼ lbs.	....
6½	10	1	Repenter.	8¼ lbs.	....	7	12	1	Repute.	9 lbs.	....
6½	10	0	Replait.	9 lbs.	....	7	8	0	Requirer.	9½ lbs.	....
7	8	3	Replier.	5½ lbs.	....	7	10	0	Rescript.	11½ lbs.	....
7	6	2	Repour.	6 lbs.	....	7	12	0	Reseizer.	10¼ lbs.	....
7	8	2	Repress.	6¼ lbs.	....	7	14	0	Reserver.	12 lbs.	....
Twisted Links extra over Straight Links.................................per pair									Resident.	....	....
Straight Links with T Bar Hook extra.................................per pair									Resin.	....	....
Twisted Links with T Bar Hook extra ....per pair									Resolute.	....	....
Repair Links, ¼ inch, packed in ½ gross boxes.......................per gross									Resonant.	....	....
Repair Links, 5-16 inch, packed in ½ gross boxes.......................per gross									Respire.	....	....

B. F. AVERY & SONS. LOUISVILLE, KY.

MALLEABLE CLEVISES.

ONE HORSE.
Used on Wood Beam.

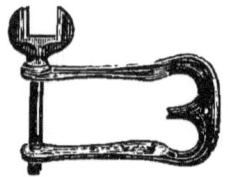

Number.	Thickness of Beam.	Center of Wrench to End of Beam	Approximate Weight.	Code Word.	Price per pound.
101	2 inch.	4 inch.	0.9 lbs.	Restant.	10 cents.

Used on		Used on	
Advance	Nos. ½, 1.	Georgia Stocks	Nos. 1, 2.
Big Bolt	No. 107.	Lone Star Stock	No. 17.
Cadet	Nos. 6, 7.	New Series Cast Plows	Nos. ½, 1.
Carolina Stock	No. 10.	Old Series Cast Plows	No. 8.
Chilled Plow	No. 8.	Pony Series	Nos. Pony, A.O.
Chilled Hillside	No. 7.	Red Pony	
Combination Scraper and Sweep	Nos. 1, 2, 3, 4, 6, 7.	Single Shovel	No. 1.
Cotton Scrapers	Nos. 5, 5½, 6, 7, 7½.	Texas Stock	Nos. 6, 7.
Cotton Sweep	Nos. 8, 9, 10.	Tiny Tim	
Delta Cultivator		Universal Stock	No. 5.
Double Shovels	Nos. 2, 3, 4, 7.	Veteran	Nos. 6½, 7.
Double or V Plow Stock	No. 8.	Wing Shovel	

TWO HORSE.
Used on Wood Beam.

Number.	Thickness of Beam.	Center of Wrench to Center of Pin.	Approximate Weight.	Code Word.	Price per pound.
102	2 inch.	3½ inch.	1.0 lb.	Restless.	10 cents.
103	2¼ inch.	3½ inch.	1.5 lbs.	Restraint.	10 cents.
104	2½ inch.	3⅝ inch.	1.6 lbs.	Resume.	10 cents.

No. 102 Used on		No. 103 Used on		No. 104 Used on	
Big Bolt	Nos. 108, 109.	American	Nos. A, B, 10.	Dandy	No. 8X.
Blackland	Nos. 61X, 20-O.	Chilled Plow	No. 12.		
New Series Cast Plow	No. 2.	Dandy	Nos. 6½, 7.		
Orange Plow	No. 11.	New Series Cast Plow	No. 3.		
Pony Series	No. B.O.	Old Series Cast Plow	No. 12.		
Rainbow	No. 407.				
Western	No. B.O.				

TWO HORSE. WITH SHACKLE.
Used on Wood Beam.

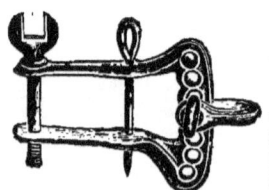

No.	Thickness of Beam.	Center of Wrench to Center of Pin.	Holes	Approximate Weight.	Code Word.	Price per pound.
110	2¼ inch.	3¼ inch.	7	1.6 lbs.	Retainer.	10 cents.
120	2½ inch.	3⅝ inch.	7	2.4 lbs.	Retarder.	10 cents.
130	2¼ inch.	4¼ inch.	8	3.2 lbs.	Retiform.	10 cents.
132	2⅝ inch.	4¼ inch.	7	3.0 lbs.	Retorter.	10 cents.

No. 110 Used on		No. 120 Used on		No. 130 Used on		No. 132 Used on	
Granite	No. 14.	Granite	Nos. 14½, 15.	Ohio Valley, Nos. 10, 11, 12		American, Nos. 13,19,20,40	
		Granite Vineyard	No. 15.	Potato Digger	No. 12.	Dandy	Nos. 9,10.
		Ideal	No. 26.			Ideal	No. 28.
		Lone Star Stock	No. 18.				
		Ohio Valley	Nos. 8, 9.				
		Old Style New Ground	No. 1.				

B. F. AVERY & SONS. LOUISVILLE, KY.

MALLEABLE CLEVISES.

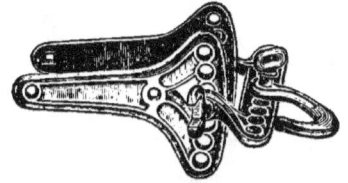

JAW CLEVIS. USED ON WOOD BEAM.

Number.	Thickness of Beam.	Center to Center of Beam Holes.	Holes in Jaw.	Holes in Cross Clevis.	Approximate Weight.	Code Word.	Price per pound.
370	2¾ inch.	3¾ inch.	7	8	4 lbs.	Retribute.	10 cents.
380	3 inch.	4¾ inch.	7	9	4.7 lbs.	Retroflex.	10 cents.
310	3 inch.	5½ inch.	6	10	6.2 lbs.	Retrovert.	10 cents.

No. 370 Used On	No. 380 Used On
Blackland .... Nos. 62X, 62¼X, 63X, 30-0, 40-0.	Blackland .... Nos. 64X, 65X.
New Clipper .... Nos. 10, 12.	New Clipper .... Nos. 14, 16.
Pony Series .... Nos. C. O., D. O.	Pony Series .... No. E. O.
Rainbow .... Nos. 408, 409, 410.	Western .... No. E. O.
Western .... Nos. C. O., D. O.	

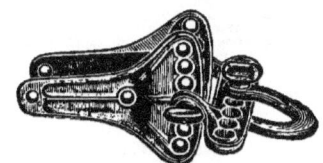

JAW CLEVIS. USED ON STEEL BEAM.

Number.	Thickness of Beam.	Center to Center of Beam Holes.	Holes in Jaw.	Holes in Cross Clevis.	Approximate Weight.	Code Word.	Price per pound.
R. B. S. B.	½ or ⅝ inch.	3¾ inch.	6	6	3.6 lbs.	Revealer.	10 cents.
220	½ or ⅝ inch.	3⅝ inch.	6	8	4.5 lbs.	Revenger.	10 cents.

No. R. B. S. B. Used On	No. 220 Used On
Big Bolt .... Nos. 107, 108, 109.	American .... Nos. B, 10, 13, 19, 20, 40.
Blackland .... Nos. 61X, 20-0.	Blackland .... Nos. 62X, 62¼X, 63X, 64X, 65X, 65X.
Middle Burster .... Nos. 9, 10, 12.	Blackland .... Nos. 30-0, 40-0.
Ohio Valley .... No. 8.	Imprvd Blackland .. Nos 7, 8, 9, 10, 11, 12.
Pony Series .... Nos. Pony A. O., B. O.	Middle Burster ..... Nos. 14, 16.
Western .... Nos. Pony A. O., B. O.	New Clipper .... Nos. 10, 12.
	Ohio Valley .... Nos. 9, 10, 11, 12.
	Pony Series .... Nos. C. O., D. O., E. O.
	Rainbow .... Nos. 407, 408, 409, 410.
	Western .... Nos. C. O., D. O., E. O.

JAW CLEVIS—THREE HORSE. USED ON STEEL BEAM.

Number.	Thickness of Beam.	Center to Center of Beam Holes.	Holes in Jaw.	Holes in Cross Clevis.	Approximate Weight.	Code Word.	Price per pound.
321	⅝ inch.	3¼ inch.	6	11	6.5 lbs.	Reverer.	10 cents.

Used on New Clipper Steel Beam Plows Nos. 14, 16.

CROSS HEADS AND PINS.

Number.	For Clevis Number.	Holes in Cross Clevis.	Distance Between Jaws Inside.	Diameter of Pin.	Approximate Weight.	Code Word.	Price per pound.
370	370	8	3¼ inch.	½ inch.	1.5 lbs.	Revert.	10 cents.
380	380	9	3 13-16 inch.	9-16 inch.	1.6 lbs.	Revest.	10 cents.
310	310	10	4 15-16 inch.	9-16 inch.	1.8 lbs.	Review.	10 cents.
R. B. S. B.	R. B. S. B.	6	2 3-16 inch.	½ inch.	1 lb.	Revile.	10 cents.
220	220	8	3 inch.	½ inch.	1.4 lbs.	Reviser.	10 cents.

B. F. AVERY & SONS.   LOUISVILLE, KY.

MALLEABLE AND WROUGHT CLEVISES.

DOUBLE SHOVEL CLEVISES.
Used on Steel Beam.

Number.	Center to Center of Beam Holes.	Approximate Wt.	Code Word.	Price per lb.
I.B.D.S., 5 Hole, with Straight Shackle	1¾ inch.	1.2 lbs.	Revival.	10 cents
I.B.D.S., 5 Hole, with Hook Shackle	1¾ inch.	1.4 lbs.	Reviver.	10 cents
K. 49, with Hook	1¾ inch.	0.8 lb.	Revolt.	10 cents

I.B.D.S., 5 Hole, with Straight Shackle, used on Double Shovels Nos. 5, 6, and 7.
I.B.D.S., 5 Hole, with Hook Shackle, used on Double Shovel No. 10.
K. 49, with Hook, used on Wallis Steel Frame Side Harrow.

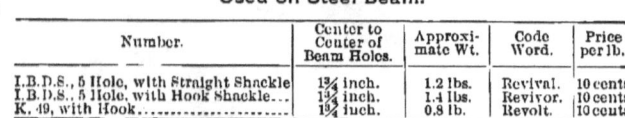

SHACKLE CLEVISES.

Number.	Size Inside.	Approximate Weight.	Code Word.	Price per lb.
94, Straight	¾ x 1¾ inch.	0.5 lb.	Revolve.	10 cents.
95, Straight	⅞ x 2 inch.	0.6 lb.	Reward.	10 cents.
130, Straight	1 x 2 inch.	0.7 lb.	Reynard.	10 cents.
180, Straight	1 x 2½ inch.	1.0 lb.	Rhetian.	10 cents.
99, Twisted	⅞ x 2½ inch.	0.8 lb.	Rhino.	10 cents.
E. 216, Twisted	¾ x 2½ inch.	1.0 lb.	Rhodium.	10 cents.
K. 68, Hook			Rhombic.	10 cents.
K. 149, Hook			Rhus.	10 cents.

No. 94. Used on Clevises Nos. I.B.D.S. and 110, Planter's Friend No. 9, and Louisville Planters.
No. 95. Used on Clevises Nos. 120, 130, and 132.
No. 180. Used on Clevis No. 180.
No. 99. Used on Clevises Nos. R. B. S. B., and 220.
No. E. 216. Used on Clevises Nos. 370, 380, and 321.
No. K. 68. Used on Truckers' Cultivators.
No. K. 149. Used on I.B.D.S. Clevis, 5 Hole, with Hook Shackle.

DOUBLETREE CLEVISES.

Number.	Size Inside.	Approximate Weight.	Code Word.	Price per lb.
K.108, with Screw Pin	1⅝ x 3 inch.	0.7 lb.	Rial.	10 cents.
K.104, with Screw Pin	2 x 5 inch.	1.2 lb.	Riban.	10 cents.
K.110, with Plain Pin	1⅝ x 3 inch.	0.7 lbs.	Ribwort.	10 cents.
K.106, with Plain Pin	2 x 5 inch.	1.2 lbs.	Riches.	10 cents.

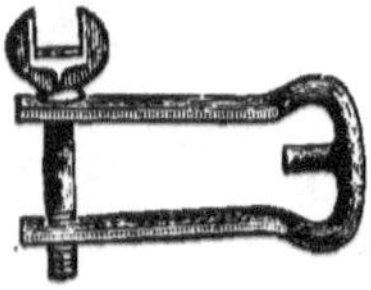

WROUGHT CLEVIS. ONE HORSE.

Number.	Thickness of Beam.	Center of Wrench to End of Beam.	Approximate Weight.	Code Word.	Price per lb.
1	2 inch.	4 inch.	1.2 lbs.	Ricochet.	12 cents.

WROUGHT CLEVIS. TWO HORSE.

Number.	Thickness of Beam.	Center of Wrench to Center of Pin.	Approximate Weight.	Code Word.	Price per lb.
2	2½ inch.	4¼ inch.	2.0 lbs.	Riddler.	12 cents.
3	2¾ inch.	4½ inch.	2.8 lbs.	Ridicule.	12 cents.

No. 2. Used on Improved New Ground Plows Nos. 1 and 2.
No. 2. Used on Samson New Ground Plows Nos. 8 and 9.
No. 2. Used on Jumping Shovel Plows Nos. 15 and 16.

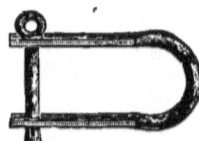

KENTUCKY WROUGHT BULL-TONGUE CLEVIS.

Number.	Thickness of Beam.	Center of Pin to End of Beam.	Approximate Weight.	Code Word.	Price per lb.
1	2½ inch.	4¼ inch.	1.3 lbs.	Ridotto.	12 cents.

Used on Side Harrow.

STEEL PLOW SHAPES.

On the following pages we give a complete list of sizes, styles, and shapes of our stock blades. Outlines showing the curves of each blade are given, so that every dealer will have the means of accurately selecting just what is wanted, avoiding the annoyance and delay occasioned by getting unsuitable shapes through errors in ordering.

The approximate weight of each size of blade is given as a guide to dealers, both in ordering and in fixing their selling price per piece, but we invariably sell and invoice all blades sold by the pound at their ACTUAL weight.

All small and medium-weight blades are wired twelve (12) to a bundle; large, heavy blades six (6) to a bundle.

SPECIAL NOTE—Specify in each and every order whether BLACK (unpolished) or POLISHED blades are wanted.

All orders for stock blades as herein enumerated can be promptly filled.

We are in position to make any special blades required by the trade, if quantity is sufficient and ample time is given us to make them.

LIST OF EXTRAS.

BLACK FINISHED STEEL PLOW SHAPES.

SCOOTERS.

Page.			Advance.
128.	No. 13.	Over 2½ in. wide, 10 in. or longer,	Base Price.
		Over 2½ in. wide, under 10 in. long..	¼c.
		2½ in. wide, 10 in. or longer..........	½c.
		2½ in. wide, under 10 in. long	¾c.
		Under 2½ in. wide, 10 in. or longer	1c.
		Under 2½ in. wide, under 10 in. long	1¼c.

SOLIO SWEEPS.

122.	No. 1, Magnolia	
122.	No. 2, Mississippi	
122.	No. 3, Alabama	¼c.
123.	No. 101, Tarver..............................	
123.	No. 104, Star..............................	
123.	No. 111, Texas..............................	

WING SWEEPS.

124.	No. 4, Dixon	2½c.
123.	No. 5, Farquhar..............................	1c.

HEEL SWEEPS.

124.	No. 6, Curved	1½c.
124.	No. 112, Georgia..............................	

STRAIGHT SHOVELS.

125.	No. 7, Avery,	under 9 in. long..........	¾c.
125.	No. 7, Memphis,	9 in. or longer............	½c.
125.	No. 8, Mississippi,		

CORN SHOVELS.

125.	No. 113, Texas,	under 9 in. long....	1¼c.
125.	No. 9, Georgia,	9 in. or longer.......	1c.
126.	No. 10, Narrow Point,		
126.	No. 11, Round Point		
126.	No. 114, Stapler..............................		1c.
127.	No. 115, Barney		
127.	No. 103, Mountain		

BULL TONGUES.

127.	No. 102, Mountain..............................	¾c.
127.	No. 107, Star, } See below.	
128.	No. 12, Regular, }	
	Over 2½ in. wide, 10 in. or longer	¾c.
	Over 2½ in. wide, under 10 in. long	1c.
	2½ in. wide, 10 in. or longer.......	1¼c.
	2½ in. wide, under 10 in. long...	1½c.
	Under 2½ in. wide, 10 in. or longer..............................	1¾c.
	Under 2½ in. wide, under 10 in. long	2c.

TURNING SHOVELS.

129.	No. 106, Star..............................	1½c.
129.	No. 14, No Wing..............................	¾c.
129.	No. 17, Taper..............................	
130.	No. 15, Brown..............................	
130.	No. 16, Southwestern	
130.	No. 117, Barber	1¼c.
131.	No. 118, Texas..............................	
131.	No. 136, Perfect	

SCRAPER BLADES—POLISHED.

Page.		Advance.
131.	No. 19A, Avery	2c.
131.	No. 19, Improved..............................	2¼c.
131.	No. 119, Mitchell	2c.

DOUBLE SHOVEL BLADES—POLISHED.

132.	No. 120, Malta,		
132.	No. 108, Diamond Point,	With bolts	2c.
132.	No. 121, Blackland,	No bolts.............	1½c.
132.	No. 122, Universal,		

DOUBLE SHOVEL CALF TONGUES—POLISHED.

133.	No. 41, Oval Point,	With bolts	2¼c.
133.	No. 124, Diamond Point,	No bolts.............	2c.
133.	No. 125, Universal,		

CULTIVATOR WING SWEEPS—POLISHED.

137.	No. 46, Drane-Dixon	With bolts..................	2¾c.
		No bolts....................	2½c.

SINGLE SHOVEL BLADES—POLISHED.

134.	No. 130, W. B., Single Shovel Blades	
134.	No. 131, W. B., Single Shovel Bull Tongues	Special.
134.	No. 132, Wing Shovel Blades, Hinged	
134.	No. 133, Jumping Shovel Blades..............	

DOUBLE MOLDBOARD BLADES—POLISHED.

135.	No. 134, Lone Star Burster........................	Special.
135.	No. 135, Holz Lone Star Burster	

CULTIVATOR BLANKS—POLISHED.

135.	Nos. 137, 138, Diamond Point......................	Special.

WHEELED CULTIVATOR BLADES—POLISHED.

135.	No. 25, Plain Diamond Point Blades.......	
135.	No. 36, Plain Diamond Point Blades........	
136.	Nos. 26, 27, Twisted Dia. Pt. Blades.........	
136.	No. 35, Corn Shovel..............................	
136.	No. 28, Oval Blades	
136.	Nos. 47, 48, Wallis Combination Shovel...	
137.	No. 37, Dia. Point Calf Tongues..............	
137.	No. 29, Oval Calf Tongues.....................	
137.	No. 38, Dia. Point Calf Tongues..............	Special.
138.	No. 39, Solid Cultivator Sweeps..............	
138.	Nos. 42, 43, Wallis, jr., Combinat'n Sweeps	
138.	Nos. 44, 45, Wallis, jr., Shovel Sweeps......	
138.	Nos. 33, 34, Wallis, jr., Turn. Shovels.......	
139.	Nos. 40, 41, Wallis, jr., Turning Shovels (Diamond Point)	
139.	Nos. 31, 32, Wallis, jr., Scraper Blades	
139.	Nos. 23, 24, Improved Scraper Blades......	

TRUCKERS' CULTIVATOR BLADES—POLISHED.

140.	Nos. 1, 2, 3A, Diamond Point Shovels......	
140.	Nos. 4, 5A, Half Dixon Sweeps (small)....	
140.	Nos. 6, 7A, Half Dixon Sweeps (large).....	Special.
140.	No. 8A, Dixon Sweeps............................	
140.	No. 10A, Rear Hilling Blades...................	
140.	No. 11, 12A, Side Hilling Blades.	

Extra for Bluing Black Shapes..............................	¼c. Advance.
Extra for Polishing and Bluing Black Shapes	½c. "
Extra for Painting Backs Red..............................	¼c. "

SOLID SWEEPS.

MAGNOLIA SWEEP.

(One ¾ in. square hole.)

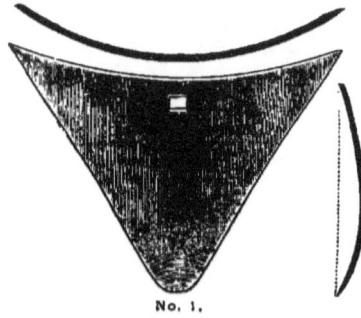

No. 1.

SIZE.	APPROXIMATE WEIGHT.	CODE WORD.
10 x 9 x 3/16	2.5 lbs	Sabian.
12 x 9 x 3/16	3.1 "	Saccule.
12 x 10 x 3/16	3.5 "	Sackage.
14 x 9 x 3/16	3.5 "	Sacrat.
14 x 10 x 3/16	4 "	Sacrist.
16 x 9 x 3/16	4.2 "	Saddler.
16 x 10 x 3/16	4.7 "	Safelier.
16 x 12 x 3/16	6.1 "	Sagamore.
18 x 9 x 3/16	5 "	Sago.
18 x 10 x 3/16	6.2 "	Sailor.
18 x 12 x 3/16	7 "	Saker.
20 x 10 x 3/16	6.7 "	Saleratus.
20 x 12 x 3/16	7.6 "	Salinous.
22 x 12 x 3/16	8.1 "	Sally.
24 x 12 x 3/16	8.6 "	Salsilla.

MISSISSIPPI SWEEP.

(One ¾ in. square hole.)

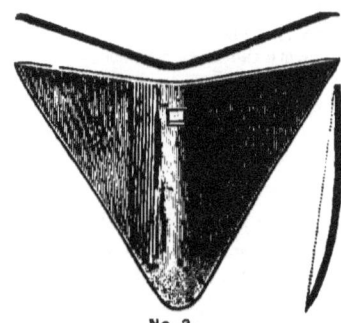

No. 2.

SIZE.	APPROXIMATE WEIGHT.	CODE WORD.
12 x 10 x 3/16	3.5 lbs	Saltern.
14 x 10 x 3/16	4.1 "	Salty.
16 x 10 x 3/16	4.5 "	Salvage.
16 x 11 x 3/16	5 "	Sambo.
18 x 11 x 3/16	5.8 "	Sampler.
20 x 12 x 3/16	7.2 "	Sanction.

ALABAMA SWEEP.

(One ¾ in. square hole.)

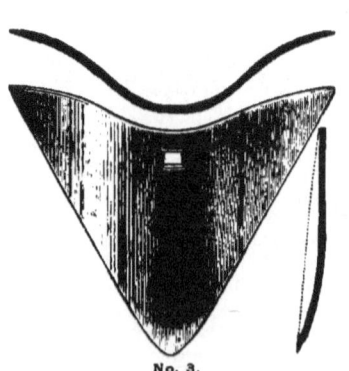

No. 3.

SIZE.	APPROXIMATE WEIGHT.	CODE WORD.
10 x 9 x 3/16	2.8 lbs	Sanded.
12 x 8 x 3/16	2.7 "	Saneness.
12 x 9 x 3/16	3.3 "	Sanicle.
14 x 9 x 3/16	3.7 "	Sapajo.
14 x 10 x 3/16	4.2 "	Sapphire.
16 x 9 x 3/16	4.3 "	Sarcenet.
16 x 10 x 3/16	4.9 "	Sardonic.
16 x 11 x 3/16	5.2 "	Sashoon.
18 x 10 x 3/16	5.4 "	Satellite.
18 x 11 x 3/16	6.2 "	Satirist.
18 x 12 x 3/16	6.7 "	Sative.
20 x 11 x 3/16	7 "	Saturnist.
20 x 12 x 3/16	7.4 "	Saunter.
22 x 12 x 3/16	8 "	Savant.
24 x 12 x 3/16	8.6 "	Savor.

B. F. AVERY & SONS. LOUISVILLE, KY.

SOLID SWEEPS.

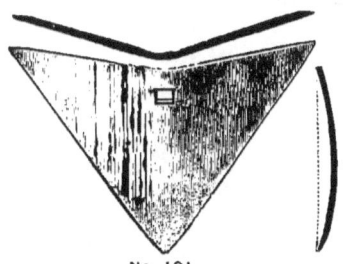

No. 101.

TARVER SWEEP.

(One ¾ in. square hole.)

SIZE.	APPROXIMATE WEIGHT.	CODE WORD.
10 x 9 x $\frac{3}{16}$	2.4 lbs	Sawdust.
12 x 9 x $\frac{3}{16}$	2.8 "	Saxon.
14 x 9 x $\frac{3}{16}$	3.4 "	Scabbard.
16 x 9 x $\frac{3}{16}$	3.8 "	Scaglia.
18 x 9 x $\frac{3}{16}$	4.4 "	Scalene.

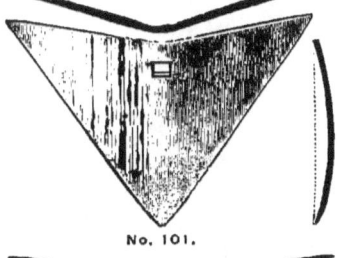

No. 104.

STAR SWEEP.

(One ¾ in. square hole.)

SIZE.	APPROXIMATE WEIGHT.	CODE WORD.
10 x 7½ x ¼	2.7 lbs	Scalper.
12 x 7½ x ¼	3.4 "	Scandal.
14 x 8½ x ¼	4.3 "	Scantle.
16 x 9½ x ¼	5.5 "	Scaphite.
18 x 10½ x ¼	6.8 "	Scared.

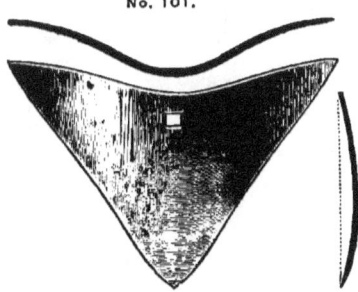

No. 111.

TEXAS (Coleman) SWEEP.

(One ¾ in. square hole.)

SIZE.	APPROXIMATE WEIGHT.	CODE WORD.
12 x 9 x $\frac{3}{16}$	3.3 lbs	Scarlet.
14 x 9 x $\frac{3}{16}$	3.8 "	Scatter.
16 x 9 x $\frac{3}{16}$	4.3 "	Scenery.
18 x 9 x $\frac{3}{16}$	4.8 "	Sceptred.
20 x 10 x $\frac{3}{16}$	5.5 "	Schene.

WING SWEEPS.

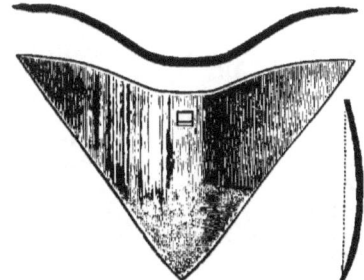

No. 5.

FARQUHAR SWEEP.

(One ¾ in. square hole.)

SIZE.	APPROXIMATE WEIGHT.	CODE WORD.
10 x 9 x $\frac{3}{16}$	2.6 lbs	Scholar.
12 x 9 x $\frac{3}{16}$	3 "	Scholium.
14 x 9 x $\frac{3}{16}$	3.5 "	Schooner.
14 x 10 x $\frac{3}{16}$	4 "	Scincoid.
16 x 10 x $\frac{3}{16}$	4.5 "	Scissile.
16 x 11 x $\frac{3}{16}$	5.1 "	Scoffer.
18 x 11 x $\frac{3}{16}$	5.5 "	Sconce.
18 x 12 x $\frac{3}{16}$	6.2 "	Scorch.
20 x 12 x $\frac{3}{16}$	6.9 "	Scorner.

B. F. AVERY & SONS. LOUISVILLE, KY.

WING SWEEPS.

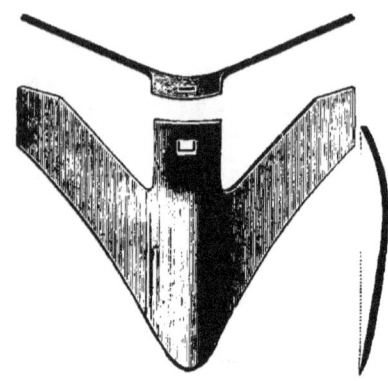

No. 4.

DIXON SWEEP.

(One ¾ in. square hole.)

SIZE.	APPROXIMATE WEIGHT.	CODE WORD.
10 x 9 x ³⁄₁₆	2.7 lbs	Scorza.
12 x 9 x ³⁄₁₆	3.1 "	Scotist.
12 x 10 x ³⁄₁₆	3.6 "	Scourer.
14 x 10 x ³⁄₁₆	4.2 "	Scrabble.
14 x 12 x ³⁄₁₆	5 "	Scrannel.
16 x 10 x ³⁄₁₆	4.8 "	Scratcher.
16 x 12 x ³⁄₁₆	5.6 "	Screen.
18 x 12 x ³⁄₁₆	6.1 "	Scribbler.
18 x 14 x ³⁄₁₆	6.8 "	Scrivener.
20 x 14 x ³⁄₁₆	7.5 "	Scruple.
22 x 15 x ³⁄₁₆	8.4 "	Scrutiny.
24 x 15 x ³⁄₁₆	9.2 "	Sculler.

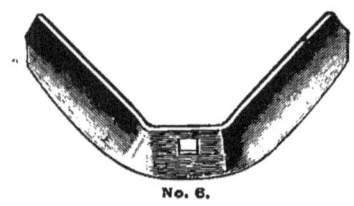

No. 6.

CURVED HEEL SWEEP.

(One ¾ in. square hole.)

SIZE.	APPROXIMATE WEIGHT.	CODE WORD.
8 x 2½ x ¼	1.2 lbs	Scurrile.
10 x 2½ x ¼	1.7 "	Scuttle.
12 x 2½ x ¼	2.4 "	Seafaring.
14 x 2½ x ¼	2.8 "	Seamew.
16 x 2½ x ¼	3.2 "	Searuff.
18 x 2½ x ¼	3.6 "	Seaward.
20 x 2½ x ¼	4 "	Seance.
22 x 2½ x ¼	4.4 "	Season.
24 x 2½ x ¼	5 "	Sebacic.
26 x 2½ x ¼	5.5 "	Seconder.

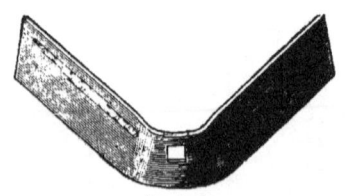

No. 112.

GEORGIA HEEL SWEEP.

(One ¾ in. square hole.)

SIZE.	APPROXIMATE WEIGHT.	CODE WORD.
8 x 3 x ³⁄₁₆	1.1 lbs	Secretary.
10 x 3 x ³⁄₁₆	1.6 "	Sectator.
12 x 3 x ³⁄₁₆	2.3 "	Securer.
14 x 3 x ³⁄₁₆	2.7 "	Sedulous.
16 x 3 x ³⁄₁₆	3 "	Seedling.
18 x 3 x ³⁄₁₆	3.4 "	Seemer.
20 x 3 x ³⁄₁₆	3.8 "	Segment.
22 x 3 x ³⁄₁₆	4.2 "	Seine.
24 x 3 x ³⁄₁₆	4.8 "	Selector.
26 x 3 x ³⁄₁₆	5.3 "	Selfish.

B. F. AVERY & SONS  LOUISVILLE, KY.

STRAIGHT SHOVELS.

AVERY OR MEMPHIS SHOVEL.
(One ¾ in. square hole.)

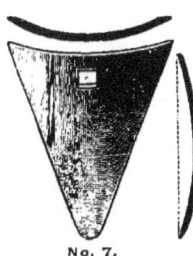

No. 7.

SIZE.	APPROXIMATE WEIGHT.	CODE WORD.
6 x 8 x ¼	1.7 lbs	Semblance.
6 x 9 x ¼	2 "	Semilunar.
7 x 8 x ¼	2.1 "	Semiotic.
7 x 9 x ¼	2.4 "	Semoule.
8 x 8 x ¼	2.4 "	Senior.
8 x 9 x ¼	2.7 "	Sensorial.
8 x 10 x ¼	3 "	Sentient.
10 x 8 x ¼	3 "	Sepiment.
10 x 9 x ¼	3.4 "	Septical.
10 x 10 x ¼	3.7 "	Septum.
12 x 10 x ¼	4.5 "	Sequester.

MISSISSIPPI SHOVEL.
(One ¾ in. square hole.)

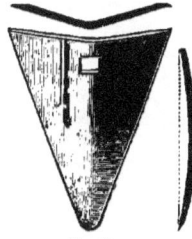

No. 8.

SIZE.	APPROXIMATE WEIGHT.	CODE WORD.
6 x 8 x ¼	1.8 lbs	Seraphim.
8 x 9 x ¼	2.7 "	Serfdom.
8 x 10 x ¼	3 "	Serin.
10 x 10 x ¼	3.6 "	Serpent.
12 x 10 x ¼	4.4 "	Serried.

CORN SHOVELS.

GEORGIA SHOVEL.
(One ¾ in. square hole.)

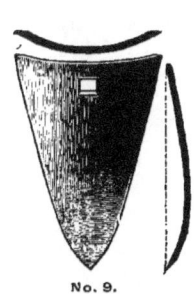

No. 9.

SIZE.	APPROXIMATE WEIGHT.	CODE WORD.
5 x 8 x ¼	1.7 lbs	Servitor.
6 x 8 x ¼	2.1 "	Session.
6 x 9 x ¼	2.3 "	Settee.
7 x 9 x ¼	2.6 "	Severance.
7 x 10 x ¼	2.9 "	Sexangle.
8 x 9 x ¼	3 "	Shabrack.
8 x 10 x ¼	3.2 "	Shaffle.
8 x 11 x ¼	3.5 "	Shaker.
9 x 11 x ¼	3.9 "	Shaly.
10 x 10 x ¼	3.7 "	Shamer.
10 x 11 x ¼	4 "	Shapely.
10 x 12 x ¼	4.5 "	Sharer.

TEXAS SHOVEL.
(One ¾ in. square hole.)

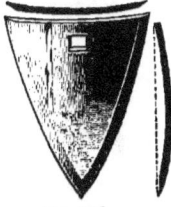

No. 113.

SIZE.	APPROXIMATE WEIGHT.	CODE WORD.
5 x 8 x ¼	1.6 lbs	Shatter.
5 x 9 x ¼	2 "	Shawn.
6 x 9 x ¼	2.4 "	Shearer.
7 x 9 x ¼	3 "	Sheen.
8 x 9 x ¼	3.8 "	Shekei.

B. F. AVERY & SONS.  LOUISVILLE, KY.

CORN SHOVELS.

NARROW POINT SHOVEL.

(One ¾ in. square hole.)

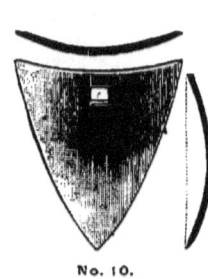

No. 10.

SIZE.	APPROXIMATE WEIGHT.	CODE WORD.
5 x 8 x ¼	1.9 lbs	Shellac.
5 x 9 x ¼	2.1 "	Shemite.
6 x 8 x ¼	2.2 "	Sherry.
6 x 9 x ¼	2.5 "	Shilling.
6 x 10 x ¼	2.8 "	Shipless.
7 x 8 x ¼	2.4 "	Shirley.
7 x 9 x ¼	2.8 "	Shivery.
7 x 10 x ¼	3.2 "	Shoer.
7 x 11 x ¼	3.7 "	Shore.
8 x 9 x ¼	3.2 "	Shortner.
8 x 10 x ¼	3.6 "	Shotted.
8 x 11 x ¼	4 "	Shoveler.
9 x 11 x ¼	4.5 "	Shred.
10 x 11 x ¼	5 "	Shrieker.
11 x 12 x ¼	6.2 "	Shrivel.
12 x 12 x ¼	6.8 "	Shrubby.

ROUND POINT SHOVEL.

(One ¾ in. square hole.)

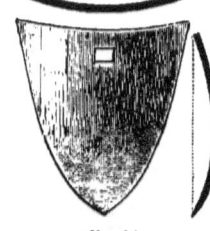

No. 11.

SIZE.	APPROXIMATE WEIGHT.	CODE WORD.
5 x 8 x ¼	2.2 lbs	Shuffle.
5 x 9 x ¼	2.4 "	Shutter.
6 x 9 x ¼	2.8 "	Siccative.
7 x 9 x ¼	3.2 "	Sideling.
7 x 10 x ¼	3.6 "	Siege.
8 x 9 x ¼	3.7 "	Sigma.
8 x 10 x ¼	4.1 "	Signally.
9 x 10 x ¼	4.7 "	Silence.
10 x 11 x ¼	5.7 "	Silicify.

STAPLER SHOVEL.

(One ¾ in. square hole.)

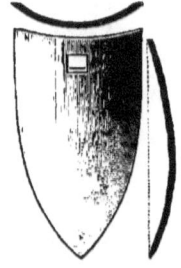

No. 114.

SIZE.	APPROXIMATE WEIGHT.	CODE WORD.
5 x 11 x ¼	3.3 lbs	Sillabub.
6 x 11 x ¼	3.8 "	Silvered.
6 x 12 x ¼	4.2 "	Simious.
7 x 12 x ¼	4.7 "	Simpleton.
8 x 12 x ¼	5 "	Sinaitic.
9 x 12 x ¼	5.5 "	Sinew.
10 x 13 x ¼	6.5 "	Singling.

CORN SHOVELS.

MOUNTAIN SHOVEL.

(One ¾ in. square hole.)

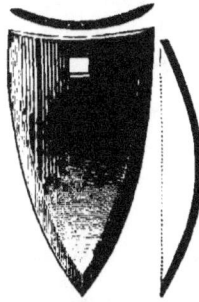

No. 103.

SIZE.	APPROXIMATE WEIGHT.	CODE WORD.
6 x 12 x 5/16	3.9 lbs	Sinistrous.
7 x 12 x 5/16	4.5 "	Sinter.
7 x 13 x 5/16	5 "	Sirdar.
7 x 14 x 5/16	5.7 "	Siskin.
8 x 12 x 5/16	5.2 "	Siva.
8 x 13 x 5/16	5.7 "	Sizel.
8 x 14 x 5/16	6.2 "	Skelly.
9 x 13 x 5/16	6.3 "	Skewer.
9 x 14 x 5/16	7 "	Skimmer.
9 x 15 x 5/16	7.8 "	Skipper.

BARNEY SHOVEL.

(One ¾ in. square hole.)

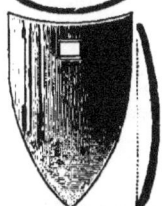

No. 115.

SIZE.	APPROXIMATE WEIGHT.	CODE WORD.
5 x 9 x ¼	2.6 lbs	Skirting.
6 x 9 x ¼	3 "	Skyey.
6 x 10 x ¼	3.4 "	Slaggy.
7 x 9 x ¼	3.5 "	Slank.
7 x 10 x ¼	3.9 "	Slater.
8 x 9 x ¼	4 "	Slavonic.
8 x 10 x ¼	4.4 "	Sleeky.
9 x 10 x ¼	4.8 "	Sleid.

BULL TONGUES.

STAR BULL TONGUE.

(One ¾ in. square hole.)

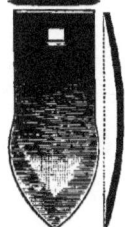

No. 107.

SIZE.	APPROXIMATE WEIGHT.	CODE WORD.
2½ x 8 x ⅜	1.5 lbs	Slice.
3 x 8 x ⅜	2 "	Slighter.
3 x 9 x ⅜	2.4 "	Slipper.
3 x 10 x ⅜	2.8 "	Slogan.
3½ x 9 x ⅜	2.9 "	Slough.
4 x 9 x ⅜	3.2 "	Sluggard.
4 x 10 x ⅜	3.4 "	Slush.

MOUNTAIN BULL TONGUE.

(One ¾ in. square hole.)

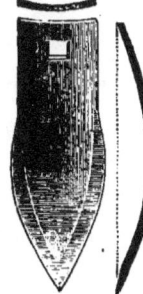

No. 102.

SIZE.	APPROXIMATE WEIGHT.	CODE WORD.
3½ x 12 x ½	4.5 lbs	Smallish.
3½ x 13 x ½	5 "	Smarter.
4 x 12 x ½	5.4 "	Smelter.
4 x 13 x ½	5.9 "	Smite.
4 x 14 x ½	6.5 "	Smoker.
4½ x 13 x ½	6.5 "	Smoother.
4½ x 14 x ½	7 "	Smuggler.

B. F. AVERY & SONS. LOUISVILLE, KY.

BULL TONGUES.
REGULAR.
(One ¾ in. square hole.)

SIZE.	APPROXIMATE WEIGHT.	CODE WORD.
2 x 8 x ⅜	1.4 lbs	Snail.
2½ x 9 x ⅜	1.9 "	Snarer.
3 x 8 x ⅜	2.2 "	Sneaker.
3 x 9 x ⁵⁄₁₆	2 "	Snicker.
3 x 9 x ⅜	2.4 "	Sniveler.
3 x 10 x ⁵⁄₁₆	2.2 "	Snorer.
3 x 10 x ⅜	2.6 "	Snuffler.
3 x 11 x ⁵⁄₁₆	2.3 "	Soapsuds.
3½ x 9 x ⅜	2.6 "	Socager.
3½ x 10 x ⁵⁄₁₆	2.4 "	Socle.
3½ x 10 x ⅜	2.9 "	Sodium.
3½ x 11 x ⁵⁄₁₆	2.7 "	Softish.
3½ x 11 x ⅜	3.2 "	Soiree.
3½ x 12 x ⅜	3.7 "	Solano.
4 x 9 x ⅜	3 "	Solecist.
4 x 10 x ⅜	3.3 "	Solfa.
4 x 11 x ⁵⁄₁₆	3.1 "	Solidify.
4 x 11 x ⅜	3.7 "	Solo.
4 x 12 x ⁵⁄₁₆	3.5 "	Solver.
4 x 12 x ⅜	4.2 "	Somnific.
4½ x 10 x ⅜	3.9 "	Sonorous.
4½ x 12 x ⁵⁄₁₆	4 "	Soother.
4½ x 12 x ⅜	4.8 "	Sophister.

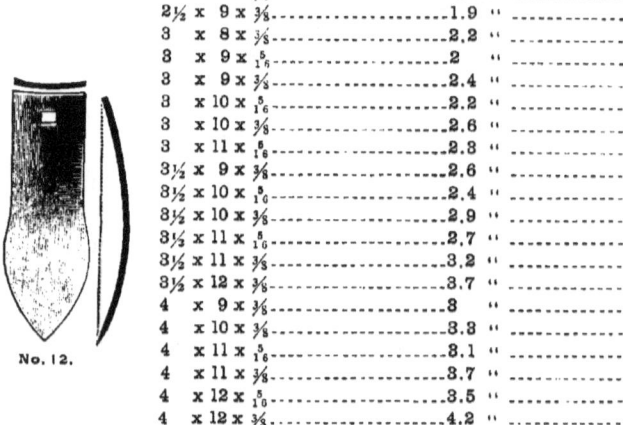

No. 12.

SCOOTERS.
(One ¾ in. square hole.)

SIZE.	APPROXIMATE WEIGHT.	CODE WORD.
3 x 9 x ⅜	2.4 lbs	Soprano.
3 x 11 x ⁵⁄₁₆	2.5 "	Sorgo.
3 x 11 x ⅜	3 "	Sortable.
3½ x 9 x ⅜	2.8 "	Sough.
3½ x 10 x ⅜	3.2 "	Sounded.
3½ x 11 x ⁵⁄₁₆	2.9 "	Souse.
3½ x 11 x ⅜	3.5 "	Sovereign.
3½ x 12 x ⅜	3.8 "	Spacious.
4 x 9 x ⅜	3.2 "	Spandrel.
4 x 10 x ⅜	3.6 "	Spanker.
4 x 11 x ⁵⁄₁₆	3.3 "	Sparing.
4 x 11 x ⅜	3.9 "	Sparoid.
4 x 12 x ⅜	4.2 "	Spathic.
4½ x 11 x ⅜	4.3 "	Spavin.
4½ x 12 x ⅜	4.6 "	Speaker.
5 x 12 x ⅜	5 "	Specie.

No. 13.

B. F. AVERY & SONS. LOUISVILLE, KY.

TURNING SHOVELS.

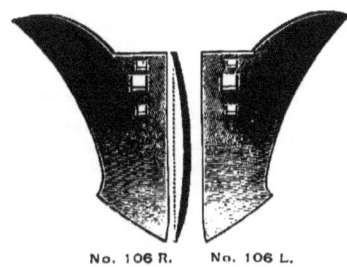

No. 106 R. No. 106 L.

STAR TURNING SHOVEL.

(One ¾ in. square hole.)

(Two ₁⁷₆ in. holes, 2¼ in. from center to center.)

SIZE.	APPROXIMATE WEIGHT.	CODE WORD.
3¼ x 9 x ₁⁵₆ R	3.5 lbs	Specimen.
3¼ x 9 x ₁⁵₆ L	3.5 "	Spectator.

NO WING TURNING SHOVEL.

(One ¾ in. square hole.)

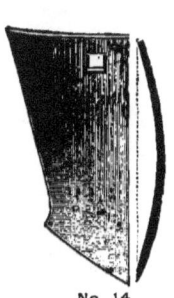

No. 14.

SIZE.	APPROXIMATE WEIGHT.	CODE WORD.
3½ x 11 x ¼	2.7 lbs.	Speculum.
3½ x 12 x ₁⁵₆	3.6 "	Speiss.
4 x 11 x ¼	3.7 "	Spelter.
4 x 12 x ₁⁵₆	4.8 "	Spewer.
4½ x 11 x ¼	3.2 "	Spherical.
4½ x 12 x ₁⁵₆	4.4 "	Spiccato.
5 x 10 x ₁⁵₆	4.3 "	Spider.
5 x 11 x ¼	3.8 "	Spiky.
5 x 11 x ₁⁵₆	4.7 "	Spine.
5 x 12 x ₁⁵₆	5.1 "	Spinster.
5½ x 11 x ₁⁵₆	5.5 "	Spire.
5½ x 12 x ₁⁵₆	6 "	Spirtle.
6 x 12 x ₁⁵₆	6.5 "	Spitted.

TAPER TURNING SHOVEL.

(One ¾ in. square hole.)

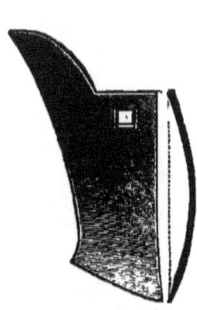

No. 17.

SIZE.	APPROXIMATE WEIGHT.	CODE WORD.
3 x 11 x ¼	3.3 lbs	Spleen.
3½ x 10 x ₁⁷₆	4.2 "	Splice.
3½ x 11 x ₁⁵₆	4.6 "	Splitter.
3½ x 12 x ¼	4.2 "	Sponge.
4 x 10 x ₁³₆	4.8 "	Sponsor.
4 x 11 x ¼	4.2 "	Sporadic.
4 x 12 x ₁⁵₆	5.7 "	Spotless.
4½ x 10 x ₁⁵₆	5.1 "	Spouted.
4½ x 11 x ¼	4.4 "	Sprig.
4½ x 12 x ₁⁵₆	6 "	Springer.
5 x 10 x ₁⁵₆	5.5 "	Sprite.
5 x 11 x ¼	4.8 "	Spume.
5 x 12 x ₁³₆	6.5 "	Spurious.
5½ x 10 x ₁⁵₆	6 "	Sputter.
5½ x 11 x ¼	5.1 "	Squabbler.
5½ x 12 x ₁⁵₆	7 "	Squander.
6 x 10 x ₁⁵₆	6.4 "	Squash.
6 x 12 x ₁⁵₆	7.5 "	Squeeze.
7 x 12 x ₁⁵₆	8.5 "	Squint.

B. F. AVERY & SONS.  LOUISVILLE, KY.

TURNING SHOVELS.

BROWN TURNING SHOVEL.

(One ¾ in. square hole.)

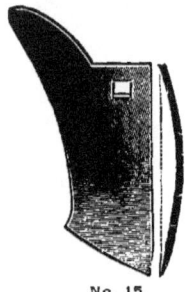

No. 15.

SIZE.	APPROXIMATE WEIGHT.	CODE WORD.
4 x 9 x 5/16	3.9 lbs	Squirter.
4 x 10 x 5/16	4.2 "	Stable.
4½ x 9 x 5/16	4.2 "	Stack.
4½ x 10 x 5/16	4.5 "	Staffier.
5 x 9 x 5/16	5.2 "	Stagirite.
5 x 10 x 5/16	5.4 "	Staith.
5½ x 9 x 5/16	5.9 "	Stale.
5½ x 10 x 5/16	6.1 "	Stall.
6 x 9 x 5/16	6.5 "	Stammer.
6 x 10 x 5/16	6.8 "	Stanch.
6 x 11 x 5/16	7 "	Stang.
6½ x 10 x 5/16	7.2 "	Starfish.
6½ x 11 x 5/16	7.5 "	Starch.
7 x 10 x 5/16	7.5 "	Stark.
7 x 11 x 5/16	7.8 "	Starter.
8 x 11 x 5/16	8 "	Starve.

SOUTHWESTERN TURNING SHOVEL.

(One ¾ in. square hole.)

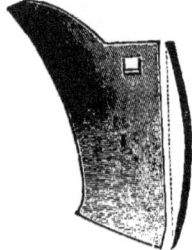

No. 16.

SIZE.	APPROXIMATE WEIGHT.	CODE WORD.
3½ x 9 x 5/16	3.6 lbs	Stately.
4 x 10 x 5/16	4.3 "	Statics.
4½ x 10 x 5/16	4.6 "	Statuary.
5 x 10 x 5/16	5.2 "	Stave.
5 x 11 x 5/16	5.6 "	Steadily.
5½ x 10 x 5/16	5.8 "	Steam.
5½ x 12 x 5/16	6.2 "	Steatite.
6 x 10 x 5/16	6.3 "	Steening.
6 x 12 x 5/16	7 "	Steepy.
7 x 10 x 5/16	7.4 "	Stela.
7 x 12 x 5/16	8.2 "	Stellite.
8 x 12 x 5/16	9 "	Stentor.

BARBER TURNING SHOVEL.

(One ¾ in. square hole.)

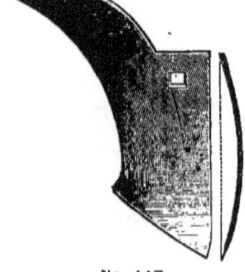

No. 117.

SIZE.	APPROXIMATE WEIGHT.	CODE WORD.
4½ x 9 x 5/16	4.6 lbs	Sterile.
5 x 9 x 5/16	5 "	Sternly.
5 x 11 x 5/16	5.8 "	Steward.
5½ x 10 x 5/16	5.8 "	Stickle.
6 x 10 x 5/16	6.4 "	Stifle.
6 x 11 x 5/16	7 "	Stilar.
6½ x 11 x 5/16	7.6 "	Stilling.
7 x 11 x 5/16	8.2 "	Stimulus.

B. F. AVERY & SONS. LOUISVILLE, KY.

TURNING SHOVELS.

TEXAS TURNING SHOVEL.
(One ¾ in. square hole.)

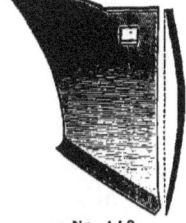

No. 118.

SIZE.	APPROXIMATE WEIGHT.	CODE WORD.
3½ x 9 x $\tfrac{5}{16}$	2.7 lbs	Stinter.
4 x 9 x $\tfrac{5}{16}$	2.9 "	Stipuled.
4½ x 9 x $\tfrac{5}{16}$	3.2 "	Stitch.
5 x 9 x $\tfrac{5}{16}$	3.6 "	Stockade.
5½ x 9 x $\tfrac{5}{16}$	4.4 "	Stoicism.
6 x 9 x $\tfrac{5}{16}$	5 "	Stomachic.

PERFECT TURNING SHOVEL.
(One ¾ in. square hole.)

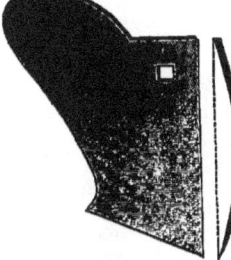

No. 136.

SIZE.	APPROXIMATE WEIGHT.	CODE WORD.
4 x 10 x $\tfrac{5}{16}$	5.2 lbs	Stoned.
4½ x 10 x $\tfrac{5}{16}$	5.8 "	Stooper.
5 x 10 x $\tfrac{5}{16}$	5.9 "	Storax.
5½ x 10 x $\tfrac{5}{16}$	6.3 "	Storming.
6 x 10 x $\tfrac{5}{16}$	6.7 "	Stoutness.
6½ x 10 x $\tfrac{5}{16}$	7 "	Straggler.

SCRAPERS.

AVERY SCRAPER BLADE.
No. 19 A.
(Holes 2¼ inches from center to center. ½ inch, square countersunk.)

SIZE.	APPROXIMATE WEIGHT.	CODE WORD.
14 x 10 x $\tfrac{3}{16}$	6.5 lbs	Strainer.

IMPROVED SCRAPER BLADE.
No. 19.
(Holes 2¼ inches from center to center. ½ inch, square countersunk.)

SIZE.	APPROXIMATE WEIGHT.	CODE WORD.
17 x 11 x $\tfrac{3}{16}$	8.5 lbs	Stranded.

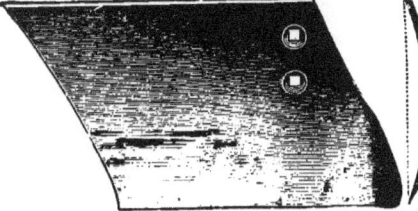

MITCHELL SCRAPER BLADE.
No. 119.
(Holes 2¼ inches from center to center. ½ inch, square countersunk.)

SIZE.	APPROXIMATE WEIGHT.	CODE WORD.
14 x 10 x $\tfrac{3}{16}$	8.1 lbs	Strass.

B. F. AVERY & SONS. LOUISVILLE, KY.

DOUBLE SHOVEL BLADES.

MALTA DOUBLE SHOVEL BLADE.
With either one or two holes.

(Two bolts 2¼ x ⅜, 2¼ in. from center to center. Polished and bolts ground in.)

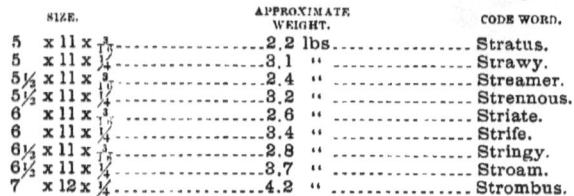

SIZE.	APPROXIMATE WEIGHT.	CODE WORD.
5 x 11 x 3/16	2.2 lbs	Stratus.
5 x 11 x ¼	3.1 "	Strawy.
5½ x 11 x 3/16	2.4 "	Streamer.
5½ x 11 x ¼	3.2 "	Strennous.
6 x 11 x 3/16	2.6 "	Striate.
6 x 11 x ¼	3.4 "	Strife.
6½ x 11 x 3/16	2.8 "	Stringy.
6½ x 11 x ¼	3.7 "	Stroam.
7 x 12 x ¼	4.2 "	Strombus.

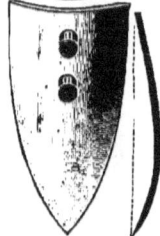

No. 120.
Polished only.

DIAMOND POINT DOUBLE SHOVEL BLADE.
With either one or two holes.

(Two bolts 2¼ x ⅜, 2¼ in. from center to center. Polished and bolts ground in.)

SIZE.	APPROXIMATE WEIGHT.	CODE WORD.
5 x 11 x 3/16	2.4 lbs	Strophe.
5 x 11 x ¼	3.2 "	Struma.
5½ x 11 x 3/16	2.7 "	Stubborn.
5½ x 11 x ¼	3.6 "	Studio.
6 x 11 x ¼	3.7 "	Stumble.

No. 108.
Polished only.

BLACKLAND DOUBLE SHOVEL BLADE.

(Two bolts 2¼ x ⅜, 2¼ in. from center to center. Polished and bolts ground in.)

SIZE.	APPROXIMATE WEIGHT.	CODE WORD.
5½ x 11 x ¼	3.6 lbs	Stupe.

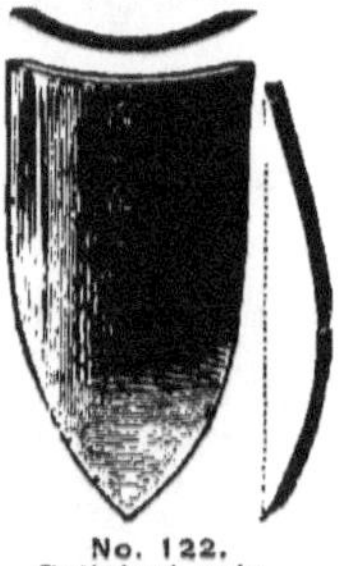

No. 121.
Polished only.

UNIVERSAL DOUBLE SHOVEL BLADE.

(Two bolts 2¼ x ⅜, 2¼ in. from center to center. Polished and bolts ground in.)

SIZE.	APPROXIMATE WEIGHT.	CODE WORD.
6 x 11 x ¼	3.2 lbs	Sturdy.

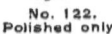

No. 122.
Polished only.

NOTE.—In ordering, specify whether with one or two holes; and whether with or without bolts. When not specified, we ship blades with two holes and bolts.
Bolts for One Hole Blades are 3 x 7-16, round countersunk.

DOUBLE SHOVEL CALF TONGUES.

OVAL POINT DOUBLE SHOVEL CALF TONGUE.
With either one or two holes.

(Two bolts 2¼ x ⅜, 2¼ in. from center to center. Polished and bolts ground in.)

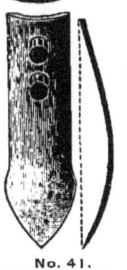

No. 41.
Polished only.

SIZE.	APPROXIMATE WEIGHT.	CODE WORD.
2 x 11 x ¼	1.4 lbs	Stylite.
2 x 11 x ⅜	2.2 "	Suasory.
2½ x 11 x ¼	1.7 "	Subcaudal.
2½ x 11 x 5/16	2 "	Subdolous.
2½ x 11 x ⅜	2.6 "	Suberic.
3 x 11 x ¼	2 "	Subjugate.
3 x 11 x 5/16	2.8 "	Sublime.
3 x 11 x ⅜	3.2 "	Submitter.
3 x 12 x ¼	2.3 "	Suborn.
3½ x 11 x ¼	2.2 "	Subrogate.
3½ x 11 x 5/16	3.2 "	Subserve.
3½ x 12 x ¼	2.5 "	Subsist.
4 x 11 x ¼	2.5 "	Substrate.
4 x 11 x 5/16	3.6 "	Subster.
4 x 12 x ¼	2.8 "	Subtly.

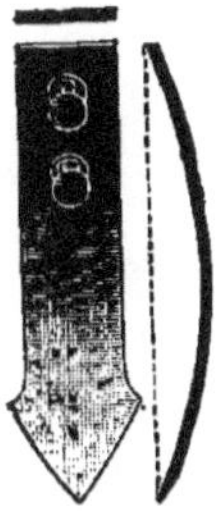

DIAMOND POINT DOUBLE SHOVEL CALF TONGUE.
With either one or two holes.

(Two bolts 2¼ x ⅜, 2¼ in. from center to center. Polished and bolts ground in.)

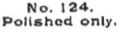

No. 124.
Polished only.

SIZE.	APPROXIMATE WEIGHT.	CODE WORD.
2½ x 11 x ¼	2 lbs	Subvert.
3 x 11 x ¼	2.2 "	Succentor.

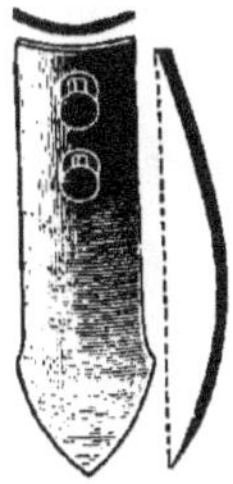

UNIVERSAL DOUBLE SHOVEL CALF TONGUE.

(Two bolts 2¾ x ⅜, 2¼ in. from center to center. Polished and bolts ground in.)

No. 125.
Polished only.

SIZE.	APPROXIMATE WEIGHT.	CODE WORD.
3 x 11 x ¼	2.9 lbs	Succinate.

NOTE.—In ordering, specify whether with one or two holes; and whether with or without bolts. When not specified, we ship blades with two holes and bolts.
Bolts for One Hole Blades are 3 x 7-16, round countersunk.

B. F. AVERY & SONS.　　　　　　LOUISVILLE, KY.

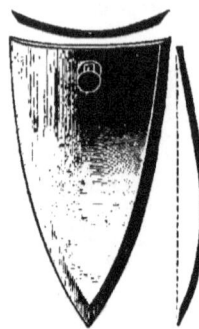

SINGLE SHOVEL BLADES.

WOOD BEAM SINGLE SHOVEL BLADE.

No. 130, Polished only.

(One 4¼ x ⅝ in. bolt, round countersunk. Polished and bolt ground in.)

SIZE.	APPROXIMATE WEIGHT.	CODE WORD.
7 x 14 x ₁⁵⁄₁₆	5.8 lbs	Succory.
8 x 14 x ₁⁵⁄₁₆	6.5 "	Sucket.

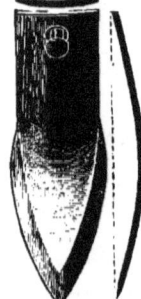

W. B. SINGLE SHOVEL BULL TONGUE.

No. 131, Polished only.

(One 4¼ x ⅝ in. bolt, round countersunk. Polished and bolt ground in.)

SIZE.	APPROXIMATE WEIGHT.	CODE WORD.
4 x 14 x ½	7 lbs	Sudatory.

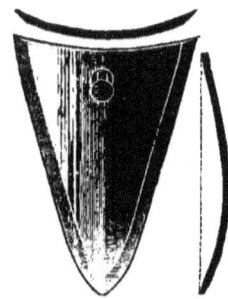

JUMPING SHOVEL BLADE.

No. 133, Polished only.

(One 5 x ⅝ in. bolt, round countersunk. Polished and bolt ground in.)

SIZE.	APPROXIMATE WEIGHT.	CODE WORD.
9 x 12 x ₁⁵⁄₁₆	6 lbs	Sufferer.
12 x 15 x ₁⁵⁄₁₆	9 "	Suffocate.

WING SHOVEL BLADE.
HINGED.
No. 132, Polished only.

(Two 4 x ⅜ in. bolts, 2¼ in. from center to center. Polished and bolts ground in.)

SIZE.	APPROXIMATE WEIGHT.	CODE WORD.
30 in. spread	12 lbs	Sugared.

B. F. AVERY & SONS. LOUISVILLE, KY.

DOUBLE MOLDBOARD BLADES.

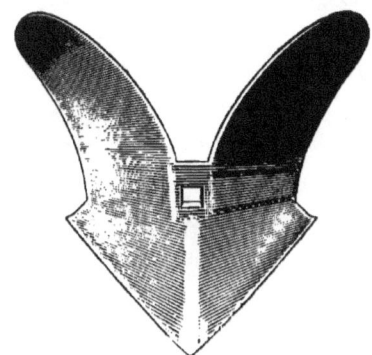

LONE STAR BURSTER BLADE.
No. 134. Polished only.
(One ¾ inch square hole.)

SIZE.	APPROXIMATE WEIGHT.	CODE WORD.
12-inch cut	11½ lbs	Suicidal.

"HOLZ" LONE STAR BURSTER BLADE.
No. 135. Polished only.
(One ¾ inch square hole.)

SIZE.	APPROXIMATE WEIGHT.	CODE WORD.
10 x 16 x 3/16	10 lbs	Suitor.
12 x 16 x 3/16	13.6 "	Sully.

CULTIVATOR BLANKS.

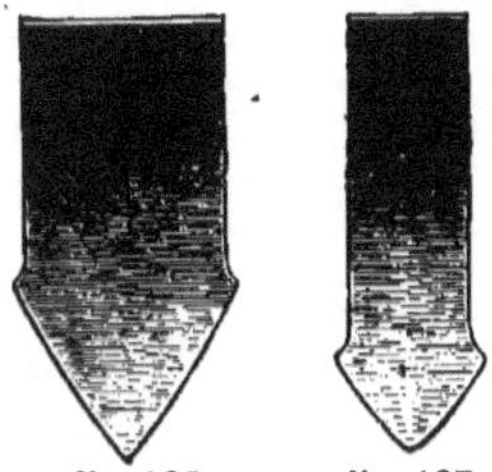

DIAMOND POINT.

	SIZE.	APPROXIMATE WEIGHT.	CODE WORD.
No. 137.	2½ x 7 x ¼	1.2 lbs	Sulphuric.
No. 137.	2½ x 11 x ¼	2 "	Sumless.
No. 137.	3 x 7 x ¼	1.4 "	Summoner.
No. 137.	3 x 11 x ¼	2.2 "	Sunbeam.
No. 138.	5 x 11 x ¼	3.2 "	Sunder.

No. 138. No. 137.
Polished only.

CULTIVATOR BLADES.

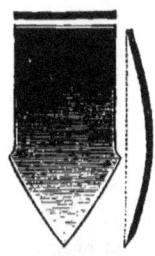

PLAIN DIAMOND POINT BLADE.
With Block.

(Used on Avery Comet and Western Cultivator.)

SIZE.	APPROXIMATE WEIGHT.	CODE WORD.
5 x 10½ x ¼	3.8 lbs	Sunlight.

No. 25. Polished only.

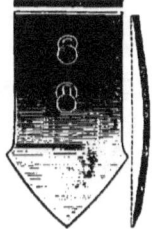

PLAIN DIAMOND POINT BLADE.

(Two 2½ x ⅜ bolts, 2¼ inches from center to center. Used on Avery New South Cultivator.)

SIZE.	APPROXIMATE WEIGHT.	CODE WORD.
5½ x 10½ x ¼	3.3 lbs	Sunset.

No. 36. Polished only.

B. F. AVERY & SONS.   LOUISVILLE, KY.

CULTIVATOR BLADES.

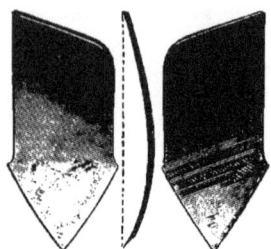

No. 26—R. H.   No. 27—L. H.
Polished only.

TWISTED DIAMOND POINT BLADE.
With Block.

(Used on Avery Comet and Western Cultivators.)

SIZE.	APPROXIMATE WEIGHT.	CODE WORD.
5 x 10½ x ¼ Right	4 lbs	Subperb.
5 x 10½ x ¼ Left	4 lbs	Supernal.

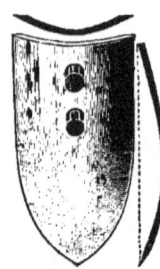

No. 28. Polished only.

OVAL BLADE.

(Holes 2¼ inches from center to center. Bolts 2½ x ⅜, round countersunk. Used on all Avery Cultivators.)

SIZE.	APPROXIMATE WEIGHT.	CODE WORD.
6 x 11 x ¼	4 lbs	Supervene.

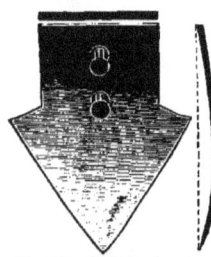

No. 35. Polished only.

CORN SHOVEL.

(Two 2½ x ⅜ bolts, 2¼ inches from center to center. Used on Avery New South Cultivator.)

SIZE.	APPROXIMATE WEIGHT.	CODE WORD.
5½ x 9 x 11 x ¼	4 lbs	Supple.

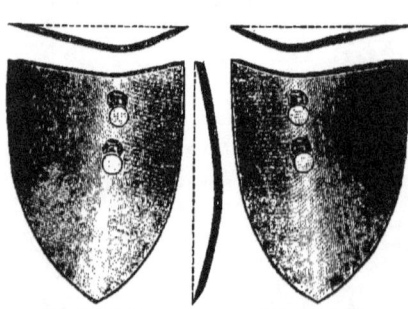

No. 47—R. H.   No. 48—L. H.
Polished only.

WALLIS COMBINATION SHOVEL.

(Holes 2¼ inches from center to center. Bolts 2¼ x $\frac{7}{16}$, round countersunk.)

Used on Avery's Comet Cultivator Nos. 104 and 104X, and on Avery's Revolution Six-Shovel Cultivator.

(No. 47 is also used on No. 7 Double Shovel Cultivator.)

	SIZE.	APPROXIMATE WEIGHT.	CODE WORD.
No. 47, 2	3 x 10 x ¼	3.2 lbs	Suppliant.
No. 47, 2½	4 x 10 x ¼	4 lbs	Support.
No. 47, 3	5 x 10 x ¼	4.4 lbs	Supposer.
No. 48, 2	3 x 10 x ¼	3.2 lbs	Supra.
No. 48, 2½	4 x 10 x ¼	4 lbs	Supreme.
No. 48, 3	5 x 10 x ¼	4.4 lbs	Surole.

B. F. AVERY & SONS.  LOUISVILLE, KY.

CULTIVATOR BLADES.

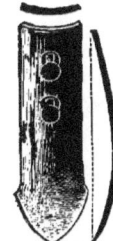

OVAL CALF TONGUE.

(Holes 2¼ in. from center to center. Bolts 2½ x ⅜, round countersunk. Used on all Avery Cultivators.)

SIZE.	APPROXIMATE WEIGHT.	CODE WORD.
3 x 10½ x ¼	2.2 lbs	Surgeon.

No. 29. Polished only.

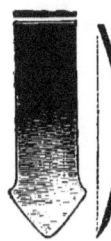

DIAMOND POINT CALF TONGUE.
With Block.

(Used on Avery Comet and Western Cultivators.)

SIZE.	APPROXIMATE WEIGHT.	CODE WORD.
3 x 10½ x ¼	8.2 lbs	Surmiser.

No. 37. Polished only.

DIAMOND POINT CALF TONGUE.

(Two 2½ x ⅜ bolts, 2¼ in. from center to center. Used on Avery New South Cultivator.)

SIZE.	APPROXIMATE WEIGHT.	CODE WORD.
3 x 10½ x ¼	2.2 lbs	Surplice.

No. 38. Polished only.

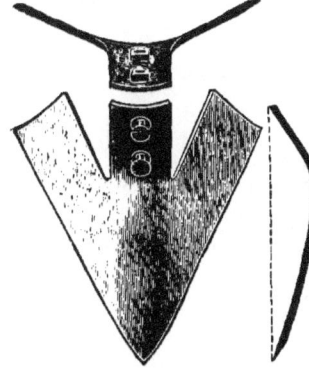

DRANE-DIXON CULTIVATOR SWEEP.

(Holes 2¼ in. from center to center. Bolts 2½ x ⅜, round countersunk.)
(Used on all Avery Cultivators.)

SIZE.	APPROXIMATE WEIGHT.	CODE WORD.
8 x 12 x 3/16	2.5 lbs	Surrendry.
9 x 12 x 3/16	3 "	Surveyor.
10 x 12 x 3/16	3.5 "	Survivor.
12 x 12 x 3/16	4.1 "	Suspecter.
14 x 12 x 3/16	4.8 "	Suspiral.
16 x 12 x 3/16	5.6 "	Suttle.

No. 46. Polished only.

B. F. AVERY & SONS. LOUISVILLE, KY.

CULTIVATOR BLADES.

SOLID CULTIVATOR SWEEP.

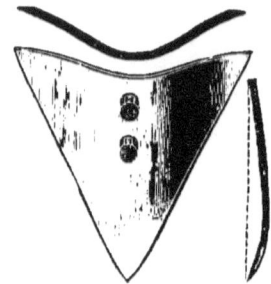

(Holes 2¼ in. from center to center. Bolts 2½ x ⅜, round countersunk.)
(Used on Avery Comet and Western Cultivators.)

SIZE.	APPROXIMATE WEIGHT.	CODE WORD.
10 x 10 x 3/16	3 lbs	Swaddle.
12 x 10 x 3/16	3.5 "	Swallet.
14 x 10 x 3/16	4.2 "	Swamp.
16 x 10 x 3/16	5 "	Swarm.
18 x 12 x 3/16	6.8 "	Swash.
20 x 12 x 3/16	7.5 "	Sweater.

No. 39, Polished only.

WALLIS, Jr., COMBINATION SWEEP.

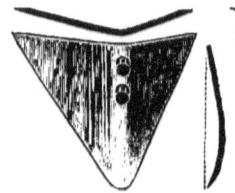

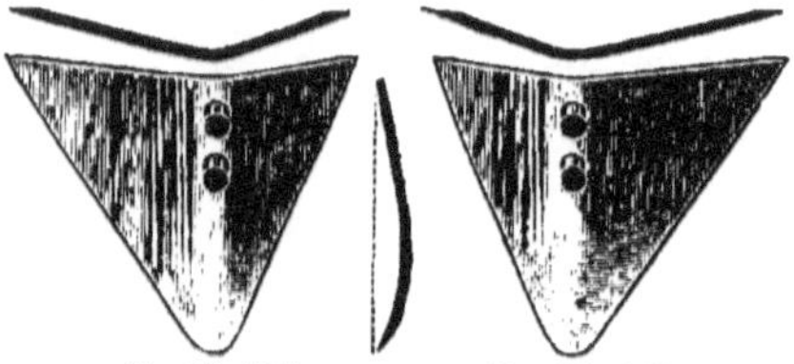

No. 42—R.H.   No. 43—L.H.
Polished only.

(Two 2¼ x 7/16 bolts, 2¼ in. from center to center.)
(Used on Avery Comet and Western Cultivators.)

SIZE.	APPROXIMATE WEIGHT.	CODE WORD.
6–8 x 10 x 3/16 R	5 lbs	Sweeper.
6–8 x 10 x 3/16 L	5 "	Sweetener.
7–9 x 10 x 3/16 R	5.6 "	Swelter.
7–9 x 10 x 3/16 L	5.6 "	Swifter.

WALLIS, Jr., SHOVEL SWEEP.

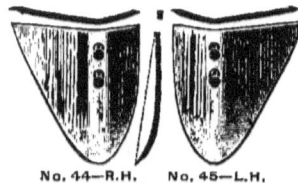

No. 44—R.H.   No. 45—L.H.
Polished only.

(Two 2¼ x 7/16 bolts, 2¼ in. from center to center.)
(Used on Avery Comet and Western Cultivators.)

SIZE.	APPROXIMATE WEIGHT.	CODE WORD.
2 –6 x 10 x 3/16 R	3.5 lbs	Swimmer.
2 –6 x 10 x 3/16 L	3.5 "	Swingel.
2½–7 x 10 x 3/16 R	3.8 "	Swinker.
2½–7 x 10 x 3/16 L	3.8 "	Swosber.
3 –8 x 10 x 3/16 R	4.2 "	Sybarite.
3 –8 x 10 x 3/16 L	4.2 "	Syenite.

WALLIS, Jr., CULTIVATOR TURNING SHOVELS.

(For Double Shovel also.)

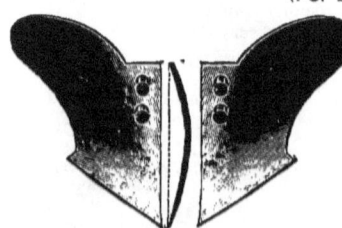

No. 33—R.H.   No. 34—L.H.
Polished only.

(Holes 2¼ in. from center to center. Bolts 2¼ x 7/16 in., round countersunk.)
(Used on Avery Comet and Western Cultivators.)

SIZE.	APPROXIMATE WEIGHT.	CODE WORD.
5 x 11 x ¼ R	6 lbs	Sylph.
5 x 11 x ¼ L	6 "	Symbolics.
6 x 11 x ¼ R	7 "	Symmetry.
6 x 11 x ¼ L	7 "	Symposiac
7 x 12 x ¼ R	8 "	Synaxis.
7 x 12 x ¼ L	8 "	Synclinal.

B. F. AVERY & SONS.   LOUISVILLE, KY.

CULTIVATOR BLADES.

WALLIS, Jr., DIAMOND POINT CULTIVATOR TURNING SHOVELS.

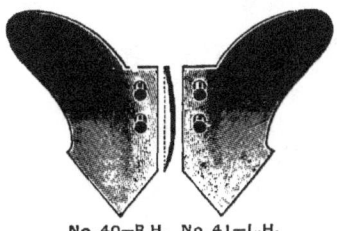

No. 40—R.H.   No. 41—L.H.
Polished only.

(Used on Avery Comet and Western Cultivators.)
(For Double Shovel also.)
(Holes 2¼ in. from center to center. Bolts 2¼ x 7⁄16 in., round countersunk.)

SIZE	APPROXIMATE WEIGHT	CODE WORD
5 x 11 x ¼ R	6 lbs	Syncope.
5 x 11 x ¼ L	6 "	Syncopize.
6 x 11 x ¼ R	7 "	Syncretist.
6 x 11 x ¼ L	7 "	Syndactyl.
7 x 12 x ¼ R	8 "	Syndic.
7 x 12 x ¼ L	8 "	Synechia.

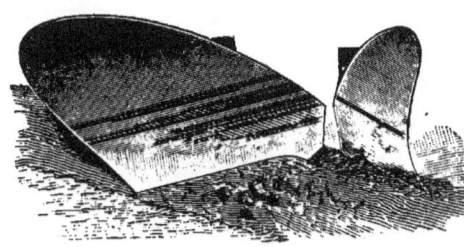

No. 31.   No. 32.
Polished only.

WALLIS, Jr., CULTIVATOR SCRAPER BLADES.
With Blocks.

(Used on Avery Comet and Western Cultivators.)

SIZE	APPROXIMATE WEIGHT	CODE WORD
9 x 8 x 3⁄16	18 lbs. pr pair	Synergist.
11 x 9 x 3⁄16	21 " "	Syngraph.

No. 23—R.H.   No. 24—L.H.
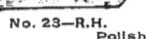
Polished only.

IMPROVED SCRAPER BLADES.
With Block.

(Used on Avery Comet and Western Cultivators.)

SIZE	APPROXIMATE WEIGHT	CODE WORD
10 x 10 x 3⁄16 R	7 lbs	Synochus.
10 x 10 x 1⁄16 L	7 "	Synodal.

CULTIVATOR BLADE BLOCKS.

J90.   J91.   J92.   J95.   J96.

NO.	USED ON	CODE WORD
J90	Straight Shovel No. 25	Synonym.
J91	Twisted Shovel No. 26, R.H	Synonymist.
J92	Twisted Shovel No. 27, L.H	Synonymous.
J95	Improved Scraper Blade No. 23, R.H	Synonymy.
J96	Improved Scraper Blade No. 24, L.H	Synopsis.

B. F. AVERY & SONS. LOUISVILLE, KY.

TRUCKER CULTIVATOR BLADES.

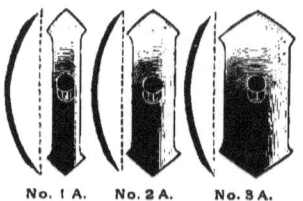

No. 1 A.   No. 2 A.   No. 3 A.

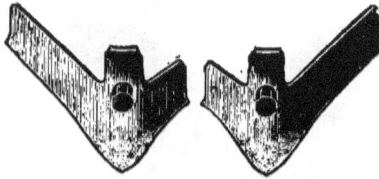

No. 4 A—R.H.   No. 5 A—L.H.

No. 6 A—R.H.

No. 7 A—L.H.

No. 8 A.

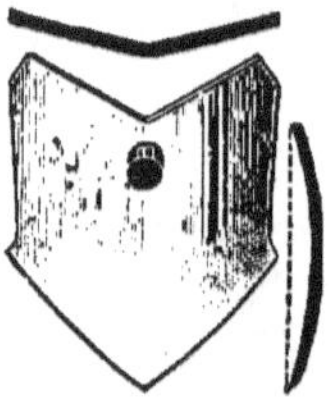

No. 10 A.

No. 11 A—R.H.   No. 12 A—L.H.

Polished Only. (With 1½ x ⅝ Bolt, Round Countersunk.)

No.	Name.	Size.	Approximate Weight.	Code Word.
1 A.	Diamond Point Shovel, Reversible	1¼ x 8 x ⅝	1 lb.	Synovia.
2 A.	Diamond Point Shovel, Reversible	2 x 8 x ¼	1.1 lbs.	Syntax.
3 A.	Diamond Point Shovel, Reversible	3 x 8 x ¼	1.2 lbs.	Syntaxis.
4 A.	Half Dixon Sweep, small, right hand	9 x 6 x 3/16	1.6 lbs.	Syntetic.
5 A.	Half Dixon Sweep, small, left hand	9 x 6 x 3/16	1.6 lbs.	Syntomy.
6 A.	Half Dixon Sweep, large, right hand	12 x 6 x 3/16	2 lbs.	Syntonic.
7 A.	Half Dixon Sweep, large, left hand	12 x 6 x 3/16	2 lbs.	Syphon.
8 A.	Dixon Sweep, small	8 x 6 x 3/16	1.8 lbs.	Syriac.
8 A.	Dixon Sweep, medium	10 x 6 x 3/16	2 lbs.	Syringa.
8 A.	Dixon Sweep, large	12 x 6 x 3/16	2.2 lbs.	Syrma.
10 A.	Rear Hilling Blade	6¼ x 6¼ x 3/16	2 lbs.	Systasis.
11 A.	Side Hilling Blade, right hand	8¼ x 6 x 3/16	4 lbs.	Systole.
12 A.	Side Hilling Blade, left hand	8¼ x 6 x 3/16	4 lbs.	Systyl.

REPAIR PRICE LIST FOR MOON COULTERS.

Cut of Coulter on pages 104 and 105.

No. 1.	Price.
Blade, 8-inch	$1 00
Standard or Rod	50
No. 1 Shoe	1 00
No. 1 Journal	60
Journal Box, R. H	20
Journal Box, L. H	20
No. C. Journal Clamp, R.H	15
No. D. Journal Clamp, L.H	15
Hub (countersunk), R. H	20
Hub (threaded), L. H	20
No. K 101. Beam Clamp Bottom	40
No. K 102. Beam Clamp Center	40
No. K 103. Beam Clamp Wedge	15
No. 2.	
Blade, 10-inch	1 25
Standard or Rod	50
No. 2 Shoe	1 25
No. 2 Journal	60
Journal Box, R. H	20
Journal Box, L. H	20
No. G. Journal Clamp, R. H	15
No. H. Journal Clamp, L. H	$0 15
Hub (countersunk), R. H	20
Hub (threaded), L. H	20
No. K 101. Beam Clamp Bottom	40
No. K 102. Beam Clamp Center	40
No. K 103. Beam Clamp Wedge	15
No. 3.	
Blade, 12-inch	1 50
Standard or Rod	50
No. 3 Shoe	1 50
No. 3 Journal	60
Journal Box, R. H	20
Journal Box, L. H	20
No. K. Journal Clamp, R. H	15
No. L. Journal Clamp, L. H	15
Hub (countersunk), R. H	20
Hub (threaded), L. H	20
No. K 101. Beam Clamp Bottom	40
No. K 102. Beam Clamp Center	40
No. K 103. Beam Clamp Wedge	15

Repair Price List for Truckers' Cultivators and Attachments.

Cut of Implements on pages 84 and 85.

No.		Price.
K 68.	Clevis Hook and Link for Nos. A, B, C, D	$0 30
K 69.	Cross Pieces for Nos. A, B, C, D, per set	30
K 70.	Expanding Clip, less hand screw, for Nos. A, B	25
K 116.	Quadrant for Nos. C, D	25
K 117.	Expanding Slide for Nos. C, D	25
K 120.	Expanding Hand Screw for Nos. A, B	20
K 189.	Wrench for Nos. A, B, C, D	10
J 118.	Pawl, steel, for Nos. C, D	30
324.	Trigger for Nos. C, D	15
	Lever, complete, for Nos. C, D	80
	Standard, with Bolts, for Nos. A, B, C, D	40
	Handle Braces, long, per pair	$0 50
	Handle Braces, short, per pair	30
	Finished Handles, per pair	75

No. For Horse Hoe Attachment.

No.		Price.
K 133.	Blade Dial	25
K 134.	Standard	25

For Gauge Wheel Attachment.

No.		Price.
K 71.	Gauge Wheel Arm, R. H	35
K 72.	Gauge Wheel Arm, L. H	35
	Gauge Wheel	40

Repair Price List for Orchard Harrows and Attachments.

Cut of Implements on page 86.

No.		Price.
K 68.	Clevis Hook and Link for Nos. F, G	$0 30
K 69.	Cross Pieces for Nos. F, G, per pair	30
K 70.	Expansion Clip for No. F	25
K 95.	Tooth Clamp for Nos. F, G	15
K 96.	Expansion Hinge for No. G	15
K 116.	Quadrant for No. G	25
K 117.	Expansion Slide for No. G	25
K 120.	Hand Screw for No. F	20
K 189.	Wrench for Nos. F, G	10
K 213.	Expansion Hinge for No. F	15
J 118.	Pawl, steel, for No. G	30
324.	Trigger for No. G	$0 15
	Lever, complete, for No. G	80
	Handle Braces, long, per pair	50
	Handle Braces, short, per pair	30
	Finished Handles, per pair	75

For Gauge Wheel Attachment.

No.		Price.
K 71.	Gauge Wheel Arm, R. H	35
K 72.	Gauge Wheel Arm, L. H	35
	Gauge Wheel	40

REPAIR PRICE LIST FOR U BAR STEEL FRAME LEVER HARROWS.

Cut of Implement on page 59.

No.		Price.
K 68.	Hook and Link, each	$0 50
K 87.	Quadrant, old style, each	50
K 88.	Pawl Case, old style, each	10
K 89.	Pawl for K88, old style, each	10
K 90.	Lever Socket, old style, each	35
K 91.	Lever Bar Clamp, with arm, each	25
K 92.	Tooth Clamp, without Bolts, for ½x½ teeth, each	10
K 93.	Runners without Bolts, each	25
K 94.	Clamp Collar for Cross Bars, each	10
K 112.	Tooth Clamp, without Bolts, for ½x⅝ and ⅝x⅝ teeth, each	10
K 220.	Drawhead, each	25
K 221.	Quadrant, each	50
K 222.	Lever Socket, each	35
E 209.	Trigger for Lever, each	15
J 118.	Pawl, each	30
324.	Trigger for Lever, old style, each	10
	U Bars, each	1 00
	End Cross Bars, each	$1 00
	Center Cross Bars, each	75
	Cross Bar that lever fastens to, each	50
	Levers, complete, each	1 00
	Front or A Braces, per set	70
	Teeth ½x½x9 inches, each	10
	Teeth ⅝x⅝x9 inches, each	15
	Bolts for Tooth Clamps, each	05
	Bolts for Runners, each	05
	Spreader Irons for (2) section draw bar, old style	50
	Spreader Irons for (3) section draw bar, old style	85
	Spreader Irons for (4) section draw bar, old style	1 25
	Chain Spreader with adjustable hitch for (2) section draw bar	1 00
	Chain Spreader with adjustable hitch for (3) section draw bar	1 25
	Chain Spreader with adjustable hitch for (4) section draw bar	1 50

	Price
Drawbar for 1 Section, ironed, complete, in one piece, 2x3½ in. by 3 feet 5 in., with ½-in. irons, old style	$1 70
Drawbar for 2 Sections, ironed, complete, in one piece, 2x3½ in. by 8 feet 6 in., with ½-in. irons, old style	2 50
Drawbar for 3 Sections, ironed, complete, in one piece, 2x5 in. by 13 feet 6 in., with 9-16-in. irons, old style	3 00
Drawbar for 4 Sections, ironed, complete, in one piece, 2x6 in. by 18 feet 4 in., with 9-16-in. irons, old style	4 50
Drawbar for 1 30 tooth Section, complete, with spreader chains, etc., 3 feet 7 inches long	1 70
Drawbar for 1 60 tooth Section, complete, with spreader chains, etc., 8 feet 7 inches long	2 50
Drawbar for 1 90 tooth Section, complete, with spreader chains, etc	3 00
Drawbar for 1 120 tooth Section, complete, with spreader chains, etc	4 50
Drawbar for 1 25 tooth Section, complete, with spreader chains, etc , 3 feet 2 inches long	1 70
Drawbar for 1 50 tooth Section, complete, with spreader chains, etc., 6 feet 10¾ inches long	2 50
Drawbar for 1 75 tooth Section, complete, with spreader chains, etc	3 00
Drawbar for 1 100 tooth Section, complete, with spreader chains, etc	4 50

REPAIR PRICE LIST FOR COMMON SENSE HARROW.

Cut of Implement on page 59.

	Price
Wood Cross Bars, 2½x2½ inches, each	$0 20
Wood Bars, 2½x2½ inches, each	70
Iron Rod, with nut and washer, each	$1 00
Teeth, ⅝x12 inches, per dozen	1 00

B. F. AVERY & SONS.  LOUISVILLE, KY.

REPAIR PRICE LIST

FOR "INVINCIBLE" SULKY PLOWS.

Cut of Implements on page 42. Cut of Repairs on page 143.
When ordering right or left-hand repairs, do so from operator's position or rear of Sulky.
Order repairs by letter and number given.

No. of Part.	Articles.	Price.
E 209.	Trigger for lifting pawl	$0 15
E 226.	Coulter hub (half)	30
E 270.	Coulter yoke head	20
E 271.	Coulter sand shield	15
E 288.	Pawl (old style)	15
E 294.	Pawl case (old style)	25
E 297.	Dial clevis follower	25
E 321.	Wood bushing for E 226	10
E 343.	Coulter blade, 15-inch	2 00
E 346.	Coulter stem	60
E 349.	Coulter arm, R. H.	35
E 350.	Coulter arm, L. H.	35
E 357.	Draft rod slide	60
E 410.	Pawl (no cut shown)	50
E 500.	Dial clevis head	50
E 501.	Draft rod casting	35
E 503.	Furrow wheel axle bearing, L H	50
E 504.	Furrow wheel axle bearing, R. H. (old style)	50
E 505.	Connecting rod arm with rivet on furrow axle, R. H.	30
E 506.	Land wheel axle bearing, R. H.	60
E 508.	Land axle lever socket with rivet	50
E 510.	Rear axle swivel socket, R. H.	80
E 511.	Rear axle clutch collar with rivet, R. H.	30
E 515.	Rear axle land shield collar (old style)	25
E 516.	Rear axle land shield collar cap	15
E 517.	Weed hook washer	15
E 518.	Furrow wheel sand shield collar	20
E 519.	Furrow wheel sand shield collar cap	20
E 520.	Swivel pole casting on pole	35
E 521.	Swivel pole casting on frame	25
E 522.	Rear axle swivel socket, L. H	80
E 523.	Rear axle clutch collar with rivet, L. H.	30
E 524.	Connecting rod arm on furrow axle, L. H.	60
E 525.	Quadrant washer	10
E 527.	Coulter clamp with bolts	70
E 528.	Land wheel axle bearing and seat rest	75
E 529.	Trash shield complete with bolts and washer for rear wheel (old style)	75
E 530.	Trash shield washer for rear wheel	05
E 531.	Rear axle swivel socket with lever, R. H., for No. 5 (no cut shown)	1 75
F 532.	Rear axle swivel socket with lever, L. H., for No. 5 (no cut shown)	1 75
E 533.	Rear lever quadrant bracket, R. H., for No. 5 (no cut shown)	35
E 534.	Rear lever quadrant bracket, L. H., for No. 5 (no cut shown)	35
E 535.	Rear wheel sand shield collar, R. H., for No. 5 (no cut shown)	25
E 536.	Rear wheel sand shield collar, L. H., for No. 5 (no cut shown)	25
E 537.	Furrow wheel axle bearing (no cut shown)	50
E 577.	Quadrant for compound lever, R. H., for No. 5 (no cut shown)	50
E 582.	Quadrant for compound lever, L. H., for No. 5 (no cut shown)	50
E 800.	Beam for furrow side, for either R. or L. H. plow	4 00
E 801.	Beam for landside, for either R. or L. H. plow	4 00
E 802.	Land wheel axle	2 75
E 803.	Furrow wheel axle for 10 and 12 inch bottoms	2 50
E 804.	Furrow wheel axle for 12 and 14 inch bottoms	2 50
E 805.	Furrow wheel axle for 14 and 16 inch bottoms	2 50
E 806.	Rear furrow wheel axle	2 00
E 807.	Plow standard (state name and size of plow)	$3 00
E 808.	Furrow lever complete	1 75
E 809.	Land lever complete	1 50
E 810.	Seat spring	2 00
E 811.	Seat spring leaf	75
E 812.	Quadrant for land lever	80
E 813.	Quadrant for furrow lever	80
E 814.	Draft rod	80
E 815.	Knuckle brace (state name and size of plow)	1 50
E 816.	Furrow wheel scraper	50
E 817.	Rear wheel scraper	40
E 820.	Chain to lock rear wheel	60
E 821.	Lifting spring hook	25
E 823.	Spiral lifting spring	1 00
E 824.	Land lever trigger rod	20
E 825.	Furrow lever trigger rod	20
E 826.	Steel landside for 10 in. bottom { State if	1 25
E 836.	Steel landside for 12 in. bottom } for New	1 50
E 826.	Steel landside for 14 in. bottom { Clipper	1 75
E 826.	Steel landside for 16 in. bottom { or Texas }	2 00
E 827.	Seat	85
E 828.	Foot rest	75
E 829.	Connecting rod, furrow lever to axle	40
E 831.	Frog for 10, 12, 14 inch bottom (state if for New Clipper or Texas), each	2 00
E 831.	Frog for 16 inch bottom (state if for New Clipper or Texas), each	2 50
E 832.	Weed hook	60
E 833.	Furrow wheel sand shield stirrup	20
E 834.	Tool box clamp washer	05
E 835.	Point and mold clip (state name and size of plow)	10
E 836.	Land quadrant washer	10
E 837.	Swivel arm for pole	1 00
E 839.	Stirrup for foot rest	20
E 840.	Bolt for coulter clamp	15
E 841.	Spring for pawl E 288 and E 410.	15
E 842.	Monkey wrench	75
E 843.	Land lever, without attachment	70
E 844.	Furrow lever, without attachment	1 00
E 845.	Pole, painted (no cut shown)	2 50
E 846.	Pawl cover for E 410 (no cut shown)	20
E 847.	Pawl cover for J 118 (no cut shown)	20
E 848.	Compound lever complete (no cut shown)	75
E 849.	Rear lever complete (no cut shown)	75
E 850.	Rear quadrant, R. H. (no cut shown)	50
E 851.	Rear quadrant, L. H. (no cut shown)	50
E 852.	Rear quadrant brace (no cut shown)	25
E 853.	Steel neckyoke, 36 inch (no cut shown)	1 00
J 108.	Tool box	60
J 118.	Steel pawl for rear lever for No. 5 (no cut shown)	30
J 812.	Spring for J 118 (no cut shown)	15
T 69.	Land wheel sand shield	20
T 74.	Axle washer for land and furrow wheels	10
T 100.	Axle washer, rear wheel	10
S.	Land wheel, with box and nut, painted (no cut shown)	3 75
T.	Furrow wheel, with box and nut, painted (no cut shown)	3 50
R.	Rear furrow wheel, with box and nut, painted (no cut shown)	2 50
OB 508.	Wheel box for S and T wheels (no cut shown)	1 00
OB 507.	Wheel box for R wheel (no cut shown)	75
N 54.	Wheel box nut for S and T wheels (no cut shown)	40
N 14.	Wheel box nut for R wheel (no cut shown)	35
66.	Wrench (no cut)	20

B. F. AVERY & SONS.      LOUISVILLE, KY.

Repairs for "Invincible" Sulky Plow.

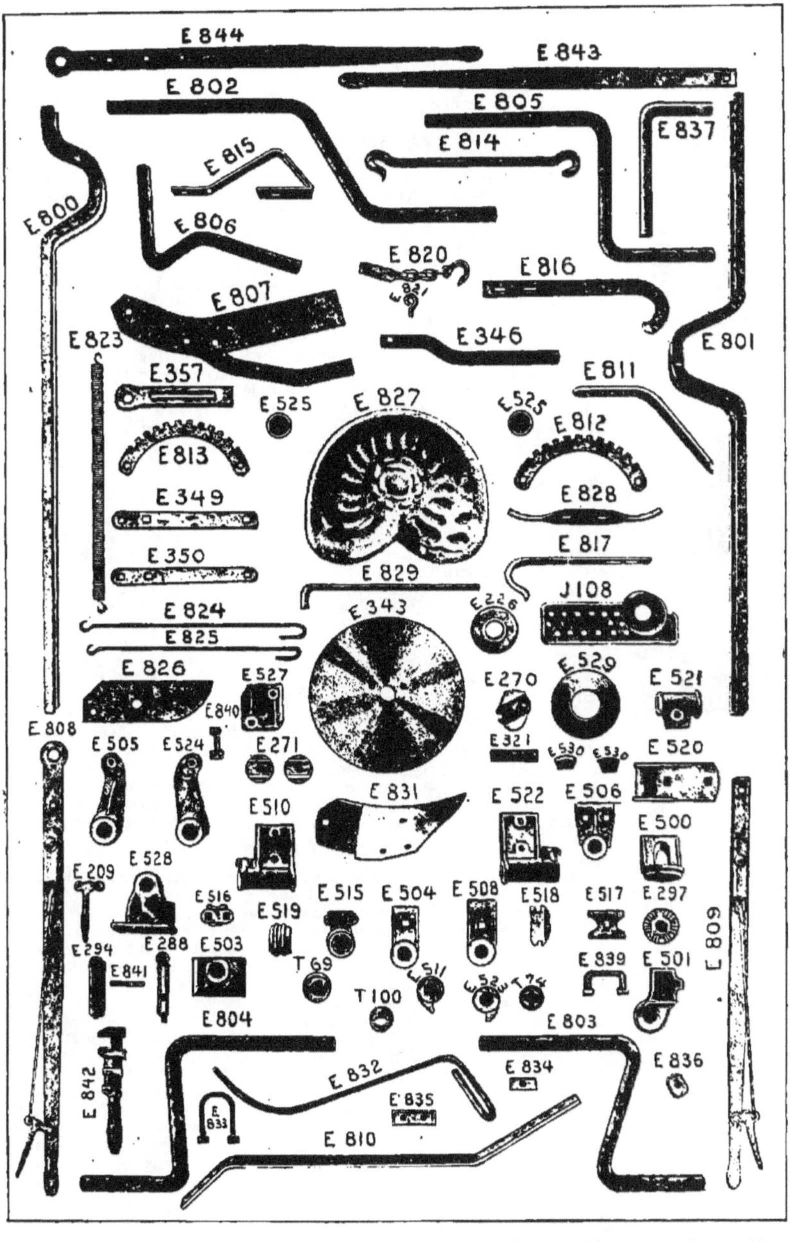

Cut of Implement on Page 42.   Prices of Repairs on Page 142.

B. F. AVERY & SONS. LOUISVILLE, KY.

DIRECTIONS
FOR SETTING UP AND OPERATING AVERY'S INVINCIBLE SULKY PLOW.
Cut of Implements on Page 42.

Before setting up Sulky see that all bearings are free from dirt or grit and are thoroughly oiled.

Put the land axle (which is the longest one) from left side through land wheel axle bearing, E 506 (reverse if L. H. Sulky).

Bolt land wheel axle bearing and seat rest, E 528, to frame, but do not tighten.

Place pawl of land lever (the medium length lever) in third notch from rear in land lever quadrant, then hold bolt head of bolt to be used to fasten lever against nut, fastening land wheel axle bearing, E 506, to frame, and push land axle through to the right until land wheel lever socket, E 508, is in its place, then bolt securely to lever.

Put bottom end of furrow lever (longest one) over end of land axle on right hand side of frame and secure with cotter.

Tighten bolt in land wheel axle bearing and seat rest, E 528.

Insert end of furrow axle in furrow wheel axle bearing, E 503, then bolt furrow wheel axle bearing, E 537 (old No. E 504), to frame.

Bolt connecting rod, E 829, to furrow lever.

Place on land axle the 28-inch wheel, on front furrow axle the 24-inch wheel, and the 18-inch wheel on rear axle with small side of hubs inward.

On Invincible Sulky No. 5, which has the back furrowing attachment, remove bolts in rear wheel swivel socket E 531 on right hand plow and E 532 on left hand plow and fit lever in groove of swivel socket, and bolt back to frame; be careful not to tighten the bolt too tight, as the casting must swivel in frame when back-furrowing.

Remove weed hook washer, E 517, fit the weed hook in washer, and rebolt to frame.

Attach spiral lifting spring to hook in weed hook washer, E 517, and to small hook near top end of furrow lever.

Loosen key bolts in coulter clamp E 527 and push coulter stem up through clamp until coulter plays clear of point of plow and about $\frac{7}{8}$ inch to land, then tighten key bolts.

Bolt seat spring to land wheel axle bearing and seat rest, E 528.

Place the foot rest just above angle in seat spring, driving the stirrup that holds foot rest from under side of seat spring through foot rest.

Bolt tool box on top of frame, just forward of standard.

The Invincible Sulky will open a furrow from one to seven inches deep, by throwing both levers forward to the proper notch to obtain the desired depth (if the ground is extremely hard, the land or leveling lever should be pushed forward sufficient to let the plow lean to the land). After the first furrow has been opened and the required depth obtained, pull the lifting lever back to the sixth or central notch in quadrant, then level the plow by shifting the land or leveling lever. When the team is walking right, then adjust the clevis to or from the land **until the front furrow wheel tracks against the wall of the furrow previously plowed.** There are absolutely no adjustments to make on this plow except the clevis. The width of cut is varied by moving the front furrow wheel in or out on axle.

Have the clevis adjusted as high as it can be used without having a tendency to pull the rear wheel off the ground.

To back-furrow and turn a square corner with the plow in the ground, tighten the set screw in swivel socket E 531 R on right hand plow or E 532 L on left hand plow. When the plow gets to the end of furrow and as the front furrow wheel starts to climb on the land, move the lifting lever forward; this elevates the wheel, and the plow maintains a uniform depth. Before turning raise the rear wheel by means of lever back of seat, then turn the team square around until the lead horse is in the furrow; do not let the team move the plow until they are in that position, when the plow will turn a perfect corner with the plow in the ground; when the team starts up, pull both levers back into position. If plowing very deep and lever has to be pushed very far forward, it is advisable to remove the coil lifting spring on furrow lever. In turning "haw" with the right hand plow or "gee" with the left hand plow, loosen the set screw on swivel socket E 531 R or E 532 L, when the plow will turn a perfect square corner with the plow in the ground without touching any of the levers.

NOTE.—Reference herein to set screw **E 531 R and E 532 L applies only to the No. 5 Invincible Sulky, which is made to turn in the ground either to the right or left,** whereas the No. 1 will only turn in the ground one way.

DIRECTIONS

FOR SETTING UP AND OPERATING AVERY'S INVINCIBLE DISC PLOW.

Cut of Implement on Page 40.

E. 506.

E. 528.

E. 508.

E. 504.

E. 829.

J. 108.

Remember that it is important that all bearings should be free from grit and dirt, and oiled thoroughly.

Put the land axle (which is the longest one) from left side through land wheel axle bearing E. 506.

Bolt land wheel axle bearing and seat rest E. 528 to frame, but do not tighten.

Place pawl of land lever (shortest lever) in third notch from rear in land lever quadrant, then hold bolt head of bolt to be used to fasten lever against nut fastening land wheel axle bearing E. 506 to frame, and push land axle through to the right until land wheel lever socket E. 508 is in place, then bolt securely to lever.

Put bottom end of furrow lever over end of land axle on right hand side of frame and insert cotter.

Tighten bolt in land wheel axle bearing and seat rest E. 528.

Insert end of furrow axle in furrow wheel axle bearing E. 503, then bolt furrow wheel axle bearing E. 537 (old No. E. 504) to frame.

Bolt connecting rod E. 829 to furrow lever.

Place wheel E. 559 on land axle and wheel E. 550 on front furrow axle.

Raise rear end of machine and insert from bottom through casting E. 552 the rear axle, after securing this axle with cotter put on wheel.

Bolt front end of seat rail with two bolts on land wheel axle bearing and seat rest E. 528, and rear end on top of frame to bolt between frame directly over standard.

Attach spiral lifting spring to hook in washer, E. 517, and to small hook near top end of furrow lever.

Bolt seat spring at second and third hole from front end of seat rail. If additional weight is required on disc, bolt further back.

Place the foot rest just above angle in seat spring, driving the stirrup that holds foot rest from under side of seat spring through foot rest.

Bolt tool box on top of frame, just forward of standard.

Bolt disc securely to flange.

For ordinary work adjust scraper so that the cutting edge of same is parallel with center of the disc, and one inch inside of outer rim of disc.

The Invincible Disc Plow will open a furrow from (3) three to (8) eight inches deep by throwing both levers forward to the proper notch to obtain the desired depth. After the first furrow has been opened and the required depth obtained, pull the lifting lever back to the sixth or central notch in quadrant, then level the plow by shifting land or leveling lever. When the team is walking right, then adjust the clevis to or from the land until the front furrow wheel tracks in the mark made by the rear wheel in previous furrow.

When hitch is properly adjusted and plow is cutting proper width the front furrow wheel will always track as above.

The width of cut can be changed by moving the front furrow wheel in or out on axle.

Be sure and keep the disc hub well oiled by means of the oil pipe on inside of standard.

Wheel axles should be greased with axle grease.

B. F. AVERY & SONS. LOUISVILLE, KY.

REPAIR PRICE LIST FOR
SIMPLE SULKY PLOWS.

Cut of Implement on page 46. Cut of Repairs on page 147.
Order repairs by letter and number given.
When ordering right or left hand repairs, do so from operator's position or rear of Implement.

No. of Part.	Articles.	Price.
E 15.	Quadrant, for land lever	$0 50
E 41.	Pawl case, for land lever	20
E 43.	Pawl, for E 41 and E 200	15
E 200.	Pawl case (old style)	25
E 204.	Coulter yoke—L. H. (old style)	50
E 205.	Coulter yoke—R. H. (old style)	50
E 208.	Collar with set screw for saddle (no cut)	40
E 209.	Trigger, for levers	15
E 213.	Clevis jaw—R. H. (old style)	20
E 214.	Clevis jaw—L. H. (old style)	20
E 215.	Cross clevis, with screw pin and brace (old style)	20
E 216.	Three-horse twisted shackle and pin (old style)	10
E 217.	Clevis pin (old style)	05
E 223.	Wheel washer	10
E 226.	Coulter hub (half)	30
E 227, E 228.	Split collar, bolted (old style)	15
E 231.	Tool box (old style)	60
E 232.	Beam saddle washer	10
E 234.	Wheel box with bolt (old style)	30
E 237.	Beam link casting (old style)	30
E 250.	Quadrant, for lifting lever	80
E 251.	Quadrant, for lifting lever, left hand plow	80
E 252.	Cant washer (inside) (old style)	20
E 253.	Pole casting, with hook bolt	40
E 254.	Cant washer (outside) (old style)	25
E 258.	Saddle clamp	10
E 264.	Beam saddle	1 20
E 265.	Socket crank, with spindle (no cut)	1 75
E 266.	Wrench (old style)	25
E 267.	Socket crank, with spindle for left hand plow	1 75
E 268.	Coulter clamp, bottom—R. H.	25
E 269.	Coulter clamp, top—R. H.	25
E 270.	Coulter head (half) (no cut)	15
E 271.	Sand shield, for coulter (no cut)	15
E 280.	Coulter clamp, bottom, for left hand plow (no cut)	25
E 281.	Coulter clamp, top, for left hand plow (no cut)	25
E 282.	Grass rod washer (no cut)	20
E 288.	Pawl, for lifting lever (no cut)	15
E 292.	Arch clip, for parallel lift, complete with bolt (old style) (no cut)	35
E 293.	Turning buckle on parallel lift (no cut)	30
E 294.	Pawl case, for lifting lever (no cut)	25
E 295.	Arch clip, for parallel lift, complete with bolt (no cut)	40
E 296.	Dial clevis head (no cut)	50
E 297.	Dial clevis follower (no cut)	25
E 298.	Draft rod shackle (no cut)	15
E 305.	Moldboard brace (old style)	60
E 305.	Steel beam (old style)	7 00
E 306.	Frog (old style)	2 75
E 307.	Moldboard brace (old style)	80
E 308.	Landside, with bolts (old style)	1 25 to 2 00
E 309.	Point and mold clip	10
E 317.	Seat spring (old style)	2 00
E 318.	Coulter stem (old style)	50
E 319.	Coulter stem plate (old style)	50
E 321.	Wood bushing for coulter	10
E 330.	Spring cotter	05
E 331.	Arch for frame	3 50
E 332.	Main axle	4 50
E 333.	Short axle, with nut	1 50
E 334.	Hound	2 00
E 335.	Foot rest on hound, with stirrup	75
E 336.	Plow lever, complete	1 75
E 337.	Land lever, complete	1 50
E 338.	Grass rod	50
E 339.	Grass rod washer (old style)	10
E 340.	Beam link, with bolts, etc. (old style)	25
E 341.	Bell crank	1 00
E 342.	Lever link, with bolts, etc.	25
E 343.	Coulter blade, 15 inch	2 00

No. of Part.	Articles.	Price.
E 344.	Stirrup for beam saddle	$0 20
E 345.	Stirrup to hold steel beam walking plow to saddle	25
E 346.	Coulter stem	60
E 347.	Coulter band, with nuts	25
E 348.	Bell crank, for left hand sulky (no cut)	1 00
E 349.	Coulter arm—R. H. (no cut)	35
E 350.	Coulter arm—L. H. (no cut)	35
E 351.	Pea vine cutter blade, 18 inch, with hubs K 172 (no cut)	4 00
E 353.	Pea vine cutter blade arm—R. H., front, for E 351 (no cut)	75
E 354.	Pea vine cutter blade arm, rear, for E 351 (no cut)	50
E 355.	Bushing, for K 172 (no cut)	15
E 357.	Draft rod slide (no cut)	60
E 358.	Draft rod, with shackle E 298 (no cut)	1 00
E 401.	Pole casting (no cut)	25
E 402.	Cant washer (outside), for furrow wheel, extension arm (no cut)	25
E 403.	Cant washer (inside), for furrow wheel, extension arm (no cut)	20
E 404.	Cant washer (outside), for furrow wheel, extension arm (no cut)	25
E 405.	Cant washer (inside), for furrow wheel, extension arm (no cut)	20
E 407.	Cant washer (outside), for furrow wheel (no cut)	25
E 408.	Cant washer (inside), for furrow wheel (no cut)	20
E 409.	Cant washer (outside), for furrow wheel (no cut)	25
E 410.	Pawl (no cut)	50
E 827.	Seat (no cut)	85
E 841.	Spring, for pawl E 288 (no cut)	15
E 842.	Monkey wrench (no cut)	75
E 846.	Pawl cover, for E 410 (no cut)	20
E 856.	Steel neck yoke, 36 inch	1 00
E 900.	Hound brace—R. H. (no cut)	25
E 901.	Hound brace—L. H. (no cut)	25
E 902.	Top arm, for parallel lift (no cut)	20
E 903.	Rear arm, for parallel lift (no cut)	20
E 904.	Front arm, with turnbuckle for parallel lift (no cut)	50
E 905.	Seat spring (no cut)	2 00
E 906.	Extension arm for furrow wheel (no cut)	2 00
E 907.	Wrought piece to reinforce frame (no cut)	30
E 908.	Knuckle brace (no cut)	30
E 909.	Stirrup for pole casting E 253 (no cut)	20
E 910.	Moldboard brace (no cut)	50
E 911.	Steel plow beam (no cut)	7 00
E 912.	Frog, for 8, 10, 12, 14-inch bottom (no cut)	2 00
E 913.	Frog, for 16-inch bottom (no cut)	2 50
E 914.	Pole, painted (no cut)	2 50
E 921.	Pea vine cutter blade arm—L. H., front, for E 351 (no cut)	75
E 922.	Pea vine cutter blade arm, rear, for E 351 (no cut)	50
E 923.	Gauge shoe, with band and strap (no cut)	1 50
E 924.	Dial clevis, complete (no cut)	2 00
E 925.	Parallel lift, complete (no cut)	1 50
K 172.	Pea vine cutter hub (half), for E 351	50
EX 11.	Cant washer (outside), for furrow wheel (old style) (no cut)	25
EX 12.	Cant washer (inside), for furrow wheel (old style) (no cut)	20
A.	Steel wheels, with boxing and nuts, painted, per pair (no cut)	10 00
B 510.	Wheel box (no cut)	1 00
N 51.	Wheel box nut (no cut)	40
A 25.	Seat (old style)	1 20
J 108.	Tool box (no cut)	60

REPAIRS FOR SIMPLE SULKY PLOW.

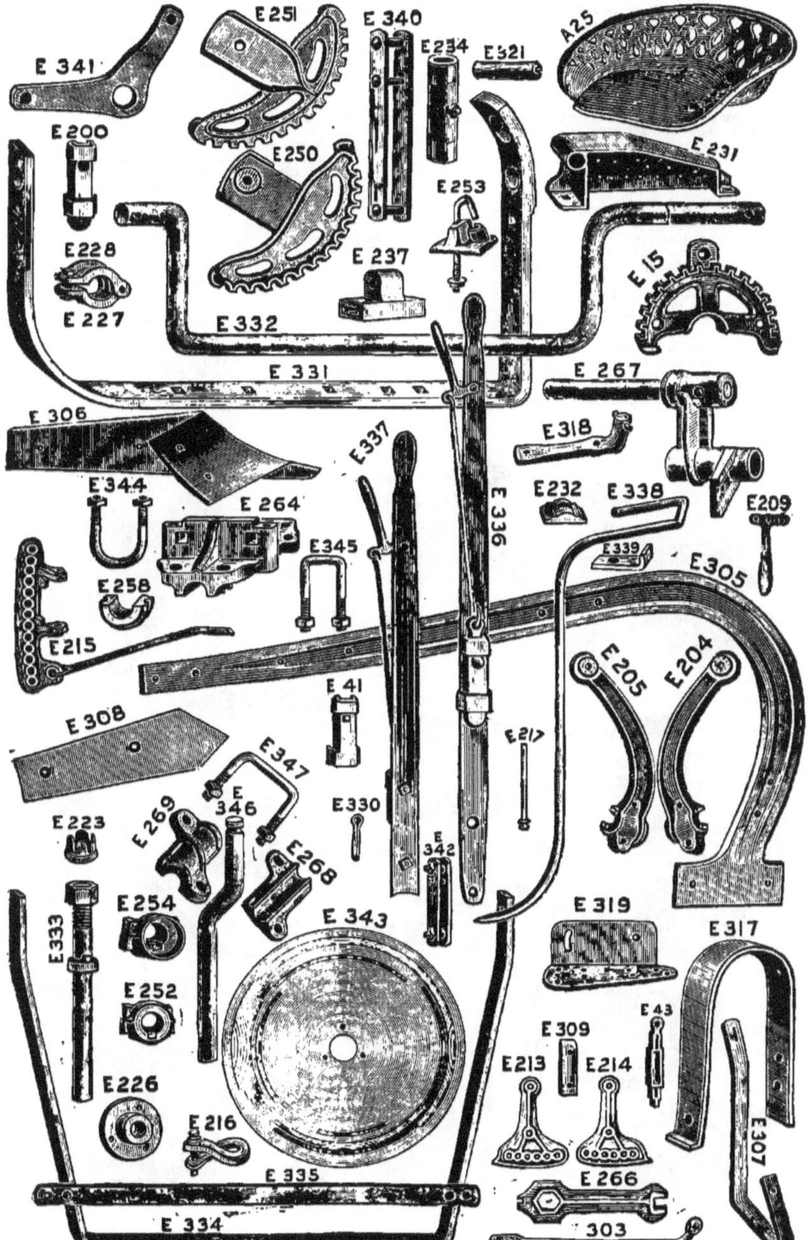

Cut of Implement on Page 46.   Prices of Repairs on Page 146.

B. F. AVERY & SONS. LOUISVILLE, KY.

Repair Price List for Middle Burster Attachment to Simple Sulky.

Cut of Implement on page 47. , Repairs for Carriage Frame on pages 146 and 147.
When ordering right or left hand repairs, do so from operator's position or rear of Implement.
Order repairs by letter and number given.

No. of Part.	Articles.	Price.
E 226.	Coulter Hub (half) for E 343	$0 30
E 258.	Saddle Clamp	15
E 264.	Saddle	1 20
E 268.	Clamp for Coulter Stem, bottom, for E 343	50
E 269.	Clamp for Coulter Stem, top, for E 343	50
E 270.	Coulter Head (half) for E 343	15
E 271.	Sand Shield Collar for E 321	15
E 296.	Dial Clevis Head	50
E 297.	Dial Clevis Follower	25
E 298.	Draft Rod Shackle	15
E 321.	Wood Bushing for Coulter Hub E 226	10
E 343.	Coulter Blade, 15-inch	2 00
E 346.	Coulter Stem for E 343	60
E 347.	Coulter Band, with Nuts, for E 343	25
E 349.	Coulter Arm, R. H., for E 343	35
E 350.	Coulter Arm, L. H., for E 343	35
E 351.	Pea Vine Cutter Blade, 18-inch, with Hub K 172	4 00
E 352.	Pea Vine Cutter Blade Arm, R.H., front, for E 351	75
E 353.	Pea Vine Cutter Blade Arm, L. H., front, for E 351	75
E 354.	Pea Vine Cutter Blade Arm, rear, for E 351	50

No. of Part.	Articles.	Price.
E 355.	Bushing for K 172	$0 15
E 356.	Moldboard Brace	35
E 357.	Draft Rod Slide	60
E 358.	Draft Rod, with shackle, E 298	1 00
E 359.	Saddle Washer	10
E 360.	Beam Saddle Stirrup for E 264 and E 258	20
E 361.	Steel Beam (state size of plow)	7 00
E 362.	Moldboard, R. H., for 14-inch	2 50
E 362.	Moldboard, R. H., for 16-inch	3 25
E 362.	Moldboard, R. H., for 18-inch	4 00
E 362.	Moldboard, R. H., for 20-inch	4 50
E 363.	Moldboard, L. H., for 14-inch	2 50
E 363.	Moldboard, L. H., for 16-inch	3 25
E 363.	Moldboard, L. H., for 18-inch	4 00
E 363.	Moldboard, L. H., for 20-inch	4 50
E 364.	Steel Point, with Bolts, for 14-inch	4 00
E 364.	Steel Point, with Bolts, for 16-inch	4 50
E 364.	Steel Point, with Bolts, for 18-inch	5 00
E 364.	Steel Point, with Bolts, for 20-inch	5 50
E 365.	Frog (state size of plow)	3 50
K 172.	Pea Vine Cutter Hub (half) for E 351 (cut marked E 172)	50
K 177.	Knuckle Brace, R. H	40
K 178.	Knuckle Brace, L. H	40

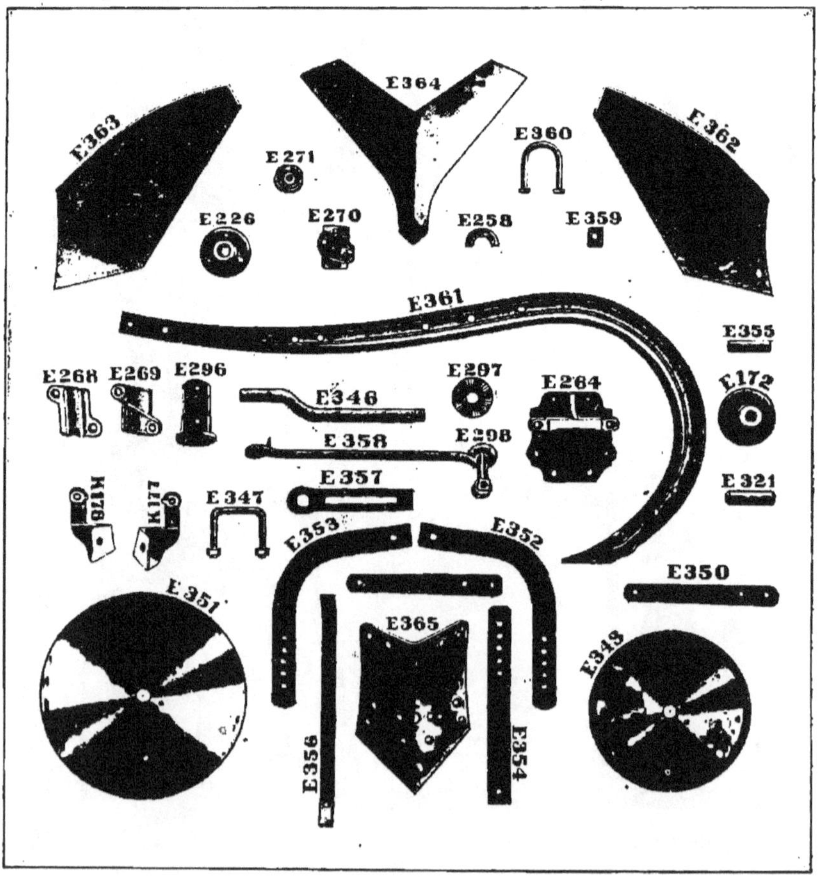

B. F. AVERY & SONS.   LOUISVILLE, KY.

REPAIR PRICE LIST FOR

Stalk Cutter Attachment to Simple Sulky.

Cut of Implement on page 48. Repairs for Carriage Frame on page 147.
When ordering right or left hand repairs, do so from operator's position or rear of Implement.
Order repairs by letter and number given.

No. of Part.	Articles.	Price.
E 209	Trigger for Lifting Lever	$0 15
E 272	Quadrant	2 00
E 273	Hitch and Drag Hook Bearing	60
E 274	Socket Crank	1 25
E 275	Half Spider, 4 arms	1 50
E 276	Half Spider, 3 arms	1 50
E 285	Pawl	20
E 286	Pawl Guide	5
E 915	Lifting Lever, complete	1 50
E 916	Strap for E 272, 1 hole	10
E 917	Strap for E 272, 2 holes	10
E 918	Chain Lever	15
E 919	Chain Lever Rest	35
E 920	Spring for E 285	15
Y 504	Drag Hook, R. H.	1 00
Y 505	Drag Hook, L. H.	1 00
95	Shackle for E 273	10

REPAIR PRICE LIST FOR

DOW-LAW COTTON PLANTERS.

Cut of Implement on page 63.
Order repairs by letter and number given.
When ordering right or left hand repairs, do so from operator's position or rear of Planter.

No. of Part.	Nos. 1 and 3 (Old Style). Articles.	Price.	No. of Part.	Nos. 2 and 4 (New Style). Articles.	Price.
G 1	Wood Wheel, Axle, and Crank	$0 25	G 2	Agitator Axle	$0 20
G 2	Agitator Axle	20	G 3	Agitator	25
G 3	Agitator	25	G 4	Draw Head	40
G 4	Draw Head	40	G 7	Agitator, whole box	25
G 5	Hopper Bottom	40	G 8	Agitator, half box	25
G 6	Feed Slide	20	G 25	Eccentric Washer	20
G 7	Agitator, whole box	25	G 26	Iron Wheel, Axle, and Crank	25
G 8	Agitator, half box	25	G 27	Iron Wheel	1 00
G 9	Thumb-screw Flange	25	G 29	Hopper Bottom	40
	Thumb Screw	10		Agitator Fingers (2)	7
	Furrow Opener	40		Coverer, with Springs	1 00
	Agitator Fingers (2)	7		Feed Slide	20
	Hopper, Right-hand Side	40		Furrow Opener	40
	Hopper, Left-hand Side	40		Handles, Finished, per pair	60
	Hopper, Front End	20		Hopper, Right-hand Side	40
	Hopper, Rear End	20		Hopper, Left-hand Side	40
	Hounds, Right	15		Hopper, Front End	20
	Hounds, Left	15		Hopper, Rear End	20
	Pitman	8		Hounds, Right	15
	Handles, Finished, per pair	60		Hounds, Left	15
	Handle Rods, with Spool	10		Handle Rods, with Spool	10
	Wood Wheel	1 00		Pitman	8
	Coverer, with Springs	1 00		Sheet-iron Spout	30
	Wheel Axle Boxing	5		Wheel Axle Boxing	5
	Sheet-iron Spout	30			

	Corn Planting Attachment.			**Corn Planting Attachment.**	
L 1	Bottom Plate	35	L 1	Bottom Plate	35
L 2	Cut-off Coverer	20	L 2	Cut-off Coverer	20
L 3	Drop Slide	20	L 3	Drop Slide	20
L 4	Cut-off	20	L 4	Cut-off	20
L 5	Agitator	40	L 5	Agitator	40
L 6	Agitator Axle	40	L 6	Agitator Axle	40
L 7	Agitator Clamp	25	L 7	Agitator Clamp	25

B. F. AVERY & SONS. LOUISVILLE, KY.

DIRECTIONS

FOR SETTING UP AND OPERATING AVERY'S SIMPLE SULKY.

Cut of Implements on pages 46, 47, and 48.

All Simple Sulky Plows leave the factory as Cant Wheel Sulky.

To Use Cant Wheel Sulky With Two Horses.—Bolt the seat at the fifth hole in arch from the right hand or furrow side; place the tongue over the hound and bolt to the UNDER SIDE of arch in the fourth hole from the right hand or furrow side. Then adjust the front of tongue until it plays freely between the horses. Then clamp tight to the hound by means of the stirrup in the tongue.

To Use Cant Wheel Sulky With Three Horses.—Bolt the tongue in the third hole from the furrow side and adjust as above.

To Fasten Plow To Carriage.—Place the beam over the bale and on top of saddle; then place the lower end of leveling device on the left hand side of saddle (with the turnbuckle toward the front); put the saddle bolts through the end of leveling device and saddle and beam, E345 then tighten. Place the two stirrups (E-345) over beam through holes provided in saddle and tighten. Then clamp the double casting (E-295) around on top of arch. Move the saddle on the bale until it measures from landside or point bar to the inside of rim at bottom of wheel about one-half inch less than the plow cuts; then fasten the collars firmly on the bale on each side of the saddle, which will hold the plow in position.

To Change From Cant Wheel To Straight Wheel.—Remove the nut on the right hand or furrow wheel axle, then reverse the two beveled washers on the same, replace the nut and tighten.

To Use Straight Wheel Sulky With Two Horses.—Place the tongue over the hound and bolt to the INSIDE of arch, in the third hole from the right hand or furrow side, then adjust front of tongue until it plays freely between the horses.

For Three Horses.—Bolt the tongue in the first hole from furrow side and tighten the tongue, as above.

To Fasten Plow To Straight Wheel Carriage.—Use same instructions as for Cant Wheel.

To plow in hog-wallow land and across corn ridges, have the leveling device properly attached and adjust the line of draft at the clevis, as you would a walking plow, then tie the latch on the main (or right-hand) lever, and it will act the same as a walking plow.

FOR ATTACHING STALK CUTTER ATTACHMENT TO SIMPLE SULKY.

Remove right hand lever and quadrant, and bolt bell crank in hole at side of arch. Bolt malleable quadrant E-272 to lower right hand side of arch, then slip socket crank E-274 with lever over the spindle part of quadrant E-272 and insert cotter.

Oil the axles and put on the wheels, with the small side of the hubs inward.

E 264 Remove beam saddle E-264 and slip collars E-208 to bend in axle. Attach spiders E-275 and E-276 to main axle. Bolt the knives to smooth surface on spider arms, and see that knives are back of arms when they touch the ground; then slip collars back against hubs of spiders and tighten set screws.

Bolt drag hook lever casting G-79 to top of pole, with front bolt fastening drag hook casting E-273. Fasten drag hook lever rest with wood screws to pole; see that slot in top of rest is back of rear bolt in drag hook lever.

Attach drag hook casting E-273 with shackle in front, to pole forward of hound. Insert end of longest drag hook from right hand side through front hole of drag hook casting E-273, and the shorter one from left hand side through rear hole, fastening them with cotters. Slip the rings of chains over drag hooks and attach the links to end of drag hook lever.

FOR ATTACHING MIDDLE BURSTER ATTACHMENT TO SIMPLE SULKY.

Remove arch clip E-295 from around arch, unbolt leveling device at beam and remove plow. Place beam of middle burster on saddle, place lower ends of leveling device on left side of beam at saddle with turnbuckle toward the front, put saddle bolts through saddle beam and ends of E345 leveling device and tighten bolts. Place two stirrups E-345 over beam through holes provided in saddle and tighten. Then rebolt arch clip E-295 to arch. Move the saddle on main axle until within about three inches of left bend in axle, then bolt the tongue underneath and seat on top the arch in fourth hole from the right; move the tongue on hound to a position pointing slightly to the right, then secure to hound with stirrup.

When using middle burster always turn to the left when the plow is in the ground, as a turn to the right with plow in ground is apt to strain the cant wheel.

B. F. AVERY & SONS.   LOUISVILLE, KY.

DIRECTIONS

FOR SETTING UP AND OPERATING AVERY'S "INVINCIBLE" GANG PLOW.

Bolt land lever between flanges of casting EX-206 between frames, and slip casting EX-206 (with lifting lever attached) over end of land axle and insert cotters.

Attach connecting rod to hole in point of furrow lever, and to casting EX-203 on furrow axle, and insert cotters.

Attach coil spring to hook at angle of frame and to end of connecting rod.

Oil axles well, and put on wheels, with small side of hubs inside.

Adjust draft rod slide and draft rods to suit team and work.

Bolt coulter stems to coulter clamps EX-214. Adjust coulters clear of point of plows and about ⅜ inch to land.

Fit weed hooks in grooves of weed hook clamps E-517, and bolt to frame.

Bolt seat spring to seat spring casting EX-217.

Place foot rest just above angle in seat spring, driving the stirrups that hold foot rest from under side of seat spring through foot rest, then clamp securely.

Bolt tool box on top of frame just forward of rear standard brace.

Most gangs will only work when horses are hitched two abreast. In the Invincible, four horses can be hitched abreast, and have the lead horse walk in the furrow and the others on the land by adjusting clevis far enough to the left on a right hand plow, and to the right on a left hand plow.

It will open a furrow from two to six inches deep, which is done by moving the two levers forward to the proper notch to obtain the required depth (if the ground is extremely hard the land or leveling lever should be pushed forward sufficient to let the plow lean to the land). After the furrow has been opened to the depth desired, pull the lifting lever back to the third notch from front of quadrant, and level plow with land or leveling lever.

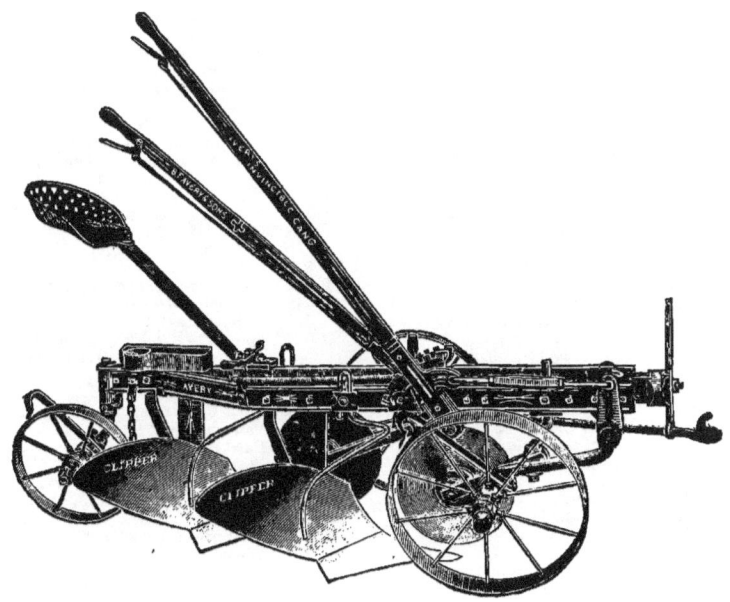

B. F. AVERY & SONS. LOUISVILLE, KY.

DIRECTIONS
FOR SETTING UP THE "LOUISVILLE" DOUBLE-EDGE STALK CUTTER.

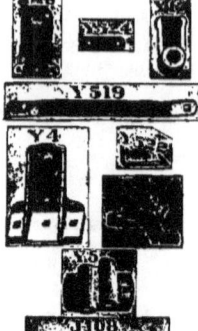

Bolt arch Y529 to end casting Y18 on bale or axle.

Bolt lifting lever Y508 to lever socket Y17.

Bolt hood arches Y517 and Y518 to main arch with clips Y524.

Bolt the braces Y519 at end holes in main arch Y529, and to hood arches Y517 and Y518.

Bolt pole to pole and arch casting Y4.

Bolt spring hook for foot lever Y522 at front hole of pole and arch casting Y4.

Place foot lever with end that contains bolt in front over hammer strap Y10.

Insert end of longest drag hook from right hand side through front hole of drag hook casting Y5, and the shorter one from left hand side through rear hole and fasten with cotters. Slip the rings of chains over drag hooks and attach the links to bolt in foot lever.

Bolt tool box under seat, to front side of weight box.

NOTE.—Be sure and keep the bolt that bolts lever to lever socket Y17 tight.

REPAIR PRICE LIST FOR
"LOUISVILLE" DOUBLE-EDGE STALK CUTTER.

Cut of Implement on page 39. Cut of Repairs on page 153.
Order repairs by letter and number given.
When ordering right or left repairs, do so from operator's position or rear of Stalk Cutter.

No. of Part.	Articles.	Price.	No. of Part.	Articles.	Price.
Y 1.	Spider for spiral knives	$2 50	Y 516.	Trash cleaner stirrups, each	$0 20
Y 2.	Box (half) for spiders Y 1 and Y 19	25	Y 517.	Hood arch—R. H.	50
Y 4.	Tongue and arch casting	1 00	Y 518.	Hood arch—L. H.	50
Y 5.	Drag hook casting	1 00	Y 519.	Hood arch braces, each	30
Y 6.	Lever socket with rivet (old style)	80	Y 520.	Foot lever with plate for drag hooks	30
Y 8.	Axle collar	30	Y 521.	Chains—from foot lever to drag hooks, each	20
Y 9.	Cleaning arm casting	30	Y 522.	Spring hook, for foot lever	20
Y 10.	Hammer strap	50	Y 523.	Rub iron, for foot lever	10
Y 11.	Pivot washer for drag hook lift	10	Y 524.	Clips for hood arch, each	10
Y 12.	Sand shield collar or axle	20	Y 525.	Rub iron, for pole	10
Y 13.	End piece for weight box—R. H.	50	Y 526.	Rub iron, for doubletree	10
Y 14.	End piece for weight box—L. H.	50	Y 527.	Ferrule, for doubletree	10
Y 15.	Neckyoke casting—top	10	Y 528.	Coil spring, for pawl E 288 and E 410	15
Y 16.	Neckyoke casting —bottom	10	Y 529.	Arch	3 00
Y 17.	Lever socket with rivet	80	Y 530.	Tongue, painted (not illustrated)	2 50
Y 18.	End casting for arch	60	Y 531.	Doubletree (wood), finished (not illustrated)	1 20
Y 19.	Spider for straight knives	2 50	D	Steel wheel, with box and nut, painted (not illustrated), each	4 50
Y 501.	Steel axle	4 00	B 512.	Wheel box	1 00
Y 502.	Foot rest	70	E 209.	Lever trigger	25
Y 503.	Quadrant	1 00	E 288.	Pawl (old style)	15
Y 504.	Drag hook—R. H	80	E 294.	Pawl case (old style)	25
Y 505.	Drag hook—L. H.	80	E 410.	Pawl	50
Y 506.	Pole and arch brace—R. H	40	E 827.	Seat	85
Y 507.	Pole and arch brace—L. H	40	E 846.	Pawl cover for E 410	20
Y 508.	Lifting lever, complete	1 50	J 97.	Wrench	20
Y 509.	Lifting lever, without attachment	75	J 108.	Tool box	60
Y 510.	Spiral knife blade	1 50	J 872.	Steel neckyoke, 48 inch	1 25
Y 511.	Straight knife blade	1 50	N 51.	Wheel box nut	40
Y 512.	Trigger rods	30	T 74.	Axle washer	15
Y 513.	Seat spring	1 50			
Y 514.	Seat spring leaf	75			
Y 515.	Arms for trash cleaner, each	20			

B. F. AVERY & SONS.  LOUISVILLE, KY.

REPAIRS FOR
LOUISVILLE DOUBLE EDGE STALK CUTTER.

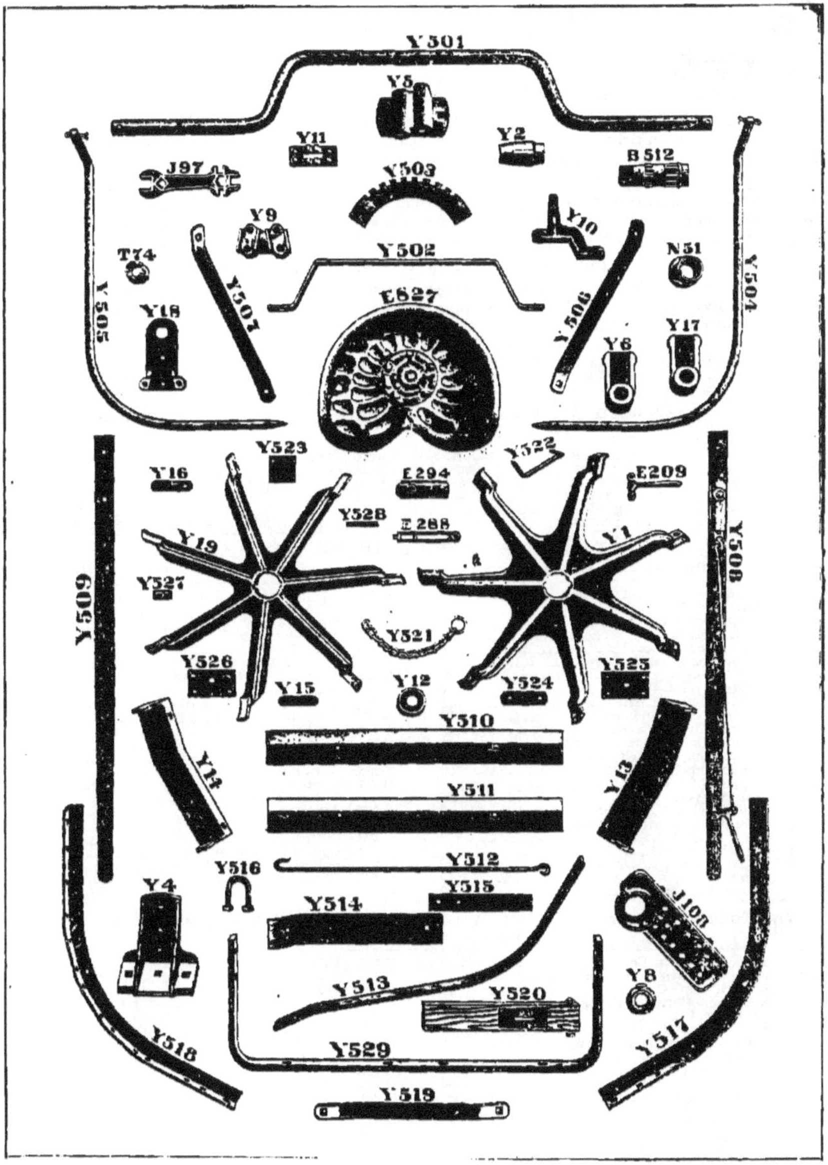

Cut of Implement on Page 39.   Prices of Repairs on Page 152.

B. F. AVERY & SONS. LOUISVILLE, KY.

DIRECTIONS
FOR SETTING UP AND OPERATING AVERY'S "LOUISVILLE" PLANTER.

G 90

Attach tin spout and opener standard to lugs on hopper bottom G 90.

Place front end of cut-off lever over boss on clutch sleeve G 119 under hopper and bolt to angle brace, being careful to have lever spring on top of angle brace.

Place sheet iron hopper so that the large hole in same will be in the rear, then bolt to cast iron hopper bottom.

Bolt handles to frame and the handle braces from frame spreader rod to inside of handles.

To Plant Corn.—Place the twelve (12) tooth chain wheel on hopper axle and the eight (8) tooth chain wheel on drive wheel axle, then oil planter well and put in corn plate, then bolt brush cut-off inside of hopper, then press the brush casting lightly against corn plate and tighten wing nut.

To Plant Cotton.—Place the twelve (12) tooth chain wheel on main wheel axle and the eight (8) tooth chain wheel on hopper axle. Remove the corn brush cut-off castings from hopper and substitute the cotton plate and thin steel cotton cut-off. Adjust the steel cut-off or gate up or down until the planter distributes the desired amount of cotton seed.

NOTE.—The corn cut-off should never be used when planting cotton.

Will plant corn from one to three grains at various distances apart as per table given below. We supply five (5) planting plates for dropping corn. The following table shows the number of grains of corn and the distance apart they will drop.

WHEN USING SMALL CHAIN WHEEL ON DRIVE WHEEL AXLE AND LARGE CHAIN WHEEL ON HOPPER AXLE.			WHEN USING LARGE CHAIN WHEEL ON DRIVE WHEEL AXLE AND SMALL CHAIN WHEEL ON HOPPER AXLE.		
When Using	Corn Will Drop	Distance Apart.	When Using	Corn Will Drop	Distance Apart.
8 hole plate	1 to 2 grains	9 inches.	8 hole plate	1 to 2 grains	4½ inches.
6 hole plate	1 to 2 grains	12 inches.	6 hole plate	1 to 2 grains	6 inches.
4 hole plate	2 to 3 grains	18 inches.	4 hole plate	2 to 3 grains	9 inches.
3 hole plate	2 to 3 grains	24 inches.	3 hole plate	2 to 3 grains	12 inches.
2 hole plate	2 to 3 grains	36 inches.	2 hole plate	2 to 3 grains	18 inches.
1 hole plate	2 to 3 grains	72 inches.	1 hole plate	2 to 3 grains	36 inches.

REPAIR PRICE LIST FOR "LOUISVILLE" PLANTERS.
Cut of Implement on page 63.   Cut of Repairs on page 155.

32.	Chain, per link	$0 03
G 45.	Malleable Foot	30
G 46.	Corrugated Washer	05
G 47.	Blade Washer	02
G 71.	Cotton Cone	40
G 72.	Cotton Cone, Cap or Cover	08
G 77.	Cone Washer	05
G 79.	Inside Beveled Wheel	20
G 80.	Outside Beveled Wheel, old style	20
G 82.	Driving Wheel, old style	1 00
G 83.	12-tooth Chain Wheel, old style	25
G 84.	8-tooth Chain Wheel, old style	20
G 86.	Brush Back, old style	20
G 88.	Hopper Bracket, right, old style	20
G 89.	Hopper Bracket, left, old style	20
G 90.	Cast Hopper	1 50
G 91.	Axle Bracket, right, old style	40
G 92.	Axle Bracket, left, old style	40
93.	Wrench	10
94.	Shackle and Pin	15
G 200.	Beam	1 00
G 201.	Beam	1 00
G 202.	Opener Standard, right	20
G 203.	Opener Standard, left	$0 20
G 204.	Wheel Scraper	25
G 205.	Opener Brace	15
G 206.	Handle Brace	15
G 207.	Hitch Strap	20
G 208.	Hopper Axle, 9-16 round, old style	25
G 209.	Wheel Axle, 9-16 round, old style	25
G 210.	Axle Pin, old style	05
G 211.	Wheel Axle Sleeve, old style	05
G 212.	Spreader Rod, with 4 Nuts	20
G 213.	Brush	30
G 215.	Seed Spout	60
G 216.	Sheet Iron Hopper, with Lid	1 20
G 218.	Spring Heel Hopper Gate	08
G 219.	Opener Standard and Brace, with Malleable Foot	1 00
G 220.	Agitator	07
G 222.	Cotton Cone Fingers	01
G 223.	Cotter	08
G 224.	Cotton Cone, complete	1 00
G 235.	Covering Blade, with Bolt	25
G 236.	Wing Nut Bolt	05

The following repairs do not appear on page 155, and are for new style Planters exclusively.

G 94.	Three-hole Corn Cone	$0 75
G 95.	Four-hole Corn Cone	75
G 96.	Six-hole Corn Cone	75
G 97.	Eight-hole Corn Cone	75
G 98.	Brush Back	30
G 99.	Hole Cleaner in Brush Back, G 98	10
G 113.	Hood for Hole Cleaner, G 99	15
G 114.	Two-hole Corn Cone	75
G 115.	Axle Bracket, right	50
G 116.	Axle Bracket, left	50
G 117.	Hopper Bracket, right	30
G 118.	Hopper Bracket, left	30
G 119.	Cut-off Clutch Sleeve	20
G 120.	Outside Bevel Wheel	30
G 121.	Twelve-tooth Chain Wheel	40
G 122.	Eight-tooth Chain Wheel	30
G 123.	Driving Wheel	$1 25
G 124.	Spring Sleeve and Spring	30
G 150.	Spring Cover Bracket	20
G 237.	Steel Hopper Axle, 11-16 round	40
G 238.	Steel Wheel Axle, 11-16 round	40
G 239.	Steel Axle Pins	10
G 240.	Steel Wheel Axle Sleeve	15
G 241.	Reversible Opener, Blade and Bolt	40
G 242.	Handles, finished, per pair	80
G 243.	Round Head Hopper Bolt	05
G 244.	Cut-off Lever, complete	75
G 245.	Spoon Covering Blade and Bolt	50
G 246.	Spoon Blade Standard, right	40
G 247.	Spoon Blade Standard, left	40
G 248.	Covering Springs, each	40
G 249.	Covering Board	15

B. F. AVERY & SONS.  LOUISVILLE, KY.

REPAIRS FOR LOUISVILLE PLANTER.

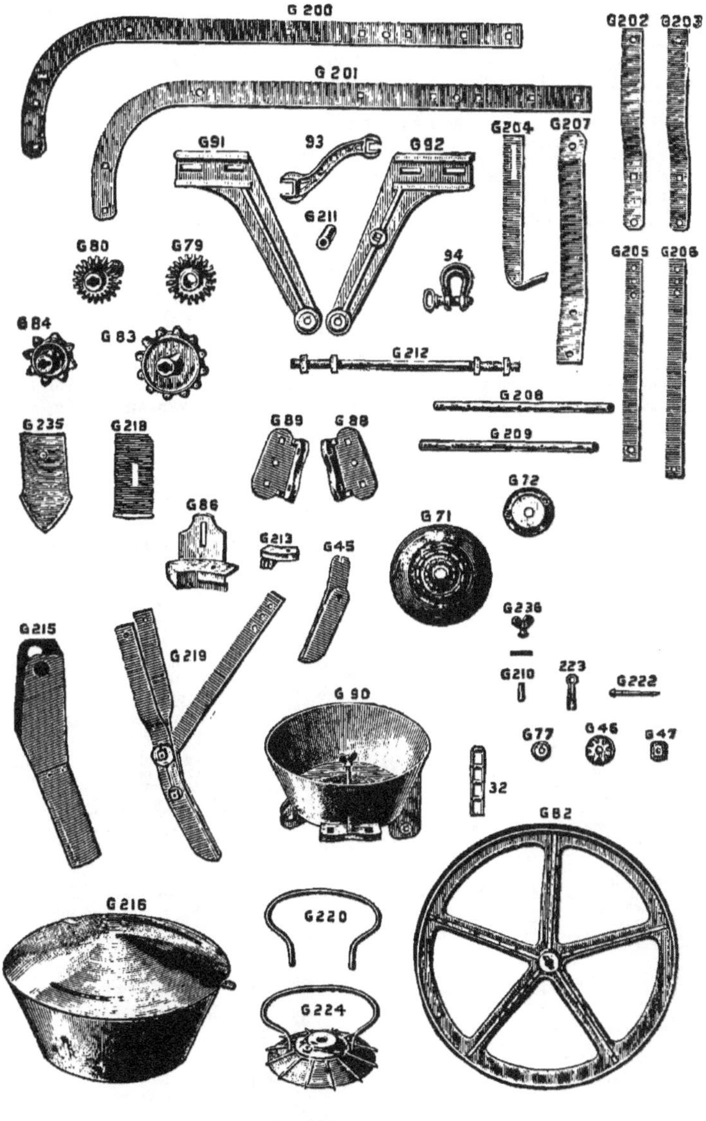

Cut of Implement on Page 63.

Prices of Repairs on Page 154.

B. F. AVERY & SONS. LOUISVILLE, KY.

DIRECTIONS

FOR SETTING UP AND OPERATING AVERY'S "MODERN" PLANTER.

Bolt handles to frame just back of hopper, using bolts extending through frame from lugs on spout. Fasten handle braces to castings G 300R and G 301L to inside of handles.

To attach roller, move standard castings G300R and G301L one hole forward on frame, then bolt castings G312 with roller braces to last hole in frames.

To attach spoon blade coverers, remove standards of shovel blade coverers from castings G300R and G301L and bolt standards of spoon blade coverers to the same castings.

TO SET FOR CORN.

Place cog wheel G350 over center bolt in hopper and on cog wheel G314 on end of main shaft; place corn plate next, then stud casting G307, then casting G310 on stud, then spool G346 on top of G368, and tighten wing nut.

We supply three planting plates, viz:

        3-hole plate, which drills corn 30 inches apart.
        6-hole plate, which drills corn 15 inches apart.
        12-hole plate, which drills corn 7 inches apart.

TO CHANGE FOR COTTON.

Remove spool G346, casting G368, stud G307, and corn plate.

Place stud G307 (with large end down) over center bolt in hopper, then cog wheel G350, then stud G307; then place cotton cone on top of stud and spool G346 in opening on top of cone, then cap G347, after which tighten wing bolt.

To regulate quantity of cotton seed, loosen slide outside of hopper, then adjust to suit. Do not fail to retighten slide bolt.

REPAIR PRICE LIST FOR
"Modern" Cotton and Corn Planters.

Cut of Implement on page 62.
Order repairs by letter and number given.
When ordering right or left hand repairs, do so from operator's position or rear of Planter.

No. of Part.	Articles.	Price.	No. of Part.	Articles.	Price.
G 300.	Covering blade standard bracket, R. H.	$0 35	G 365.	Knocker for corn plates	$0 05
G 301.	Covering blade standard bracket, L. H.	35	G 366.	Cut-off for corn plates	10
G 302.	Covering blade standard clip	10	G 367.	Housing	20
G 303.	Bevel washer for G 345	05	G 368.	Housing brace	15
G 305.	Hopper bottom	90	G 369.	Fertilizer hopper bottom	90
G 306.	Hopper bottom ring	50	G 370.	Fertilizer hopper stud	20
G 307.	Center stud in hopper	20	G 800.	Beam, R. or L	1 00
G 311.	Hopper washer	10	G 801.	Opener brace, R. or L	20
G 312.	Roller standard clip	15	G 802.	Handle brace, R. or L	15
G 313.	Cotton cone bevel wheel, 30 tooth	60	G 803.	Covering standard, R. or L	45
G 314.	Corn cone bevel wheel, 12 tooth	40	G 804.	Spoon coverer standard, R. H	30
G 316.	Drive rod bearing under hopper	15	G 805.	Spoon coverer standard, L. H	30
G 317.	Bevel clutch wheel on main axle	50	G 806.	Beam spreader	30
G 318.	Mitre wheel on G 320	50	G 807.	Opener back	15
G 319.	Mitre wheel housing	60	G 808.	Clutch lever	20
G 320.	Drive wheel	90	G 809.	Lower end for clutch lever	20
G 321.	Front axle bracket, R. H	45	G 810.	Clutch lever slide	10
G 322.	Front axle bracket, L. H	35	G 811.	Bevel wheel shaft	40
G 323.	Draw head	35	G 812.	Wheel axle	25
G 325.	Cotton cone cap	15	G 813.	Sheet iron hopper	80
G 327.	Clutch sleeve on main axle	20	G 814.	Sleeve for main axle	15
G 345.	Opener standard and spout	90	G 815.	Spring for main axle	15
G 346.	Spool	10	G 816.	Spring for cut-off	10
G 347.	Cover for G 335	15	G 817.	Sleeve for cut-off	10
G 350.	Mitre wheel inside hopper	50	G 818.	Stirrup with nuts for cut-off	10
G 351.	Cotton cone	1 00	G 819.	Feed gate	10
G 352.	Two-hole corn plate	35	G 820.	Bolt with wing nut for feed gate	10
G 353.	Three-hole corn plate	35	G 821.	Bolt with wing nut for G 305	10
G 354.	Four-hole corn plate	35	G 822.	Wood roller	60
G 355.	Five-hole corn plate	35	G 823.	Sleeve for wood roller	25
G 356.	Six-hole corn plate	35	G 824.	Standard for wood roller, R. or L	30
G 357.	One-hole corn plate	35	G 825.	Bolt for wood roller	15
G 358.	Eight-hole corn plate	35	G 826.	Wheel scraper with washer	15
G 359.	Six-hole peanut plate	35	G 827.	Bolt with wing nut for fertilizer attach.	10
G 360.	Ten-hole corn plate	35	G 828.	Fertilizer hopper (sheet iron)	80
G 361.	Eleven-hole corn plate	35	G 829.	Fertilizer feed gate complete	25
G 362.	Ten-hole sorghum plate	35	G 830.	Fertilizer axle	25
G 363.	Eleven-hole corn plate	35	G 831.	Lug for fertilizer bottom	10
G 364.	Twelve-hole corn plate	35	G 832.	Corn cut-off complete	50

B. F. AVERY & SONS.      LOUISVILLE, KY.

DIRECTIONS

FOR SETTING UP AND OPERATING AVERY'S "REVOLUTION" DISC CULTIVATOR.

Cut of Implement on Page 64.

Place rear end of pole between pole straps and in hound guide JX8 and bolt securely.

Oil the axles and put on wheels.

Attach disc standard bracket JX47 to disc standard slide JX56 on right hand side of main axle arch bar and disc, standard bracket JX48L to disc standard slide JX56 on left hand side, fastening them with steel pins with cotters at each end of pins.

Bolt spring rods between inside lugs of yoke quadrants JX53.

Bolt right hand lever on outside of right quadrant, left hand lever on outside of left quadrant.

Bolt rear ends of draw bars in draft rod clips JX98 (old No. JX61) and front ends in shackles JX56.

Bolt ends of seat bars to pivot casting JX35.

Bolt guiding lever over ferrule at end of pole irons.

Drop end of wrought pole lock JX353 in JX57 to guiding lever.

Bolt disc adjusting levers JX12 to lever arm JX96 (old No. JX52); **have vacant lugs pointing outward towards wheels.**

Place coil springs on spring rods, then throw levers down in front until spring rods have passed through trunnions JX15 far enough to admit adjusting spring sleeve JX45 above levers, then insert cotters. The disc gangs can be dropped two inches lower by putting spring sleeve underneath trunnions.

Disc gangs are branded right and left; place as branded and bolt to yoke swivel JX97 (old No. JX49) with the oil tubes in the rear.

Bolt tool box on side of left hand hound.

To change from inthrow to outthrow, remove adjusting lever JX12 and turn gangs half way around, then bolt levers to vacant lug on JX96 (old No. JX52). When these disc gangs are once bolted in position as above, they need never to be taken off for any work cultivator is supposed to do.

In using this cultivator as an eight disc harrow or for bedding lands, **the bedding bar should always be used.** The bedding bar should be clamped to disc standards just above yoke quadrant JX53. The width is adjusted by means of set screw clamp in center of bars.

Oil the ball bearings at least four times a day by removing cap over oil pipe and pouring oil in pipe. To prevent gumming coal oil should be poured in them each morning and the cultivator operated fifteen or twenty minutes, and then pour in the lubricating oil.

The disc gangs are adjusted to angle of bed by loosening the two bolts in yoke swivel JX97 (old No. JX49) and adjusting yoke to desired angle, then tighten bolts firmly. The throwing angle of the discs is obtained by means of adjusting levers JX12.

To guide the cultivator it is only necessary to keep the front end of pole over the center of row.

B. F. AVERY & SONS.      LOUISVILLE, KY.

REPAIR PRICE LIST FOR

REVOLUTION DISC CULTIVATOR No. 1.

Cut of Implement on page 64. Cut of Repairs on page 159.
When ordering right or left hand repairs, do so from operator's position or rear of Cultivator.
Order repairs by letter and number given.

No. of Part.	Articles.	Price.	No. of Part.	Articles.	Price.
J X 1.	Axle bracket	$1 00	J X 311.	Lifting lever, complete—L H	$1 50
J X 1.	Axle bracket, with spindle J X 315.	2 00	J X 312.	Lifting lever, without attachments.	1 00
J X 5.	Lifting quadrant, with spindle—		J X 318.	Disc axle bolt	40
	R. H., old style	25	J X 319.	Foot rest	30
J X 6.	Lifting quadrant, with spindle—		J X 320.	Hammer strap	10
	L. H., old style	25	J X 321.	Disc blade, 16 inch	2 00
J X 7.	Pivot casting for pole	30	J X 322.	Disc blade, 16 inch, for harrow attachment	2 00
J X 8.	Hound guide on pole	60			
J X 12.	Disc adjusting lever—without attachments.	30	J X 323.	Trigger rod	20
J X 13.	Disc adjusting lever—trigger	15	J X 324.	Ferrule for J X 24 and J X 25.	10
J X 15.	Spring rod trunnion	15	J X 325.	Ferrule for J X 304	10
J X 16.	Fender clip on hounds—L. H.	20	J X 326.	Ferrule for lifting lever	10
J X 17.	Yoke bearing	45	J X 327.	Ferrule for guiding lever	10
J X 19.	Yoke bearing sleeve	45	J X 328.	Ferrule for J X 7	10
J X 20.	Ball bearing washer	25	J X 329.	Compression spiral springs	75
J X 21.	End washer on yoke—convex.	20	J X 330.	Spring for pawl E 288.	15
J X 22.	End washer on yoke—concave.	20	J X 331.	Spring for pawl J 105	10
J X 24.	Draft rod shackle on evener—R. H.	30	J X 332.	Spring for J X 12 and J X 13	10
J X 25.	Draft rod shackle on evener—L. H.	30	J X 333.	Spring rod for J X 329	50
J X 26.	Spring rod trunnion jaw for lifting		J X 334.	Gas pipe disc oiler, with cap.	20
	lever—R. H	15	J X 335.	Sheet iron fender, R. H	85
J X 27.	Spring rod trunnion jaw for lifting		J X 336.	Sheet iron fender—L. H.	85
	lever—L. H	15	J X 337.	Sheet iron fender, chain hook.	10
J X 28.	Scraper arm with set screw	40	J X 338.	Sheet iron fender, chain	25
J X 31.	Disc yoke—R. H.	2 00	J X 339.	Disc standards (steel)	2 00
J X 32.	Disc yoke—L. H	2 00	J X 340.	Hinge pin with cotters, for J X 47, and J X 56.	50
J X 33.	Disc yoke—cap	25	J X 341.	Scraper bar	20
J X 34.	Adjusting seat casting	25	J X 342.	Scraper bar, for harrow attachment.	25
J X 35.	Pivot casting for seat	30	J X 343.	Pole and arch brace—R. H	35
J X 36.	Shackle jaw for draft rod	30	J X 344.	Pole and arch brace—L. H.	35
J X 37.	Hub for harrow attachment	60	J X 345.	Polished steel wheel spindle, for J X 1	1 00
J X 38.	Bedding bar clamp with set screw	45			
J X 39.	Scraper for R. H. disc blades, each.	20	J X 346.	Guiding lever, front pc	30
J X 44.	Hound stop, on bottom pole strap.	25	J X 347.	Guiding lever, rear pc.	30
J X 45.	Adjusting spring sleeve	20	J X 348.	Slide for J X 59	15
J X 47.	Disc standard bracket—R. H.	1 00	J X 349.	Draft rods	35
J X 48.	Disc standard bracket—L. H.	1 00	J X 350.	Bedding bar, straight pc	30
J X 49.	Yoke swivel, old style	75	J X 351.	Bedding bar, bent pc	30
J X 50.	Swivel socket on spindle	40	J X 352.	Seat rails, complete	1 50
J X 51.	Draft rod clip on yoke swivel, old style	35	J X 353.	Pole lock with J X 57	75
J X 52.	Lever arm for J X 12, old style	25	J X 354.	Monkey wrench	75
J X 53.	Yoke quadrant	75	J X 355.	Foot rest bracket	15
J X 56.	Disc standard slide on arch, with set screws	1 00	J X 356.	Steel balls for ball bearings (no cut), each	08
J X 57.	Fender clip on hound with pole lock J X 358 (new)-R. H.	75	J X 357.	Pole, painted (no cut)	2 50
J X 59.	Quadrant for guide lever	75	J X 358.	Disc adjusting lever, complete.	70
J X 60.	Seat washer for straight seat bar.	10	J X 359.	Pawl cover (no cut)	15
J X 61.	Spreader between pole straps	25	B 64.	Toggle iron seat	10
J X 62.	Socket wrench for disc standard	30	B 71.	Shackle—R. H	25
J X 96.	Lever arm for J X 12 (no cut)	25	B 72.	Shackle—L. H	25
J X 97.	Yoke swivel (no cut)	75	E 209.	Trigger for J 105 (no cut)	15
J X 98.	Draft rod clip on yoke swivel (no cut)	35	E 288.	Pawl for E 204 (old style)	15
J X 300.	Steel hounds	3 50	E 294.	Pawl case (old style)	25
J X 301.	Main axle arch bar	2 50	J 79.	Seat	75
J X 302.	Evener, top arch	1 00	J 105.	Pawl case (old style)	15
J X 303.	Evener, bottom arch	1 00	J 108.	Tool box	60
J X 304.	Eveners, each	1 50	J 118.	Steel pawl (no cut)	30
J X 305.	Evener toggle	25	J 372.	Steel neckyoke, 43 inch	1 25
J X 306.	Toggle link—R. H	20	K 89.	Pawl for J 105 (old style)	10
J X 307.	Toggle link—L. H	20	T 74.	Axle washer	10
J X 308.	Rear pole strap—top	75	V	Steel wheels, painted, with boxing and nuts (no cut), per pair.	10 00
J X 309.	Rear pole strap—bottom	85	OB 508.	Wheel box (no cut)	1 00
J X 310.	Lifting lever, complete—R. H	1 50	N 54.	Wheel box nut (no cut)	40

B. F. AVERY & SONS.  LOUISVILLE, KY.

Repairs for Avery's Revolution Disc Cultivator.

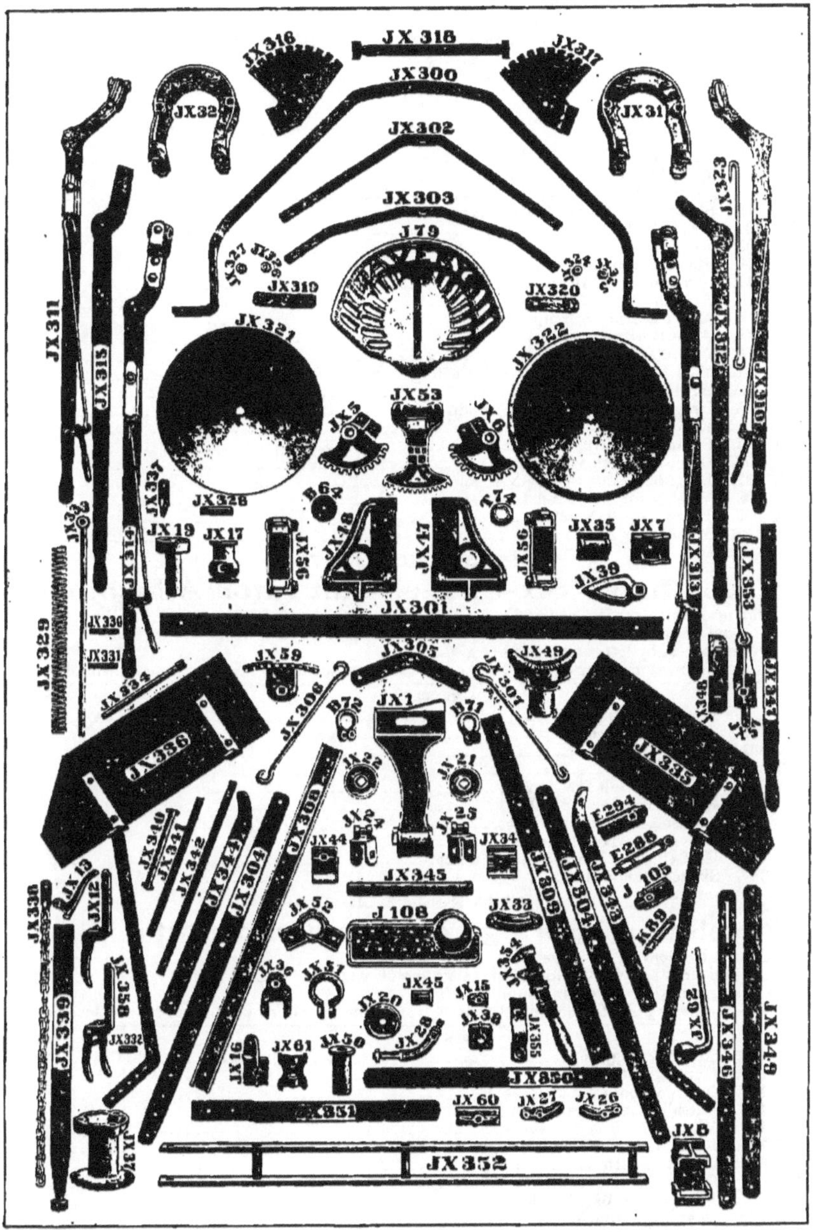

Cut of Implement on Page 64.   Prices of Repairs on Page 158.

B. F. AVERY & SONS. LOUISVILLE, KY.

REPAIR PRICE LIST FOR
"Revolution" Stalk Cutter Attachment.

Cut of repairs on page 161.
Cut of Implement on page 68.
Cut and prices on repairs for Carriage Frame, see pages 158 and 159.
Order repairs by letter and number given.
When ordering right or left hand repairs, do so from operator's position or rear of implement.

NO. OF PART.	ARTICLES.	PRICE.
Y 1.	Spider for Spiral Knives	$2 50
Y 2.	Box (half) for Spiders Y 1 and Y 19	25
Y 5.	Drag Hook Casting	1 00
Y 8.	Axle Collar	30
Y 9.	Cleaver Arm Casting	30
Y 19.	Spider for Straight Knives	2 50
Y 504.	Drag Hook, R. H	80
Y 505.	Drag Hook, L. H	80
Y 510.	Spiral Knife Blade	1 50
Y 511.	Straight Knife Blade	1 50
Y 515.	Arm for Trash Cleaner	20
Y 516.	Trash Cleaner Stirrup	20
J X 46.	Axle Bearing	50
J X 600.	Axle	3 00
J X 601.	Pole Bracket for Drag Hook Casting Y 5	90
J X 602.	Arm for Lifting Drag Hook	70
J X 603.	Drag Hook Lifting Lever, Plain	50
J X 604.	Lever Catch	15
J X 605.	Chain for Lifting Drag Hooks	30
J X 606.	Draft-bar Link with round hole	30
J X 607.	Draft-bar Link with square hole	30
J X 608.	Washer for Draft-rod Link	10
J X 609.	Ferrule for J X 602	10
J X 610.	Ferrule for J X 603	10

REPAIR PRICE LIST FOR
"Revolution" Six-Shovel Cultivator Attachment.

Cut of Implement on page 66.
Cut and prices of repairs for Carriage Frame on pages 158 and 159.
Order repairs by letter and number given.
When ordering right or left hand repairs, do so from operator's position or rear of implement.

NO. OF PART.	ARTICLES.		PRICE.
J X 58.	Beam Coupling	(No Cut)	$0 40
J X 360.	Connecting Arm	"	15
J X 361.	Gang Bar	"	25
J X 362.	Coupling	"	30
J X 363.	Clamping Bolt for B 92	"	10
B 83.	Rachet Washer for B 91	"	05
B 91.	Adjustable Break Pin Foot	"	50
B 92.	Shovel Standard Bracket	"	80
B 93.	Half Clip for Third Shovel Standard	"	20
B 840.	Shovel Standard	"	70

REPAIR PRICE LIST FOR
"Revolution" Spring Tooth Cultivator Attachment.

Cut of Implement on page 67.
Cut and prices of repairs for Carriage Frame on pages 158 and 159.
Order repairs by letter and number given.
When ordering right or left hand repairs, do so from operator's position or rear of implement.

NO. OF PART.	ARTICLES.		PRICE.
J X 99.	Side Bar Coupling	(No Cut)	$0 40
J X 100.	Center Tooth Bracket	"	20
J X 101.	Outside Tooth Bracket, R. H	"	20
J X 102.	Outside Tooth Bracket, L. H	"	20
J X 103.	Washer for J X 101 and 102	"	15
J X 364.	Blade with K 193 and Bolt, each	"	25
J X 365.	Outside Tooth	"	60
J X 366.	Center Tooth	"	60
J X 367.	Front Cross Bar, two holes	"	30
J X 368.	Rear Cross Bar, five holes	"	30
K 193.	Blade Washer	"	05

B. F. AVERY & SONS.  LOUISVILLE, KY.

Repairs for "Revolution" Stalk Cutter Attachment.
For Prices on Repairs, see page 160.

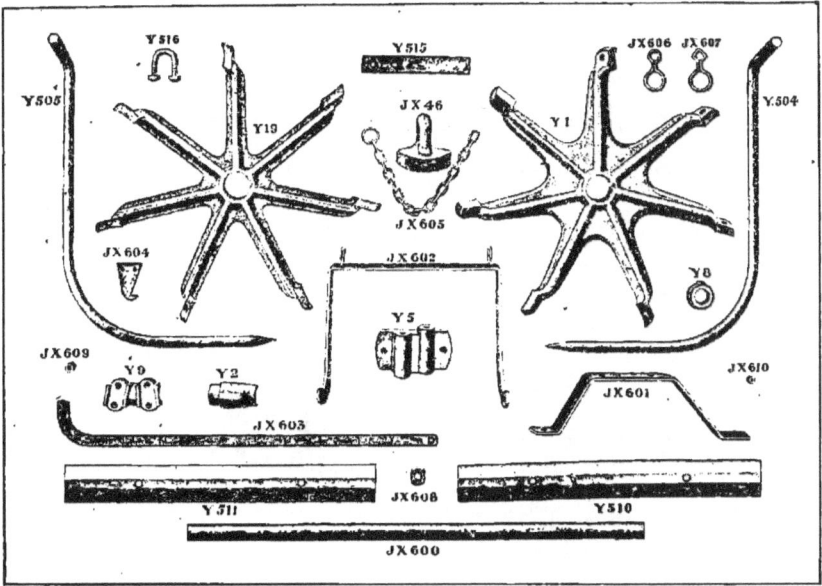

DIRECTIONS
For Attaching Stalk Cutter Attachment to Revolution Disc Cultivator.
Cut of Implement on page 68.

After detaching discs from yoke swivel, loosen bolt that fastens arch bar to axle bracket, and spread machine to its *fullest width*.

Bolt axle bearing JX 46 to yoke swivel, seeing that spider arms are in front of knives when they touch the ground.

Detach draft bars entirely from machine, then rebolt rear ends of bars between draft bar links JX 606 and JX 607, and bolt front ends to shackle jaws JX 36.

Remove short foot rests and substitute the longer ones sent with the stalk cutter attachment.

Place the arm for lifting drag hooks down over the pole with the curved ends toward rear of machine, and bolt same to fender clips JX 16 and JX 57. The drag hook lifting lever bolt to left side of arm.

Remove bolts from evener arch and hammer strap, then bolt pole bracket JX 601 for drag hook casting underneath the pole, placing the end with the largest bolt hole under arch, using bolt sent with attachment.

Insert the end of longest drag hook from right hand side through front hole of drag hook casting Y 5, and the shorter one from left hand side through rear hole and fasten with cotters. Slip the rings of chains over drag hooks, and attach the links to hooks on arm.

B. F. AVERY & SONS. LOUISVILLE, KY.

REPAIR PRICE LIST FOR
WESTERN AND NEW SOUTH CULTIVATORS.

Cut of Implements on pages 69, 70, and 71. Cut of repairs on page 164.
When ordering right or left hand repairs, do so from operator's position or rear of Cultivator.
Order repairs by letter and number given.

No. of Part.	Price.	Articles.	Used on Cultivator Number									
J 3	$0 10	Wheel washer	150	151	152	153	160	161	175	176	177	
J 51	1 50	Axle bracket, comp'e, with spindle—R. H. (old style)	150	151	152	153			175	175		
J 52	1 50	Axle bracket, comp'e, with spindle—L. H. (old style)	150	151	152	153			175	175		
J 55	1 00	Beam coupling sleeve—R. H.	150	151								
J 56	1 00	Beam coupling sleeve—L. H.	150	151								
J 61	40	Spring sleeve on spring trip (old style)										
J 62	15	Spring rod on spring trip (old style)	150			153						
J 63	05	Link on spring trip (old style)										
J 65	50	Spring trip foot (old style)										
J 69	50	Inside bracket for front shovel standard										
J 70	50	Inside bracket for rear shovel standard										
J 71	60	Shovel standard bracket—outside R. H.	150	151								
J 72	60	Shovel standard bracket—outside L. H.										
J 73	30	Beam spreader clip										
J 74	70	Tongue and hound casting	150	151	152	153	160	161	175	176	177	
J 75	35	Quadrant (old style)—R. H.	150	151	152	153			175	176		
J 76	35	Quadrant (old style)—L. H.										
J 77	40	Lifting spring rod										
J 79	85	Seat	150	151	152	153	160	161	175	176	177	
J 84	15	Beam coupling arch clip										
J 85	30	Handle clamp (bottom)	150	151			160	161				20
J 86	35	Handle clamp (top)	150	151	152	153	160	161	175	176	177	20
J 87	05	Seat washer	150	151	152	153	160	161	175	176	177	
J 88	05	Blade washer	150	151	152	153	160	161				
J 89	25	Stop to spring trip (old style)	150	151	152	153			175	176		
J 97	25	Wrench	150	151	152	153			175	176		
J 98	10	Fender dial (bottom)	150	151	152	153	160	161	175	176	177	
J 100	1 00	Beam coupling sleeve—R. H.										
J 101	1 00	Beam coupling sleeve—L. H.		152	153							
J 102	30	Gang coupling arch clip										
J 103	50	Quadrant (new style)—R. H.			152	153	160	161				
J 104	50	Quadrant (new style)—L. H.	150	151	152	153	160	161	175	176	177	
J 105	15	Pawl case										
J 106	10	Pawl case for J 105—R. H.	150	151	152	153			175	176		
J 107	10	Pawl case for J 105—L. H.										
J 108	60	Tool box (no cut)										
J 109	60	Gang coupling arch—R. H.	150	151	152	153	160	161	175	176	177	
J 110	60	Gang coupling arch—L. H.										
J 111	50	Adjustable foot for spring trip (old style)										
J 112	35	Link clip for spring trip										
J 113	25	Strap link for spring trip	No cut	150			153		161			177	
J 114	15	Trunnion for spring trip										
J 115	10	Washer for spring trip										
J 116	1 00	Beam coupling sleeve—R. H. (no cut)					160	161				
J 117	1 00	Beam coupling sleeve—L. H. (no cut)					160	161	175		177	
J 118	30	Pawl for levers—R. or L (no cut)					160	161				
J 119	30	Clip for lifting chain and foot rest (no cut)					160	161			177	
J 120	50	Adjustable foot for spring trip						161				
J 121	15	Adjusting block (no cut)					160	161				
J 200	30	Beam coupling (front)							175	176	177	
J 201	30	Beam coupling arch clip										
J 202	75	Parallel coupling (top)										
J 203	35	Rear beam coupling (bottom half)								176		
J 204	1 00	Standard bracket for beam (front)—R. H.										
J 205	1 00	Standard bracket for beam (front)—L. H.										
J 206	1 00	Standard bracket for beam (rear)							175	176	177	
J 207	35	Cap for J 204 and J 205								176		
J 208	20	Foot rest—R. H. (old style)										
J 209	20	Foot rest—L. H. (old style)							175	176		
J 210	30	Standard friction break back—R. H.										
J 211	30	Standard friction break back—L. H.							175	176	177	
J 212	10	Washer for J 210 and J 211										
J 213	85	Standard bracket for beam (front)							175		177	
J 214	25	Cap for J 206 and J 213							175	176	177	
J 215	35	Handle clamp (bottom)										
J 217	1 00	Beam coupling sleeve—R. H.										
J 218	1 00	Beam coupling sleeve—L. H.							175	176		
J 219	10	Fender dial (bottom)			152	153	160	161	175	176	177	
J 220	10	Fender dial (top)	150	151	152	153	160	161	175	176	177	
J 221	20	Parallel rod elbow								176		
J 222	40	Chain and foot rest clip							175			
J 223	50	R. H. standard friction break back (no cut)							175	176	177	
J 224	50	L. H. standard friction break back (no cut)										
J 225	1 50	Axle bracket, complete, with spindle (no cut)	150	151	152	153	160	161	175	176	177	
J 226	30	Clip for lifting chain and foot rest (no cut)							175		177	
J 227	15	Foot rest (no cut)					160	161	175			20
J 800	10	Evener rub plate on pole	150	151	152	153	160	161	175	176	177	
J 801	25	Hammer strap										
J 802	10	Pivot sleeve for doubletree										
J 803	15	Hook bolt										
J 804	1 00	Hound	150	151	152	153	160	161	175	176	177	
J 805	35	Brace—hound to axle bar										

B. F. AVERY & SONS.   LOUISVILLE, KY.

Repair Price List for Western and New South Cultivators—Continued.

No. of Part.	Price.	Articles.	Used on Cultivator Number
J 806	$0 90	Axle arch bar	150 151 152 153 160 161 175 176 177
J 807	1 25	Lever (old style), complete, for J 75—R. H.	150 151 152 153 175 176
J 808	1 25	Lever (old style), complete, for J 76—L. H.	
J 809	1 25	Lever (new style), complete, for J 103—R. H.	150 151 152 153 160 161 175 176 177
J 810	1 25	Lever (new style), complete, for J 104—L. H.	
J 811	30	Pawl and spring for 323 (old style)	150 151 152 153 175 176
J 812	10	Spring for J 105	
J 813	10	Trigger rod for J 105	150 151 152 153 160 161 175 176 177
J 814	2 00	Arch	
J 815	50	Sheet iron fender } state whether {	150 151
J 816	50	Sheet iron fender } right or left. {	152 153 160 161
J 817	50	Sheet iron fender	175 176 177
J 818	75	Seat bar—R. H.	150 151 152 153 160 161 175 176 177
J 819	75	Seat bar—L. H.	
J 820	1 50	Pipe beam (long)	176
J 821	1 00	Pipe beam (short)	
J 822	2 00	Pipe beam	175 177
J 823	80	Steel beam (short)	150 151
J 824	1 00	Steel beam (long)	
J 825	20	Steel draft pendant	
J 826	20	Connecting rod for draft pendant J 825	150 151 152 153 160 161 175 176 177
J 827	1 00	Lever, without attachment	
J 828	60	Axle bracket brace	
J 829	90	Shovel standard—outside R. H.	152 153
J 830	90	Shovel standard—outside L. H.	
J 831	1 50	Pipe beam	152 153 160 161
J 832	60	Wheel spindle	150 151 152 153 160 161 175 176 177
J 833	40	Parallel rod	176
J 834	20	Extension fender bar	175 176 177
J 835	40	Parallel bar	152 153
J 836	30	Foot rest	150 151 152 153 175 176
J 837	15	Clip for foot rest J 836	
J 838	75	Shovel standard	175 176
J 839	35	Lock, complete (old style), for gang coupling arch	150 151 152 153 175 176
J 840	30	Eye bolt for shovel standard	175 176 177
J 841	30	Lifting chain	150 151 152 153 160 161 175 176 177
J 842	10	Clip for J 98	150 151
J 843	60	Shovel standard (inside)	152 153 160 161
J 844	50	Coil lifting spring	150 151 152 153 160 161 175 176 177
J 845	2 00	Shovel standard with old style spring trip, complete	150 153
J 846	1 00	Shovel standard with break pin, complete	151 152
J 847	40	Coil spring for old style spring trip	150 153
J 849	1 25	Adjustable break pin foot and standard	152 160
J 850	15	Hook for coupling arch	150 151 152 153 160 161 175 176
J 851	2 50	Tongue, painted (no cut)	150 151 152 153 160 161 175 176 177
J 852	30	Coil spring for spring trip (no cut)	150 153 161 177
J 853	2 00	Shovel standard with spring trip, complete (no cut)	150 153 161
J 854	10	Wheel guard (no cut)	161 175
J 855	25	Wheel guard (no cut)	176
J 856	10	Link for spring trip (no cut)	150 153 177
J 857	20	Spring rod with nut for spring trip (no cut)	150 153 161 177
J 858	15	Cover for J 118 (no cut)	
J 859	05	Ferrule for J 118 (no cut)	160 161 175 177
J 860	15	Extension for third standard—R. H (no cut)	
J 861	15	Extension for third standard—L. H (no cut)	160 161
J 862	40	Outside standard extension bar (no cut)	
J 863	20	Parallel bar (no cut)	
J 864	60	Shovel standard (no cut)	177
J 865	35	Gang bar, long (no cut)	
J 866	30	Gang bar, short (no cut)	
J 867	25	Gang bar brace (no cut)	
J 868	40	Cross bar, steel (no cut)	20
J 869	60	Spring tooth (no cut)	
J 870	25	Blade with K 193 and bolt (no cut)	
J 871	15	Lifting chain clip (no cut)	
J 872	1 25	Steel neck yoke, 43-inch	150 151 152 153 160 161 175 176 177 20
B	10 00	Wheels (steel), per pair, with boxes and nuts, painted	150 151 152 153 160 161 175 176 177
B 76	1 25	Cross head—R. H.	152 153
B 77	1 25	Cross head—L. H.	
B 78	35	Front beam coupling (one half)	
B 79	60	Rear beam coupling and handle clamp	152 153 160 161
B 80	35	Rear beam coupling (bottom)	
B 81	20	Parallel rod clip	152
B 83	05	Ratchet washer for B 101	
B 101	40	Adjustable break pin foot (bottom)	152 160
B 102	25	Break pin arm	
B 103	15	Half clip for third shovel standard—R. H. (no cut)	
B 104	15	Half clip for third shovel standard—L. H. (no cut)	
B 105	1 25	Cross head—R. H. (no cut)	160 161
B 106	1 25	Cross head—L. H. (no cut)	
B 107	25	Parallel bar clip (no cut)	
B 112	40	Shovel standard clip (no cut)	
B 113	40	Shovel standard clip (no cut)	160 161
B 115	10	Adjusting block washer (no cut)	
B 116	40	Coupling head (no cut)	
B 117	40	Coupling head follower (no cut)	20
B 118	20	Spring tooth beam plate (no cut)	
B 119	15	Cross beam coupling (no cut)	

B. F. AVERY & SONS.  LOUISVILLE, KY.

Repair Price List for Western and New South Cultivators—Continued.

No. of Part.	Price.	Articles.	Used on Cultivator Number								
B 120	$0 20	Handle clip dial (no cut)									20
B 511	1 00	Wheel box (no cut)	150	151	152	153	160	161	175	176	177
B 813	30	Wood handle (no cut)									
B 813	15	Gang coupling strap—top (no cut)									20
B 819	10	Gang coupling strap—bottom (no cut)									
E 209	15	Trigger for J 807, 808, 809, 810	150	151	152	153	160	161	175	176	177
K 193	05	Blade washer (no cut)									20
N 51	40	Wheel box nut (no cut)	150	151	152	153	160	161	175	176	177
94	10	Shackle and pin	150	151	152	153	160	161	175	176	177
323	15	Pawl case (old style) for J 807 and 808	150	151	152	153			175	176	

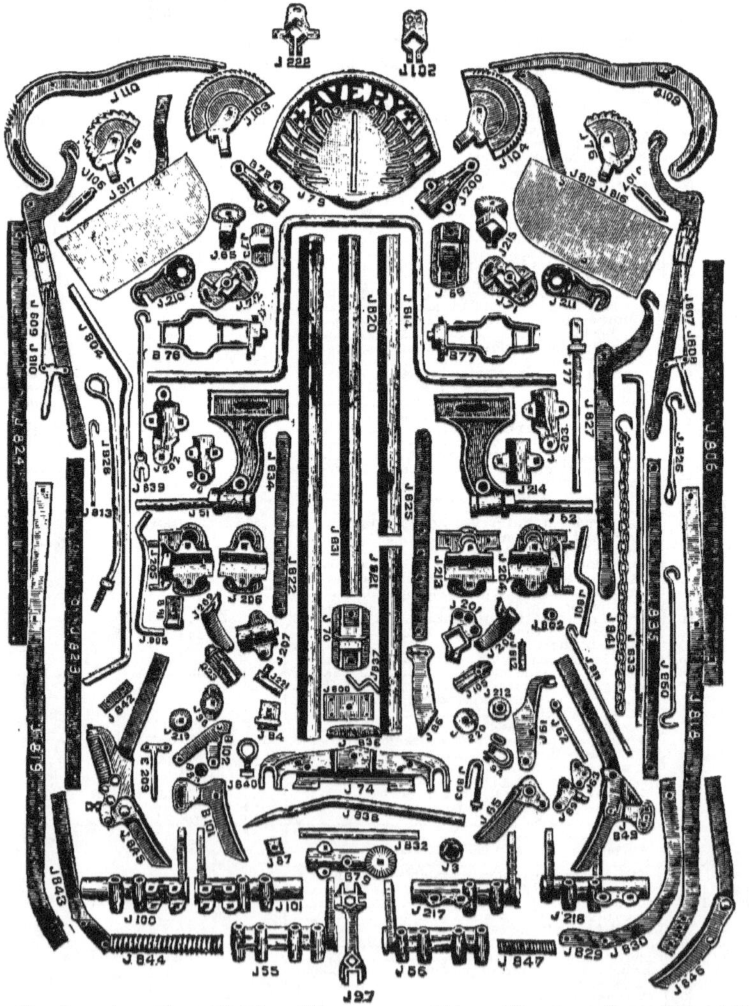

Cut of Implements on Pages 69, 70, and 71.   Prices of Repairs on Pages 162 and 163.

B. F. AVERY & SONS.  LOUISVILLE, KY.

DIRECTIONS

FOR SETTING UP THE "WESTERN" AND NEW SOUTH CULTIVATORS.

Cut of Implements on Pages 69, 70, and 71.

After oiling the axles and putting wheels on cultivators, remove the wood blocks from between the hounds and bolt the pole to hounds and to hound and tongue casting J74.

Bolt the evener between the hammer strap J801 and pole (with the draft pendants in front), and connect the lower ends of pendants to draft hook on arch.

Bolt quadrant J103R with lever attached to axle arch bar at second bolt from end on right of arch bar and secure J104L to corresponding bolt on left side.

Bolt braces for quadrants to hound and axle bar braces, then fasten seat rails with the same bolts. Adjust the seat to suit the operator. When used as a walking cultivator the seat can be thrown forward.

Fasten gangs and parallel bars of Western Cultivators to coupling sleeves J116R and J117L, with parallel bars toward inside of cultivator. In the New South fasten the gangs to coupling sleeves J217R and J218L. Each coupling sleeve is provided with two sets of hubs to fasten gangs to, which allows the placing of the gangs at two different distances apart.

NOTE.—When attaching beams to the cultivators be sure and oil around the bolts, and tighten them firm, then run the nuts back about one half turn, so that the beams will move freely laterally.

Withdraw the cotters from arch casting J74, then slip the coil springs over the spring rods and raise the rear ends of gangs, when the spring rods will enter the slots in arch casting J74, then slip the cotters back into place. The lifting tension of the springs can be adjusted at any time by holding up the rear ends of gangs and turning the nuts on spring rods up or down.

Place the beam coupling arch J109 and J110 in a horizontal position (with the numbers down and the rounded ends to the front of the cultivator), and enter the two bent ends in the holes in J201 if on the New South, or J102 if on the Western, and as the ends enter, raise the arch to a vertical position, then adjust the beams to the width desired and lock in position with hook J850 to lug on tongue and hound casting J74.

Attach lifting chains to hooks on end of levers. The depth of plowing can be regulated by lengthening or shortening the chains.

Bolt handles on right hand side of handle clamps J86, driving bolts through clamp first.

Attach fenders to dials J219 and J220 at end of extension fender bars.

Bolt tool box to center of axle arch bar.

When any nuts are loosened to make any adjustment, be sure and tighten the same before using.

B. F. AVERY & SONS. LOUISVILLE, KY.

Repair Price List for Comet Cultivators.

Cut of Implements on pages 72 to 77. Cut of repairs on page 168.
When ordering right or left hand repairs, do so from operator's position or rear of Cultivator.
Order repairs by letter and number given.

No. of Part	Price.	Articles.	Used on Cultivator Number									
B 45	$0 35	Gang coupling	100						106	107	108	
B 61	1 00	Coupling sleeve—R. H	100	101	102				106	107	108	
B 62	1 00	Coupling sleeve—L. H	100	101	102				106	107	108	
B 64	05	Seat for toggle	100	101	102	103	104	105	106	107	108	112 113
B 65	10	Axle washer	100	101	102	103		105	106	107	108	112 113
B 66	20	Spring stop										
B 67	15	Adjusting spreader block	100						106	107	108	
B 68	15	Spreader										
B 69	25	Hook-up arm	100	101	102	103		105	106	107	108	112 113
B 70	20	Handle clamp (bottom)	100						106			
B 71	15	Shackle—R. H	100	101	102	103	104	105	106	107	108	112 113
B 72	15	Shackle—L. H										
B 73	75	Pole and arch casting	100	101	102	103		105	106	107	108	112 113
B 74	1 00	Coupling sleeve—R. H										
B 75	1 00	Coupling sleeve—L. H										
B 76	1 25	Cross head—R. H			103		105					
B 77	1 25	Cross head—L. H										
B 78	35	Gang coupling (front)—one half										
B 79	50	Rear coupling and bottom handle clip			103		105				112 113	
B 80	35	Rear gang coupling (bottom)										
B 81	20	Parallel rod clip			103		105					
B 83	05	Ratchet washer—for B 91 and B 101			103	104			107		112	
B 86	75	Tongue and arch plate										
B 87	15	Lifting spring stop										
B 88	50	Gang coupling										
B 89	1 00	Gang coupling sleeve—R. H										
B 90	1 00	Gang coupling sleeve—L. H										
B 91	50	Adjustable break pin foot										
B 92	80	Shovel standard bracket				104						
B 93	20	Half clip for third shovel standard										
B 94	25	Bottom handle clip										
B 95	10	Washer for B 96										
B 96	10	Clip for B 842										
B 97	10	Fender bar clip										
B 100	25	Hook-up arm										
B 101	40	Adjustable break pin foot										
B 102	25	Adjustable break pin foot arm			103				107		112	
B 103	15	Half clip for third shovel standard—R. H										
B 104	15	Half clip for third shovel standard—L. H										
B 105	1 25	Cross head—R. H	No									
B 106	1 25	Cross head—L. H	Cut								112 113	
B 107	15	Parallel bar clip										
B 110	1 00	Coupling sleeve—R. H										
B 111	1 00	Coupling sleeve, L. H										
B 112	40	Shovel standard clamp	No						107	108	112 113	
B 113	40	Shovel standard clamp	Cut									
B 114	15	Adjusting block	No								112 113	
B 115	10	Adjusting block washer	Cut									
B 116	40	Coupling head										
B 117	40	Coupling head follower										
B 118	20	Spring tooth plate—R. or L										10
B 119	15	Cross beam coupling										
B 120	20	Handle clip dial										
B 800	10	Toggle strap										
B 801	25	Evener toggle	100	101	102	103	104	105	106	107	108	112 113
B 802	20	Extension fender bar					104					
B 803	80	Evener	100	101	102	103		105	106	107	108	112 113
B 804	15	Evener and pole brace	100	101	102	103	104	105	106	107	108	112 113
B 805	20	Extension fender bar				103		105				112
B 806	30	Evener arch (top)										
B 807	25	Evener arch (bottom)	100	101	102	103		105	106	107	108	112 113
B 808	10	Rear washer plate for pole	100	101	102	103	104	105	106	107	108	112 113
B 809	15	Arch stirrup					104					
B 810	15	Arch stirrup										
B 812	1 25	Axle arch	100	101	102	103		105	106	107	108	112 113
B 813	30	Wood handle (no cut)	100	101	102	103	104	105	106	107	108	112 113
B 814	1 40	Steel beam (long)—R. H										
B 815	1 40	Steel beam (long)—L. H										
B 816	1 25	Steel beam (short)—R. H	100						106			
B 817	1 25	Steel beam (short)—L. H										
B 818	25	Gang coupling strap (top)										
B 819	20	Gang coupling strap (bottom)	100						106	107	108	10
B 820	15	Gang hook-up										
B 821	20	Spreader rod	100						106	107	108	
B 822	05	Handle clamp strap for B 70	100						106			
B 823	50	Sheet iron fender—} state whether {	100	101	102				106	107	108	
B 824	50	Sheet iron fender—} right or left. {				103	104	105				112 113
B 826	05	Fender dial strap for J 98	100	101	102				106	107	108	
B 827	15	Bent bolt for B 69	100	101	102	103		105	106	107	108	112 113

B. F. AVERY & SONS. LOUISVILLE, KY.

Repair Price List for Comet Cultivators—Continued.

No. of Part	Price	Articles	Used on Cultivator Number
B 828	$0 15	Bent bolt for B 100	
B 829	20	Hook for B 100	104
B 830	25	Hook-up link	
B 831	20	Hook-up	101 102 103 105 112 113
B 832	20	Gang spreader strap (top)	101 102
B 833	20	Gang spreader strap (bottom)	
B 840	70	Shovel standard	104
B 841	1 00	Pipe for beam	103 105 112 113
B 842	40	Gang scraper gauge	104
B 843	1 00	Evener	
B 844	35	Parallel rod	103 105
B 845	70	Draft rod—R. H	101
B 846	70	Draft rod—L. H	
B 847	60	Draft rod—R. H	100 101 102 103 105 106 107 108 112 113
B 848	60	Draft rod—L. H	
B 849	20	Evener toggle link—R. H	100 101 102 103 104 105 106 107 108 112 113
B 850	20	Evener toggle link—L. H	
B 851	40	Evener arch (top)	104
B 852	35	Evener arch (bottom)	
B 853	15	Clamping bolt for shovel standard	101 107 108 112 113
B 854	1 50	Axle arch	
B 855	1 00	Outside gang bar (5 holes)	104
B 856	1 00	Inside gang bar (6 holes)	
B 857	1 00	Steel gang (long)—R. H	
B 858	1 00	Steel gang (long)—L. H	
B 859	85	Steel gang (short)—R. H	101 102
B 860	85	Steel gang (short)—L. H	
B 861	2 50	Tongue, painted (no cut)	100 101 102 103 104 105 106 107 108 112 113
B 862	30	Long beam	No Cut 10
B 863	25	Short beam	
B 864	40	Coupling strap and hook-up—R. H	No Cut
B 865	40	Coupling strap and hook-up—L. H	112 113
B 866	40	Coupling strap and hook-up—R. H	No Cut
B 867	40	Coupling strap and hook-up—L. H	107 108
B 868	1 50	Steel neckyoke, 43 inches (no cut)	104
J 60	40	Gang coupling	101 102
J 61	40	Spring trip sleeve (old style)	
J 62	15	Spring rod for spring trip (old style)	101 105
J 63	05	Link for spring trip (old style)	
J 65	50	Open foot for spring trip (old style)	
J 67	50	Break pin foot	100 102
J 69	50	Inside standard bracket (front)	
J 70	50	Inside standard bracket (rear)	
J 71	60	Outside standard bracket (front)	101 102
J 72	60	Outside standard bracket (rear)	
J 73	30	Outside spreader clip	
J 77	40	Lifting spring rod	100 101 102 103 104 105 106 107 108 112 113
J 85	30	Handle clamp (bottom)	101 102 107 108
J 86	35	Handle clamp (top)	101 102 103 104 105 106 107 108 112 113 10
J 88	05	Blade washer (no cut)	100 101 102 103 104 105 106 107 108 112 113
J 89	25	Stop to spring trip (old style)	101 105
J 97	20	Wrench	100 101 102 103 104 105 106 107 108 112 113
J 98	10	Fender dial (bottom)	100 101 102 106 107 108
J 108	60	Tool box (no cut)	100 101 102 103 104 105 106 107 108 112 113
J 111	50	Adjustable foot for spring trip (old style)	
J 112	35	Link clip for spring trip	
J 113	25	Strap link for spring trip	No Cut 101 105 106 108 113
J 114	15	Trunnion for spring trip	
J 115	10	Washer for spring trip	
J 120	50	Adjustable foot for spring trip (no cut)	108 113
J 219	10	Fender dial (bottom)	103 104 105 112 113
J 220	10	Fender dial (top)	100 101 102 103 104 105 106 107 108 112 113
J 829	90	Shovel standard—R. H	103 105 107 108
J 830	90	Shovel standard—L. H	
J 843	60	Standard, without attachments	101 102 103 105 107 108 112 113
J 844	50	Coil lifting spring	100 101 102 103 104 105 106 107 108 112 113
J 845	2 00	Standard, with O.S. spring trip foot, comp'e	101 105
J 846	1 00	Standard, with break pin foot, complete	102
J 847	40	Coil spring for spring trip (old style)	101 105
J 849	1 25	Standard, with adj'ble break pin foot, comp	103 107 112
J 852	30	Coil spring for spring trip	
J 853	2 00	Standard, with spring trip foot, complete	No Cut 101 105 106 108 113
J 856	10	Link for spring trip	
J 857	20	Spring rod with nut for spring trip	
J 860	15	Extension for third standard, R. H	No Cut 112 113
J 861	15	Extension for third standard. L. H	
J 862	40	Outside standard extension bar	
J 868	40	Cross bar (steel)	No Cut 10
J 869	60	Spring tooth	
J 870	25	Blade with K 103 and bolt	
J 872	1 25	Steel neckyoke, 43 inches (no cut)	107 108 112 113 10
K 193	05	Blade back or block (no cut)	104 10
T 100	10	Wheel washer	
O B 2	50	Wheel box	100 101 102 103 105 106 107 108 112 113
O B 99	75	Wheel box	104
N 4	25	Wheel box nut (no cut)	100 101 102 103 105 107 108 112 113
N 14	35	Wheel box nut (no cut)	104 106
C	4 50	Steel wheel, with box and nut, p'nt'd, per pr	100 101 102 103 105 106 107 108 112 113
Q	5 50	Steel wheel with box and nut, p'nt'd, per pr	104

B. F. AVERY & SONS. LOUISVILLE, KY.

REPAIRS FOR "COMET" WALKING CULTIVATORS.

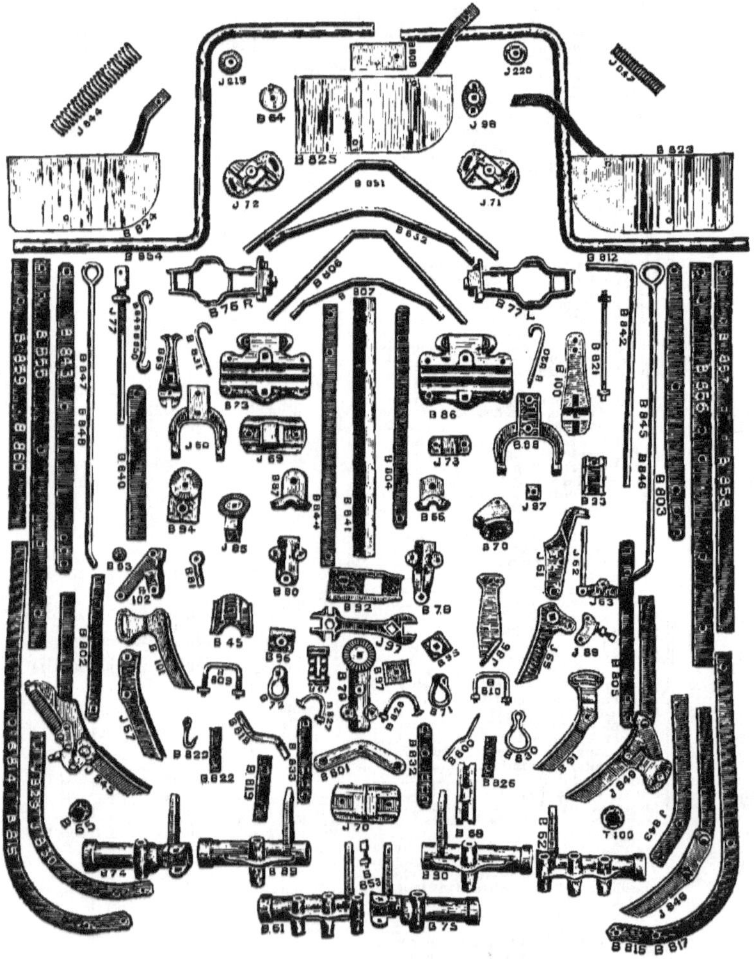

Cut of Implements on Pages 72 to 77.

Prices of Repairs on Pages 166 and 167.

DIRECTIONS

FOR SETTING UP AVERY'S COMET CULTIVATOR.

Cut of Implements on Pages 72 to 77.

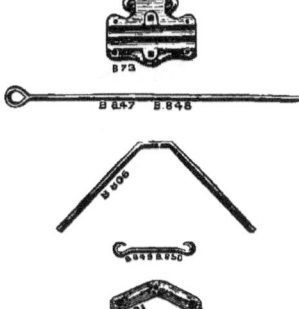

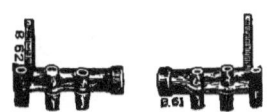

Take nuts off of long bolts in pole and arch casting B73, then place the casting so that lugs on same will be in front, and fasten pole between flanges of casting.

After removing cotters and washers from axle, slip gang coupling sleeves off of axle until slots in coupling sleeves are clear of axle, then insert the eye on end of round draft rods B847 and B848 in slots (with the bent end pointing outward), and slip coupling sleeves and rods back on axles. Loosen stirrups which pass through pole and arch casting B73, and insert ends of draft rods from bottom through evener arch B808.

Put evener toggle links B849 and B850 in evener toggle B801 and in ends of evener bar, and place center hole of evener bar over end of draft rod, then place round hole in flat brace on top of evener, and drive end of draft rod through and insert cotter, then bolt the other end to lugs on pole and arch casting B73.

Fasten tool box, with wood screws, on pole, back of evener arch.

To Attach Gangs.—If it is the Nos. 107 or 108, attach the gangs to center hubs of coupling sleeves B61 R and B62 L. If it is the Nos. 101 or 102, attach the gangs to the two inside hubs of coupling sleeves B61 R and B62 L. If it is the Nos. 112 or 113, attach the beams and parallel rods to coupling sleeves B110 R and B111 L. If it is the No. 104, attach the beams to coupling sleeves B89 R and B90 L.

Any desired distance between the gangs can be obtained by loosening the nuts of stirrup at rear end of tongue and adjusting the arch out or in, as may be desired.

NOTE.—When attaching any of these gangs to the cultivator, be sure and oil around the bolts, and tighten them firm, then run the nuts back about one half turn, so that the gangs will move freely laterally.

Slip coil springs on spring rods, raise rear of gangs until spring rods will enter spring stop B66 on the arch. The lifting tension of the springs can be adjusted by raising the rear ends of gangs until spring rods are clear of spring stops and turning the nuts on spring rods up or down.

Bolt handles on right-hand side of handle clamps J86, driving bolt through clamp first.

☞ When any nuts are loosened to make any adjustment, be sure and tighten the same before using.

B. F. AVERY & SONS. LOUISVILLE, KY.

TELEGRAPH CODE.

The following Telegraph Code will be found very convenient and useful, and we recommend its use to customers and the trade.

Great care should be taken to write each word plainly, as a change of a single letter may make a very great difference. All telegrams should be prepaid.

CODE WORDS.

STOCK QUESTIONS.

Code Word.	Signification.
Embark	How soon can you furnish?
Emblem	How soon and at what price can you furnish?
Embors	Have you in stock and can you furnish at once?
Embroil	Can you furnish within?
Empire	If so, enter order.
Empress	If not, how soon can you furnish?

STOCK ANSWERS.

Emption	We have in stock.
Emulate	We have in stock and can ship at once.
Enact	We have in stock and will ship at once.
Enacting	We have none in stock.
Enamel	We have not in stock.
Encamp	We are entirely out of ——
Enchain	If ordered immediately.
Enchanter	On receipt of order.
Enchased	After receipt of order.

PRICE QUESTIONS.

Encircle	What is your list price on?
Encompass	What is your best discount on?
Encore	What is your best cash discount from price of?
Encourage	Is price quoted net, or subject to usual discount?
Encroach	Quote us lowest net price on.
Encumber	Quote us lowest net price and best terms on.
Endow	Quote us lowest net spot cash price on.
Endrudge	Will you hold offer open?
Endwise	We are offered.
Enemy	Will you accept?
Energy	Will you allow me?

PRICE ANSWERS.

English	We quote.
Engraft	We quote on your specifications.
Engulf	We quote on your specifications as contained in your letter.
Enhance	We quote on your specifications as contained in your telegram.
Enigma	Quotations for all cash shipment.
Enjoy	Prices quoted are for prompt acceptance only.
Enkindle	All previous quotations are hereby withdrawn.
Enlight	The regular price is.
Enmity	We will sell at.
Ennoble	We will not sell at.
Enrolled	We will accept order.
Ensample	We will accept order, shall we ship?
Enshroud	We will not accept order.
Enslave	We can not accept price offered.
Entail	We can not accept contract, so please cancel.
Enthrone	Please specify quantity wanted.
Entice	Please specify size wanted.
Entomb	Please specify size and quantity wanted.
Entrap	We can not do better.
Envelope	——proposition is the very best we will do.
Envious	We will hold offer open.
Epicure	We can not hold offer open.
Epigram	We will furnish goods mentioned in your letter at.
Epilogue	We will furnish goods mentioned in your telegram at.
Epithet	F. O. B. in.
Equator	F. O. B. cars Louisville.
Erigible	F. O. B. cars your city.

B. F. AVERY & SONS. LOUISVILLE, KY.

TELEGRAPH CODE—Continued.

TERMS.

Code Word.	Signification.
Escapade	Terms are.
Escort	Terms are sixty days note or two (2) per cent cash discount ten (10) days from shipment.
Essayist	Terms are three months note or three (3) per cent cash discount ten (10) days from shipment.
Etched	Terms are four months note or two (2) per cent cash discount ten (10) days from shipment.
Etching	Terms are four months note or five (5) per cent cash discount ten (10) days from shipment.
Etiquette	Terms are October first note or five (5) per cent cash discount June first.
European	Terms are satisfactory.
Eventide	Terms are not satisfactory.
Evergreen	Terms wanted are too long; if you can not shorten up will have to decline order.
Evermore	Time payment too long.
Exactor	What terms are wanted?
Excursion	What terms may I offer?
Exhale	Net cash F. O. B.
Exhort	How much cash?
Expand	Will pay $—— cash with order.
Expansion	Or for $—— cash.
Expiate	And eight (8) per cent per annum interest.
Exploit	And ten (10) per cent per annum interest.
Explore	With lien on goods.

NUMERALS.

Code Word.	Signification.	Code Word.	Signification.
Exponent	21	Famous	66
Exporting	22	Fanatic	67
Extensor	23	Fancier	68
Extricate	24	Fanciful	69
Exude	25	Fanlight	71
Exultant	26	Fanning	72
Exundate	27	Fantastic	73
Exvato	28	Farce	74
Eyeball	29	Farcial	75
Eyebeam	31	Farm	76
Eyedrop	32	Farrago	77
Eyeglass	33	Fashion	78
Eyelet	34	Fatal	79
Eyepiece	35	Fatalism	81
Eyeshot	36	Fatten	82
Eyestring	37	Fattish	83
Eyetooth	38	Faultless	84
Eyewater	39	Favorless	85
Eyewitness	41	Fawn	86
Fable	42	Fawning	87
Fabric	43	Feather	88
Faction	44	Featherbed	89
Factotum	45	Feeder	91
Faculty	46	Fellow	92
Fagend	47	Femesole	93
Faint	48	Fencing	94
Faintness	49	Ferry	95
Fairing	51	Ferryboat	96
Fairness	52	Ferryman	97
Fairy	53	Fervent	98
Fairyland	54	Festive	99
Faithless	55	Fickle	100
Fakir	56	Fiction	200
Falcom	57	Fiddling	300
Fallacy	58	Fierce	400
Fallible	59	Fierceness	500
Falsehood	61	Fighting	600
Falsify	62	Filtering	700
Fame	63	Finally	800
Fameless	64	Financier	900
Famish	65	Flagrance	1000

B. F. AVERY & SONS. LOUISVILLE, KY.

TELEGRAPH CODE—Continued.

REFERRING TO ORDERS.

Code Word.	Signification.
Flambeau	Enter our order for.
Flame	Specifications to follow.
Flamingo	In addition to previous order.
Flanking	To complete car load add.
Flannel	You can substitute.
Flapping	To be delivered.
Flashy	We must have.
Flasket	With all fixtures complete.
Flatfish	With all fixtures except following, namely.
Flation	Prepare for immediate shipment; full instructions by letter.

REFERRING TO ORDERS—ANSWERS.

Flatness	We have entered order.
Flatterer	We have no order.
Flatulent	Shall we enter order?
Flaunting	Your order of the.
Flavor	Your order is not plain; be more explicit.
Flawless	Goods ordered will make car.
Flaxseed	We require——pounds to complete car.
Fleabite	What shall we add to complete car?
Fledgeling	Shall we fill out car with——?
Fleece	We will complete.
Fleeceless	Require addition to order.
Fleeting	May we substitute?
Fleshing	We are now loading.
Flickering	We are making.
Flight	We will do our best.
Flimsily	We can not promise definitely.
Flinching	We have been disappointed in delivery of.
Flinger	We are waiting for the——.
Flippant	We can not get the——.
Flirt	Your order is not clear; we write you to-day for full information.

REFERRING TO SHIPMENTS—QUESTIONS.

Flitter	Ship immediately.
Flix	Ship as soon as possible.
Floater	Ship what you have ready and let balance follow.
Flogged	Ship to our order at.
Flooding	Ship and draw with bill lading attached.
Floor	Ship to the care of.
Florentine	Ship by car load.
Florist	Can you ship?
Flotation	When will you ship order of the?
Flounder	Have you shipped order of the?
Flouring	If not, when will you ship?
Flouting	If you can not ship in time named advise us by wire.
Flower	Hasten shipment of the——.
Flunky	Keep shipment traced by wire.
Flurry	Send tracer for shipment.
Flushed	Telegraph number and initials of car and route shipped.
Flushness	What is rate of freight to?

REFERRING TO SHIPMENTS—ANSWERS.

Flutter	We will ship.
Fluxation	We can ship.
Fluxible	We could ship.
Flyfish	We could probably ship in.
Flyleaf	We can not ship.
Flytrap	We have shipped.
Flywheel	We have not shipped.
Foaling	We expect to ship.
Foaming	We will try to ship.
Fodder	We will ship on receipt of.
Foldage	Think we can ship.
Foldless	Yes. Shall we ship?

B. F. AVERY & SONS. LOUISVILLE, KY.

TELEGRAPH CODE—Continued.

REFERRING TO SHIPMENTS—ANSWERS—Continued.

Code Word.	Signification.
Fomenter	We have ready for shipment.
Fondled	Shall we ship?
Fondness	If ordered by telegraph promptly we could ship in.
Foodless	Can not promise positively, but think we can ship in.
Footband	We could not make and ship.
Footbridge	But we can ship promptly on receipt of order.
Footfall	Shall we ship what we have ready and let balance follow when completed?
Footless	Shall we ship or await further instructions before doing so?
Footpad	Send shipping instructions.
Footstalk	Telegraph shipping instructions.
Forage	Rate of freight is——.
Forbidden	The best obtainable rate of freight is.
Forcedly	We can not obtain through rate of freight.
Forefoot	Shall we insure at your expense shipment now ready?

SHIPPING ROUTE.

Foreground	Cheapest route.
Forehead	Express.
Forerank	Freight.
Foretaken	Steamer.
Forging	Atchison, Topeka & Santa Fe R. R.
Forgive	B. & O. S. W. R. R.
Forlorn	C., B. & Q. R. R.
Formation	C., C., C. & St. L. (Big Four) R. R.
Formic	C., I. & L. (Monon) R. R.
Forsake	C. & O. R. R.
Fossil	I. C. R. R.
Founding	L., E. & St. L. R. R.
Fourfold	L. & N. R. R.
Fowling	L., St. L. & T. R. R.
Foxhound	M., K. & T. R. R.
Fractious	Mobile & Ohio R. R.
Fragment	Mo. Pacific R. R.
Framed	P., C., C. & St. L. R. R. (Pan Handle.)
Franchise	St. L. & S. F. R. R.
Frankness	Southern Railway Co.
Frantic	St. Louis & Southwestern R. R.

SHIPPING—DATES.

Freedman	As soon as.
Freehold	As soon as we can.
Frequent	As soon as possible.
Friendless	In about.
Friendship	No sooner than.
Frightful	Not later than.
Frisky	After receipt of order.
Frolic	To-day or to-morrow.
Frontage	To-morrow or next day.
Frontier	In a day or two.
Frosted	Middle of this week.
Fuddled	In about a week.
Fulcrum	Last of this week.
Fulgent	Last of this week or early next week.
Fulsome	Last of next week.
Fumbler	Next Monday or Tuesday.
Function	Next Tuesday or Wednesday.
Furious	Next Wednesday or Thursday.
Furlong	Next Thursday or Friday.
Furnace	Next Friday or Saturday.
Furrier	Next Saturday or Monday.
Fussy	In three days.
Fustian	In five days.
Gadding	In ten days.
Gaffer	In two weeks.
Gaggling	In three weeks.
Gainsay	In four weeks.
Galecto	First week in.
Galenic	Second week in.
Galilee	Third week in.

B. F. AVERY & SONS.   LOUISVILLE, KY.

TELEGRAPH CODE—Continued.

LETTERS AND TELEGRAMS.

Code Word.	Signification.
Galiot	Your letter was received in time.
Gall	Your letter was not received in time.
Gallant	See letter.
Galley	See our letter of the——.
Gallipot	Have you received our letter of ——?
Gallop	Get our letter at——.
Gallows	Where will letter reach you?
Galore	When through go to——and get our letter.
Galvanic	Have written you to-day; wait for letter.
Gamboling	Have you written, and, if so, where did you send it?
Gamecock	We wrote you fully at——.
Gamester	Go to——immediately and get mail.
Gammon	Go to——as soon as convenient and get mail.
Gangrene	Have sent particulars by mail.
Gangway	Will send particulars by mail.
Garbage	Send particulars by mail.
Garfish	Answer by mail.
Gargle	{ Do not leave place hereafter named until you get our letter dated—— or number.
Garland	Your telegram was received in time.
Garlic	Your telegram was not received in time.
Garment	See our telegram of the——sent to——.
Garnish	Have you received our telegram of——?
Garret	Answer by telegraph immediately.
Garrison	Telegraph to-morrow early.
Gascon	Will send particulars by telegraph.
Gashing	Telegraph to——.
Gaslight	Telegraph in plain language.
Gastric	We have wired you at——.
Gasworks	We do not understand your message.
Gateway	——word of your cipher message is unintelligible.
Gauging	Please repeat order of——; the original must have been lost.
Gauntlet	Why don't you answer?
Gavel	We have not heard from you lately.
Gawky	Send all papers in the case.
Gazette	All the papers in the case have been sent you.
Gearing	Is there any thing for me to attend to before leaving the place?
Gelatin	{ There is nothing else for you to attend to; go on your route, but let us know where we can catch you by wire or mail.
Gelding	Do not make contract with——.

PRINTED MATTER.

Generic	Send me a few posters of all kinds.
Generous	Send a full supply of printed matter to me at——.
Genitor	Send me a package of catalogues by express.
Genius	Send me a package of catalogues by mail.
Gentile	Send a supply of catalogues and folders to——.
Gesture	Send a good supply of all kinds of printed matter and signboards.

B. F. AVERY & SONS. LOUISVILLE, KY.

INDEX TO CATALOGUE.

	PAGE
Bean Separator	82
Bean Thresher	82
Beat Digger and Subsoil Plows	26
Blades—	
Bull Tongue	127, 128
Cultivator	135, 136, 137, 138, 139
Cultivator Blanks	135
Double Moldboard	135
Double Shovel	132, 133
Jumping Shovel	134
List of Extras	121
Scrapers	131
Scooters	128
Shovels	125, 126, 127
Single Shovel	134
Solid Sweeps	122, 123
Trucker Cultivator	140
Turning Shovels	129, 130, 131
Wing Shovel	134
Wing Sweep	123, 124
Blackland Double Shovels	97
Gang Plow Bottoms	49, 50, 51
Hand Plows	16, 17, 18, 19, 20, 21
Sulky Plow Bottoms	42, 43, 44, 46
Bolts, Heel	115
Bolts, Plow	115
Cane Mills	80
Cast Plows	34, 35
Chilled Gang Plow Bottoms	49
Hand Plows	29, 30, 31, 32, 33
Hillside Plows	29
Sulky Plow Bottoms	42, 43, 44
Vineyard Plows	32
Clevises	118, 119, 120
Comet Cultivators	72, 73, 74, 75, 76, 77
Corn Drills	61
Corn Planters	60, 61, 62, 63
Cosmopolitan Gang Plows	52, 53
Cotton Planters	62, 63
Cotton Scrapers	103
Cotton Scraper and Sweep Combination	102
Cotton Sweeps	102
Coulters, Caster	105
Knife	106, 107
Moon	104, 105
Stiff	105
Cultivators—	
Blades, Comet, New South, Western,	135 to 139
Blades, Trucker's Cultivator	140
Comet, Shovel, Walking	72, 73, 74, 75, 77
Comet, Spring Tooth, Walking	76
Delta	88
Directions for Setting up Comet	169
New South	165
Revolution	157
Western	165
Disc, Revolution	64, 65
Double Shovel	98
Garden	89, 90, 91, 92, 93
New South, Shovel, Riding	69
Repairs, Comet	166, 167, 168
New South	162, 163, 164
Revolution	158, 159, 160
Western	162, 163, 164
Revolution, Disc, Riding	64, 65
Six Shovel	66
Spring Tooth	67
Riding, New South, Revolution, Western	64, 65, 66, 67, 69, 70, 71, 76
Shovels, Comet, New South, Western,	66, 69, 70, 71, 72, 73, 74, 75, 77
Spring Tooth Comet, Revolution, Western	76
Truckers'	84, 85
Walking, Comet	72, 73, 74, 75, 76, 77
Western, Shovel, Riding	70, 71
Western, Spring Tooth, Riding	76
Directions for Setting up—	
Comet Cultivators	169
Invincible Disc Sulky Plow	145
Invincible Moldboard Gang Plow	151
Invincible Moldboard Sulky Plow	144
Louisville Planter	154
Louisville Stalk Cutter	152
Modern Planter	156
New South Cultivator	165
Revolution Disc Cultivator	157

	PAGE
Directions for Setting up—	
Revolution Stalk Cutter	161
Simple Sulky Middle Burster	150
Simple Sulky Plow	150
Simple Sulky Stalk Cutter	150
Western Cultivators	165
Disc Cultivator, Revolution	64, 65
Harrows	54, 55, 56, 57, 58
Gang Plow	40, 41
Sulky Plows	40, 41
Double Plow Stocks	101
Spreader Rods	115
T Washers	114
Double Shovels	94, 95, 96, 97, 98
Blades	132
Calf Tongues	133
Fenders	114
Heel Slides	114
Regulating Runners	95
Spreader Rods	115
Doubletree Irons	112
Doubletrees, Steel	108
Wood	110, 111, 112
Evaporator Pans and Furnaces	81
Eveners, Four-Horse	109
Fenders, Double Shovel	114
Field Rollers	78
Fin Cutters	105
Furnaces and Evaporators	81
Gang Plows, Cosmopolitan	52, 53
Invincible Disc	40, 41
Invincible Moldboard	49
Napoleon	50, 51
Garden Tools, Cultivators	90, 91, 92, 93
Drills	89, 90, 92
Plows	91, 92, 93
Gauge Wheels	106, 107
Grading Plows	25
Grass Rods	114
Hames	116
Handles, Plow	113
Harrows, Disc	54, 55, 56, 57, 58
Orchard	86
Side, Steel Frame	87
Side, Wood Frame	68
Steel Frame, Lever	59
Teeth	114
Wood Frame	59
Hay Rakes	79
Heel Bolts	115
Heel Slides	114
Hillside Plows	28, 29
Invincible Disc Gang Plows	40, 41
Disc Sulky Plows	40, 41
Middle Burster	45
Moldboard Gang Plow	49
Moldboard Sulky Plows	42, 43, 44
Jointers	30, 31, 32, 106, 107
Jumping Coulters	106, 107
Jumping Shovel Blades	134
Jumping Shovel Plows	38
Knife Coulters	106, 107
Land Rollers	78
Lap Links	113
Lap Rings	113
Lawn Mowers	83
Louisville Stalk Cutters	39
Malleable Clevises	118, 119, 120
Middle Burster Plows	22
Sulky, Invincible	45
Sulky, Simple	47
Mississippi Scrapers	114
Napoleon Gang Plows	50, 51
Neckyokes, Steel	109
Wood	112
New Ground Plows, Grubber	38
Improved	36
Jumping Shovel	38
Old Style	36
Samson	37
New South Cultivators	69

B. F. AVERY & SONS. LOUISVILLE, KY.

INDEX TO CATALOGUE—Continued.

	PAGE
Orchard Harrows	86
Pans, Evaporator	81
Pea Hullers	82
Pea Threshers	82
Planters, Cherokee	60
Dow-Law	63
Garden	89, 90, 92
Louisville	63
Modern	62
Union	61
Plows, Cast, New Series	34
Old Series	34
Red Pony	35
Veteran	35
Plows, Chilled American	30, 31
Bottoms, Invincible Gang	49
Bottoms, Invincible Sulky	42, 43, 44
Granite	32
Hillside	29
Old Series	33
Vineyard	32
Plows, Double Stocks—	
Planter's Friend	101
V Stocks	101
Plows, Single Stocks—	
Carolina	100
Georgia	100
Lone Star	99
Texas	100
Universal	99
Plows, Steel—	
Advance	23
Big Bolt	15
Cadet	13
Cosmopolitan Gang	52, 53
Dandy	14
Double Shovels	94, 95, 96, 97, 98
El Matador	24
Garden	91, 92, 93
Grubber, New Ground	28
Hard Pan Beet Digger and Subsoil	26
Ideal Hillside	28
Improved Blackland	17
Improved New Ground	36
Invincible Disc Gang	40, 41
Invincible Disc Sulky	40, 41
Invincible Middle Burster	45
Invincible Moldboard Gang	49
Invincible Moldboard Sulky	42, 43, 44
Jumping Shovels	38
Middle Burster, Invincible Sulky	45
Middle Burster Plows	22
Middle Burster, Simple Sulky	47
Napoleon Gang	50, 51
New Clipper	4, 5
Ohio Valley	8, 9
Old Style New Ground	36
Orange	24
Ought Series Blackland	20, 21
Pony Series	10, 11, 12
Potato Digger	27
Railroad and Grading	25
Rainbow	16
Samson New Ground	37
Simple Sulky Middle Burster	47
Simple Sulky Moldboard Plow	46
Single Shovel	93
Tiny Tim	13
Western	6, 7
Wing Shovel	94
X Series Blackland	18, 19
Rakes, Hay	79
Railroad or Grading Plow	25
Repair Links, Trace Chains	117

	PAGE
Repairs—	
Comet Cultivator	166, 167, 168
Common Sense Harrows	141
Dow-Law Planters	149
Invincible Moldboard Sulky Plow	142, 143
Louisville Planter	154, 155
Louisville Stalk Cutter	152, 153
Modern Planter	156
Moon Coulters	141
New South Cultivator	162, 163, 164
Orchard Harrows	141
Revolution Disc Cultivator	158, 159
Revolution Six Shovel Attachment	160
Revolution Spring Tooth Attachment	160
Revolution Stalk Cutter Attachment	160, 161
Simple Sulky	146, 147
Simple Sulky Middle Burster Attachment	148
Simple Sulky Stalk Cutter Attachment	149
Steel Frame Lever Harrows	141
Trucker's Cultivators	141
Western Cultivators	162, 163, 164
Revolution Disc Cultivator	64, 65
Six-Shovel Cultivator	66
Spring Tooth Cultivator	67
Stalk Cutter	68
Rice Land Goods. See Special Catalogue.	
Rolling Coulters	104, 105
Rules of Business	3
Runners, Regulating	95
Scrapers, Cotton	102, 103
Mississippi	114
Seed Drills	61, 89, 90, 92
Side Harrows	87, 88
Simple Sulky	46
Simple Sulky Middle Burster	47
Simple Sulky Stalk Cutter	48
Single Plow Stocks	99, 100
Single Plow Stocks, T Washers	114
Single Shovel Blades	134
Single Shovel Plows	93
Singletree Irons	112
Singletrees, Steel	108
Wood	110, 111
Sorghum Mills	80
Spreader Rods	115
Stalk Cutters, Louisville	39
Revolution	68
Simple Sulky	48
Steel Shapes	121 to 140
Steel Trees	108, 109
Straight Knife Coulters	106, 107
Subsoil Plows	26
Sulky Plows—	
Invincible, Disc	40, 41
Invincible, Middle Burster	45
Invincible, Moldboard	42, 43, 44
Simple, Middle Burster	47
Simple, Moldboard	46
T Washers	114
Teeth, Harrow	114
Telegraph Code	170, 171, 172, 173, 174
Trace Chains and Repair Links	117
Tripletrees, Steel	109
Trucker's Cultivators	84, 85
Trucker's Cultivator Blades	140
Vineyard Plows	32
Washers, T	114
Wing Shovel Blades	134
Wing Shovel Plows	94
Wood Trees	110, 111, 112
Wrenches	117
Wrought Clevises	120
Western Cultivators	70, 71, 76

INDEX TO CODE WORDS.

E—170 to 171 inclusive.
F—171 to 173 inclusive.
G—173 to 174 inclusive.
J— 5 to 8 inclusive.
K— 9 to 12 inclusive.
L— 12 to 30 inclusive.
M—30 to 51 inclusive.
N—51 to 55 inclusive.
O— 55 to 62 inclusive.
P— 63 to 111 inclusive.
Q—112 to 113 inclusive.
R—113 to 120 inclusive.
S—122 to 140 inclusive.

www.ingramcontent.com/pod-product-compliance
Lightning Source LLC
Chambersburg PA
CBHW020257170426
43202CB00008B/402